IBPS RRB Prelims Exam

Office Assistant & Officers Scale I

Latest Edition
Practice Kit

13 Tests
10 Mock Test
03 Previous Year Paper

Based On Real Exam Pattern

✓ Thoroughly Revised and Updated

✓ Sample Papers with Answer Keys

Title	: IBPS RRB Prelims Exam Office Assistant & Officers Scale I
Author Name	: Mr. Rohit Manglik
Published By	: EduGorilla Community Pvt. Ltd.
Publishers Address	: 12/651, First Floor Opp. Arvindo Park, Near Jama Masjid, Indira Nagar, Lucknow, Uttar Pradesh-226016, India

Copyright EduGorilla

ISBN : 978-93-91464-56-1

Second Edition

Disclaimer EduGorilla

Compiled and created by EduGorilla Community Pvt. Ltd

Printed By EduGorilla Community Pvt. Ltd.

ROHIT MANGLIK
CEO, EduGorilla

Dear Applicants,

People say *"Success comes to those who work hard."* But I've seen people working hard for their exams day in and day out for marginal success. While others succeed in their examinations by putting in just half the work. So are they God Gifted? No! I believe that it's because they work *smart* and not just *hard*. Similarly, for your exams, you should strategize your preparation so as to increase the likelihood of success. Well with EduGorilla get ready to increase your *chances of selection* in your exam by *16x*.

EduGorilla helps you in not only working *hard* but also working in a *smart and strategic* manner. With EduGorilla's preparation package, you get a chance to make your exam preparation easy, and a fun learning path towards selection. Finding the right path to your preparations can be difficult if you don't know in which direction to head. Don't worry, we have you covered! EduGorilla will be your guide to success in your journey. With our Preparation Package, you can prepare strategically and beat the exam in just one attempt.

EduGorilla's Preparation Package includes-

- **Test Series**
- **Books**

Our preparation package is handcrafted as per the latest changes, expert opinions, and students' discretion. Thus, enabling you to get through each stage of the selection process for your exam.

Our Books are designed by the teachers and experts of the respective exam with a combined 150+ years of experience; to provide you with easy, efficient, and effective learning. Our books are smart, in the sense that not only do they give you the answers to the questions but also provide similar questions for practice.

EduGorilla's competent Test Series gives you real-time experience and confidence through which you can clear your offline or online exam in just one attempt. We currently host 83,000+ mock tests for 1,440+ competitive and academic exams.

Thus, EduGorilla misses no chance to assist you in your preparation and covers all stages of the exam, so that you don't have to look anywhere else.

We provide complete preparation packages for defense, banking, teaching, and other National & State-Level exams. Hence, it doesn't matter which exam you aspire to because you will reach your success.

ALL THE BEST !
Let EduGorilla be your Guide to Success.

Rohit Manglik,
Founder and CEO, EduGorilla

INTRODUCTION

EduGorilla focuses on guiding students to succeed in their examinations. With that in mind, our book, titled "IBPS RRB Prelims Exam : Office Assistant & Officers Scale I", has been drafted through the collective efforts of our distinguished experts with 150+ years of combined experience. This book consists of questions that are created following the latest changes in the syllabus and exam pattern. We compiled the book on the basis of questions that are most likely to appear in the IBPS RRB. Through EduGorilla's "IBPS RRB Prelims Exam : Office Assistant & Officers Scale I" your chances of success will increase 16x.

EduGorilla does this through our Complete Preparation Package. This package consists of well-conceptualized and structured content in the form of questions that are tailor-made according to your needs and will help you practice for exams in a smart way by pinpointing all the necessary information. It also provides smart answer sheet for your self-evaluation. You can assess your shortcomings and work accordingly on areas that may require more of your attention.

EduGorilla promises to help you succeed in your examination and accomplish your dream goals. We believe in our aspirants and see them at the top of the merit list. And the first step towards the top is to start preparing with us. EduGorilla's "IBPS RRB Prelims Exam : Office Assistant & Officers Scale I" includes the following attributes.

➤ Well-Researched Content

➤ Top-Notch Quality

➤ Smart Answer Sheet

➤ Exam Relevant Questions

Therefore, EduGorilla fortifies your preparation and makes it durable enough to help you stand tall and beat the examination.

IBPS RRB

Scan QR code for Eligibility, Exam Pattern, Syllabus and more.

Book ID: 0801

TABLE OF CONTENTS

Mock Test	1-81
Mock Test - 1	1-8
Mock Test - 2	9-15
Mock Test - 3	16-23
Mock Test - 4	24-31
Mock Test - 5	32-40
Mock Test - 6	41-48
Mock Test - 7	49-56
Mock Test - 8	57-64
Mock Test - 9	65-72
Mock Test - 10	73-81

Previous Year Paper	82-102
12 Sep 2020 (Shift - I)	82-88
12 Sep 2020 (Shift - II)	89-95

Reasoning

Q.1 According to numerical series, How many pairs of digits are there in the number "67289574" each of which has as many digits between them as in the numerical series in both forward and backward directions?

A. None   **B.** One
C. Two   **D.** Three
E. More than three

Q.2 How many such pairs of letters are there in the meaningful word "EMPLOYMENT" each of which has as many letters between them in the word as in the English alphabet?

A. None   **B.** Two
C. Three   **D.** One
E. More than three

Q.3 In the question below are given some statements followed by two conclusions numbered I and II. You have to take the given statements to be true even if they seem to be at variance with commonly known facts. Read all the conclusions and then decide which of the given conclusions logically follows from the given statements disregarding commonly known facts.

Statements:

All ice cream is chocolate.

Some mango is vanilla.

Some ice cream is vanilla.

Conclusions:

I. Some ice cream being vanilla is a possibility.

II. Some mango is chocolate.

A. Only conclusion I follow
B. Only conclusion II follows
C. Either conclusion I or II follows
D. Neither conclusion I nor II follows.
E. Both conclusions I and II follow

Q.4 Direction: In the question below are given three statements followed by four conclusions I, II and III. You have to take the given statements to be true even if they seem to be at variance from commonly known facts. Read all the conclusions and then decide which of the given conclusions logically follows from the given statements disregarding commonly known facts.

Statements:

All Clocks are Digital.

Some Watches are Calculator.

No Clock is a Watch.

Conclusions:

I. All Watches being Digital is a possibility.

II. No calculator is a Clock.

III. Some Digitals are Clocks.

A. Only II follows

B. Only III follows
C. Both I and III follow
D. Either II or III follows
E. None of these

Q.5 Direction: In the question below are given some statements followed by two conclusions numbered I and II. You have to take the given statements to be true even if they seem to be at variance with commonly known facts. Read all the conclusions and then decide which of the given conclusions logically follows from the given statements disregarding commonly known facts.

Statements:

All chairs are locks.

All locks are key.

Some key are box.

Conclusions:

I. Some chairs are key.

II. Some box are chairs.

A. Only conclusion I follow
B. Only conclusion II follows
C. Either conclusion I or II follows
D. Neither conclusion I nor II follows
E. Both conclusions I and II follow

Q.6 Direction: In the questions given below statements are followed by some conclusions. You have to take the given statements to be True even if they seem to be at variance from commonly known facts. Read all the conclusions and then decide which of the given conclusions logically follows from the given statements disregarding commonly known facts.

Statement:

Frequently Silver is Black.

None Black is White.

Occasionally Gold is Silver.

More of the White is Yellow.

Conclusion:

I) some Yellow is not Black.

II) Few silver is black.

III) All White can never be Silver.

A. Only III and II follows
B. Only I follows
C. Only I and II follows
D. All follows
E. Only II follows

Q.7 Direction: In the question below are given some statements followed by some conclusions. You have to take given statements to be true even if they seem to be at variance with commonly known facts. Read all the conclusions and then decide which of the given conclusions logically follows from the given statements disregarding commonly known facts.

Statements:

Some Painter are Artist.

Only few brush are paints.

All artists are paints.

No frame is Paints.

Conclusions:

I. Some Paints are Painter.

II. Some Brush are not Paint.

III. Some Brush are Artist.

A. Only I and II follows

B. Only I and Either II or III

C. Either II or III

D. Only III follows

E. Only I follows

Ques (8-12):Direction: Study the following information carefully and answer the questions given below.

Six friends P, Q, R, S, T and U are sitting around a hexagonal table in a restaurant. Only one person is sitting on each side of the table and they all are facing the centre. They all ordered a different food among momos, burger, noodles, biryani, pizza and ice cream but not necessary in the same order.

S is sitting 3rd to the left of the person, who orders pizza.

T order biryani and he is an immediate neighbour of the person who orders pizza.

Exactly one person is sitting between T and the person who orders momos.

The person who ordered momos is not adjacent to the person who ordered pizza.

The person who orders ice cream is sitting exactly between R and U.

Q orders ice cream and P orders burger.

P is sitting to the immediate right of S.

Q.8 Who orders Pizza?

A. P

B. Q

C. R

D. None of these

E. Cannot be determined

Q.9 How many people are sitting between Q and P in clockwise direction from P?

A. 1

B. 2

C. 3

D. None of these

E. Cannot be determine

Q.10 Which food does R order?

A. Pizza

B. Noodles

C. Momos

D. None of these

E. Either (A) or (B)

Q.11 Who is sitting opposite to the person, who orders ice cream?

A. Q

B. P

C. R

D. S

E. None of these

Q.12 Who orders momos?

A. P

B. Q

C. R

D. S

E. None of these

Q.13 How many meaningful English words can be formed, with the second, the third, the sixth and the seventh letters of the word AEROMANCY, using each letter only once in each word? (To be counted from left)

A. None   **B.** One   **C.** Two   **D.** Three

E. Four

Q.14 If in a certain code language, GOVERN is written as NREVOG. How is 'DEMAND' written in that code language?

A. DNAMED

B. NAMEDD

C. DNEMAD

D. DNAEDM

E. None of the above

Ques (15-17):Direction: Study the given information and carefully answer the questions that follow.

Seven villages A, B, C, D, E, F and G are situated as follows:

E is 2 km to the west of B. F is 2 km to the north of A. D is 2 km to the south of G. C is 1 km to the west of A. G is 2 km to the east of C. D is exactly in the middle of B and E.

Q.15 How far is E from F (in km) as the crow flies?

A. 5 km

B. 6 km

C. 4 km

D. 4.5 km

E. None of these

Q.16 Which two villages are the farthest from one another?

A. D & C

B. F & E

C. F & B

D. G & E

E. Cannot be determined

Q.17 A is in the middle of:

A. C & F

B. B & D

C. C & G

D. C & B

E. None of these

Ques (18-19):Direction: In a family there are 6 members P, Q, R, X, Y and Z. R is the sister of Z. X is the father of P and grandfather of Z. Q is the brother of Y's husband. There are three brothers, one mother and two fathers.

Q.18 Who is the father of Z?

A. P

B. R

C. Y

D. Q

E. None of these

Q.19 How many females are there in the family?

A. One

B. Two
C. Three
D. Four
E. Can't be determine exactly

Q.20 A series is given with one term missing. Select the correct alternative from the given ones that will complete the series.
ROD,XUJ, DAP, JGV, ?

A. PMB   **B.** QNC
C. QMB   **D.** PNB
E. None of these

Ques (21-25):Direction: Read the information carefully and answer the following question.

Twelve persons are sitting in two parallel rows. Six persons P, Q, R, S, T and U are facing north and other six A, B, C, D, E and F are facing south. Each person in a row is facing exactly one person of the other row but not necessarily in the same order.

E does not sit at any of the extreme ends. S and T are not immediate neighbors of each other. A and R are sitting diagonally opposite to each other. Two persons sit between R and Q. One of the immediate neighbors of Q faces C, who does not sit near A. Two persons sit between B and D. T sits second to the left of U. A is sitting on one. from the extreme end. P faces B and P is not an immediate neighbor of Q.

Q.21 Who sits third to the left of C?
A. D   **B.** F   **C.** B   **D.** A
E. E

Q.22 How many persons are there in between P and U?
A. 3   **B.** 4
C. 2   **D.** 1
E. Can't be determined

Q.23 Who faces Q?

[RBI Assistant, 2020]

A. E   **B.** C   **C.** B   **D.** A
E. F

Q.24 How many persons sits left of U?
A. 2   **B.** 3   **C.** 1   **D.** 4
E. 5

Q.25 Who faces the one who sits second to the left of U?
A. B   **B.** E   **C.** C   **D.** D
E. F

Ques (26-30):Direction: Study the following information carefully and answer the questions given below.

Q.26 In equation J ≥ F > N < H ≥ G we can determine J > N is true then in which of the following equation J > N will be definitely true
A. J ≥ F = N < H ≤ G   **B.** J ≤ F = N < H ≥ G
C. J > F = N > H ≥ G   **D.** J ≥ F ≤ N < H ≤ G
E. J = F ≥ N = H ≤ G

Q.27 Which of the following symbols should be placed in the blank spaces respectively *(in the same order, from left to right)

in order to complete the given expression in such a manner that makes the expression 'F > N' and 'U > D' definitely true?
F_O_U_N_D
A. <, <, >, =   **B.** <, =, =, >
C. >, =, =, >   **D.** ≥, =, =, ≤
E. >, >, =, <

Q.28 Which of the following should be placed in the blank spaces respectively (in the same order from left to right) in order to complete the given expression in such a manner that makes the expression 'A < P' definitely false?

___<___<___>___
A. L, N, P, A   **B.** L, A, P, N
C. A, L, P, N   **D.** N, A, P, L
E. P, N, A, L

Q.29 Statements:
R = S, L ≥ K, K ≥ R
Conclusions:
I) L > R
II) S = L
A. Only conclusion I follows
B. Only conclusion II follows
C. Either conclusion I or II follows
D. Neither conclusion I nor II follows
E. Both conclusions I and II are follow

Q.30 Statements:
R = S, K < R, L < K
Conclusions:
I) S > L
II) K < S
A. Only conclusion I is follow
B. Only conclusion II is follows
C. Either conclusion I or II is follows
D. Neither conclusion I nor II is follows
E. Both conclusions I and II are follow

Ques (31-35):Directions: These questions are based on the following information.

8 people: A, B, C, D, E, F, G and H participated in a competition and got rank from 1 to 8. They work in different companies: TCS, Reliance, ONGC, Wipro, Microsoft, HP, Infosys and ITC.

D does not work in Reliance or HP and B does not work in Reliance. The person with rank 7 works in Wipro and the one with rank 6 in ONGC. The sum of the ranks of G and H is 11 and the rank of H is higher than that of G. C's rank is 3 and he works in Infosys. G works in Microsoft. B's rank is the sum of C's and E's ranks. D's rank is the sum of B's and C's ranks. A works in TCS. E's rank is 2.

Q.31 Who works at HP?
A. A   **B.** B   **C.** C   **D.** D
E. E

Q.32 What is the rank of the person working at Wipro?
A. 5   **B.** 6

C. 7   **D.** 8
E. None of these

Q.33 Who works at ONGC?
A. A   **B.** C   **C.** D   **D.** E
E. F

Q.34 What is the sum of ranks of A and E?
A. 4   **B.** 6
C. 8   **D.** 3
E. None of these

Q.35 Where does E work?
A. HP   **B.** ONGC   **C.** Reliance   **D.** Wipro
E. ITC

Ques (36-40):Direction: Study the following information carefully to answer the given questions.

Six boxes M, N, O, P, Q, and R are placed one above the other not necessarily in same order with 6 being the topmost and 1 is the bottommost. These boxes contains different electronic items viz laptop, camera, phone, webcam, router, and charger. Only two boxes are placed between O and P, which has camera in it. Box O placed above Box P. The box which is at top contains laptop. Box O placed at even numbered position and is not placed at top. Only one box is placed between O and the one which contains router. Box Q contains webcam. Box N placed immediately below Box R, which contains charger.

Q.36 How many boxes are placed between the one which contains Phone and Box N?
A. Four   **B.** Three
C. Two   **D.** One
E. None of the above

Q.37 What is the position of Box Q?
A. Third from the bottom
B. Second from the top
C. Top most position
D. Third from the top
E. Second from bottom

Q.38 How many boxes are placed between M and N?

[IBPS Clerk, 2021]

A. Three   **B.** Two
C. One   **D.** Four
E. None of the above

Q.39 Which box contains Phone?
A. M   **B.** O   **C.** Q   **D.** P
E. N

Q.40 Box M contains which electronic item?
A. Webcam   **B.** Laptop
C. Router   **D.** Camera
E. None of the above

Quantitative Aptitude

Ques (41-45):Direction: Find the number that will come in place of the question mark '?' in the following number series.

Q.41 22, 23, 48, 147, 592, ?
A. 2875   **B.** 2665   **C.** 2965   **D.** 2605
E. 2915

Q.42 20, 24, 33, 58, 107, ?
A. 116   **B.** 168   **C.** 228   **D.** 208
E. 176

Q.43 52, 67, 84, 103, ?, 147
A. 108   **B.** 134   **C.** 139   **D.** 124
E. 122

Q.44 0.5, 2, 7, 29, 146, ?
A. 911   **B.** 765   **C.** 623   **D.** 793
E. 877

Q.45 72, 73, 69, 78, 62, ?
A. 78   **B.** 87   **C.** 83   **D.** 89
E. 76

Q.46 A number P equals 80% of the average of 12, 4, 10 and a number Q. If the average of P and Q is 26, the value of Q is:
A. 13   **B.** 26
C. 39   **D.** 40
E. None of these

Q.47 A is five years older than B who is thrice as old as C. If the total age of A, B and C be 47, then how old is B?
A. 10   **B.** 19   **C.** 12   **D.** 15
E. 18

Q.48 There is a 50% increase in an amount in 2 years at simple interest. What will be the compound interest of Rs 20000 after 2 years at the same rate?
A. Rs. 10000   **B.** Rs. 20000
C. Rs. 15620   **D.** Rs. 11250
E. Rs. 5000

Q.49 A train crosses the platform of a station in 18 seconds and crosses a man standing on the platform in 10 seconds. If the speed of the train is 108 km/hr, find the length of the platform.

[IBPS PO, 2020]

A. 225 m   **B.** 235 m   **C.** 230 m   **D.** 240 m
E. 260 m

Q.50 There are four different bags. Also, there are four different coins. In how many ways can the coins be put into bags if there are exactly two coins in exactly one of the bags?
A. 48   **B.** 96   **C.** 72   **D.** 144
E. 180

Q.51 Rohan started a garage to provide the services for the old cars and after giving the labor charges of 10% per month, he was saving 15% per car which was Rs. 15000 then and on average he was selling 20 cars per month. What was the selling price of 20 cars?
A. Rs. 1200000   **B.** Rs. 2000000
C. Rs. 3000000   **D.** Rs. 2200000

E. None of these

Q.52 Pipe C and D can fill an empty tank in 15 hours and 20 hours respectively pipe C and D opened alternatively every hour and in the first pipe C is opened. In how many times the tank will be 66.66% filled?

A. $15\frac{1}{3}$ hours   **B.** $11\frac{1}{3}$ hours

C. $17\frac{1}{3}$ hours   **D.** $18\frac{1}{3}$ hours

E. None of these

Q.53 The price of an umbrella decreased by 20%. As a result of which the sale increased by 40%. What will be the net effect on the total revenue of the shop?

A. 12% decrease   **B.** 15% increase

C. 20% decrease   **D.** 12% increase

E. 18% decrease

Q.54 Naresh sold two books for Rs. 600 each, thereby gaining 20% on one book and losing 20% on the other book. Find his overall loss or gain percent.

A. 4% loss   **B.** 4% gain

C. 10% loss   **D.** 10% gain

E. None of these

Q.55 A steamer with a speed of 15 km/h in still water travels 40 km downstream and returns in 6 hr. What is the speed of current?

A. 5 km/hr   **B.** 4.5 km/hr

C. 6 km/hr   **D.** 5.5 km/hr

E. 7 km/hr

Ques (56-60):Direction: Find the approximate value that should come in the place of question mark (?) in the following question.

Q.56 $\sqrt{2303.97} \times 11.99 \div 23.98 + \sqrt{676.16} =?$

A. 60   **B.** 40   **C.** 55   **D.** 50

E. 45

Q.57 $324.89 - 11.98 \times 8.08 + (2.93)^3 = (?)^2$

A. 14   **B.** 18   **C.** 22   **D.** 16

E. 24

Q.58 69.96% of $499.99 + \sqrt{99.99} = 4.95 \times?$

A. 72   **B.** 64   **C.** 68   **D.** 76

E. 84

Q.59 49.9% of $299.99 - 29.93\%$ of $199.99 + 19.92\%$ of $399.99 =?$

A. 10   **B.** 110   **C.** 130   **D.** 170

E. 70

Q.60 39.90% of $549.98 + \sqrt[3]{728.9} - (12.95)^2 = ?$

A. 80   **B.** 70   **C.** 50   **D.** 40

E. 60

Ques (61-65):Direction: In the given question, two equations numbered I and II are given. You have to solve both the equations and mark the appropriate answer.

Q.61 I. $x^2 - 5x + 6 = 0$

II. $y^2 + y - 6 = 0$

A. x < y   **B.** x > y   **C.** x ≤ y   **D.** x ≥ y

E. x = y

Q.62 I. $2x^2 - 12x + 18 = 0$

II. $2y^2 - 19y + 39 = 0$

A. x < y   **B.** x > y   **C.** x = y   **D.** x ≥ y

E. x ≤ y

Q.63 I. $x^2 + 13x + 42 = 0$

II. $y^2 + 19y + 90 = 0$

A. x < y   **B.** x ≤ y   **C.** x > y   **D.** x ≥ y

E. x = y

Q.64 I. $3x^2 - 23x - 8 = 0$

II. $3y^2 - 32y - 11 = 0$

A.   x < y

B.   x > y

C.   x ≤ y

D.   x ≥ y

E.   x = y OR the relationship cannot be determined

Q.65 I. $3x^2 - 14x - 5 = 0$

II. $6y^2 - 46y - 16 = 0$

A.   x < y

B.   x > y

C.   x = y OR the relationship cannot be determined

D.   x ≥ y

E.   x ≤ y

Ques (66-67):Direction: The following question is accompanied by two statements (I) and (II). You have to determine which statements(s) is/are sufficient/necessary to answer the questions.

Q.66 What is the rate of simple interest?

I. The amount was invested for 8 years.

II. The simple interest is half the investment.

A. Statement I alone is sufficient to answer the question, but statement II alone is not sufficient

B. Statement II alone is sufficient to answer the question, but statement I alone is not sufficient

C. Both the statements I and II together are needed to answer the question

D. Either statement I alone or statement II alone is sufficient to answer the question

E. Neither statement I nor statement II is sufficient to answer the question

Q.67 What is the difference between the income of a man and woman per day?

I. Two men and five women can do the work in 8 days.

II. Ratio of efficiencies of a woman and a child is 4 : 7. One day income of a man, woman and child is Rs. 925.

A. The data in both statements I and II together are necessary to answer the question

B. The data in statement I alone or in statement II alone is sufficient to answer the question

C. The data in both statements I and II together are not sufficient to answer the question

D. The data in statement II alone is sufficient to answer the question, while the data in I alone is not sufficient to answer the question

E. The data in statement I alone is sufficient to answer the question, while the data in II alone is not sufficient to answer the question

Ques (68-72):Direction: Read the given table carefully and answer the following questions.

The table shows the number of visitors to 4 parks and the number of child visitors and the number of male adult visitors.

Parks	Total Visitors	Number of Adult Male Visitors	Number of child Visitors
A	100	40	30
B	140	70	20
C	150	60	40
D	120	50	30

NOTE: Total number of visitors = Number of male visitors + Number of female visitors + Number of child visitors

Q.68 Total Female adult visitors in parks A and C are what percent of total visitors in the same parks?

A. 36%   **B.** 26%   **C.** 40%   **D.** 32%
E. 44%

Q.69 What is the ratio of the number of male adult visitors in parks A, C and D to the number of female adult visitors in all the parks?

A. 5 : 11   **B.** 11 : 13   **C.** 9 : 13   **D.** 8 : 11
E. 15 : 17

Q.70 If each female adult visiting park B is married and each couple has one child then what is the difference between the number of unmarried male adult visitors and the number of male visitors (as a couple) having no children? (Each couple visit the same park)

A. 20   **B.** 30   **C.** 10   **D.** 15
E. 25

Q.71 The number of child visitors in park A and D is what percent more/less than the number of female adult visitors in park B and C?

A. 40%   **B.** 30%   **C.** 33.33%   **D.** 25%
E. 50%

Q.72 What is the average number of child visitors visiting all the parks?

A. 25   **B.** 30   **C.** 35   **D.** 40
E. 32

Q.73 The LCM and HCF of two numbers are 168 and 6 respectively. If one of the numbers is 24, find the other.

A. 36   **B.** 38   **C.** 40   **D.** 42
E. 44

Q.74 If $A: B: C = 2: 3: 4$, then the ratio $\frac{A}{B}:\frac{B}{C}:\frac{C}{A}$ is equal to-

A. 8: 9: 16   **B.** 8: 9: 12   **C.** 4: 9: 16   **D.** 4: 9: 12
E. 8: 9: 24

Q.75 The area of a rectangle is 42sq.cm and its length is 7cm. Find its perimeter.

A. 14 cm   **B.** 21 cm   **C.** 26 cm   **D.** 24 cm
E. 18 cm

Ques (76-80):Direction: Study the following pie chart carefully & answer the question given below it.

The pie chart given below shows the break-up of the cost of construction of a house (in degrees). Assuming that the total cost of construction is Rs. 60000, answer the question given below.

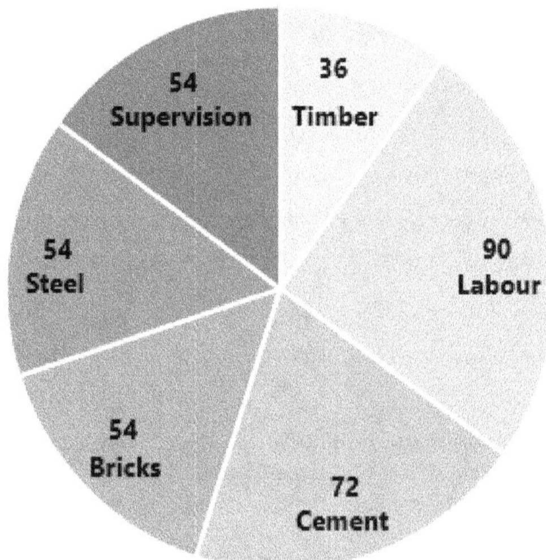

Q.76 The amount spent on cement is:
A. Rs. 20000   **B.** Rs. 16000
C. Rs. 12000   **D.** Rs. 10000
E. Rs. 11000

Q.77 The amount spent on labour exceeds the amount spent on steel by:
A. 5% of the total cost
B. 10% of the total cost
C. 12% of the total cost
D. 15% of the total cost
E. 20% of the total cost

Q.78 The amount spent on cement, steel and supervision is what percent of the total cost of construction?
A. 40%   **B.** 45%   **C.** 50%   **D.** 55%
E. 60%

Q.79 The amount spent on labour exceeds the amount spent on supervision by:
A. Rs. 200000   **B.** Rs. 160000
C. Rs. 120000   **D.** Rs. 6000
E. Rs. 8000

Q.80 What is the ratio of the combined expenditure on Supervision and Timber to the combined expenditure on Bricks and Cement?

A. 7 : 5   **B.** 3 : 4   **C.** 4 : 3   **D.** 5 : 7

E. 5 : 1

// Smart Answer Sheet //

Correct — Percentage of students who answered correctly. **Skipped** — Percentage of students who skipped.

Q.	Ans.	Correct / Skipped	Q.	Ans.	Correct / Skipped	Q.	Ans.	Correct / Skipped	Q.	Ans.	Correct / Skipped	Q.	Ans.	Correct / Skipped	Q.	Ans.	Correct / Skipped
1	E	22.45 % / 58.88 %	15	C	18.45 % / 64.21 %	29	C	8.2 % / 67.62 %	43	D	22.13 % / 66.32 %	57	D	14.46 % / 70.14 %	71	A	8.29 % / 76.11 %
2	B	13.11 % / 60.08 %	16	C	12.46 % / 64.54 %	30	E	17.94 % / 67.68 %	44	E	12.97 % / 66.74 %	58	A	17.65 % / 70.46 %	72	B	11.61 % / 76.59 %
3	D	11.32 % / 60.66 %	17	C	20.74 % / 64.7 %	31	B	11.26 % / 67.77 %	45	B	17.94 % / 66.98 %	59	D	15.68 % / 70.8 %	73	D	7.12 % / 78.73 %
4	C	16.06 % / 61.67 %	18	A	19.11 % / 64.74 %	32	C	13.15 % / 70.24 %	46	C	4.72 % / 67.14 %	60	E	12.15 % / 71.16 %	74	E	6.8 % / 79.23 %
5	A	16.99 % / 62.15 %	19	B	15.77 % / 65.15 %	33	E	10.52 % / 70.49 %	47	E	10.84 % / 67.92 %	61	D	12.52 % / 71.64 %	75	C	7.66 % / 80.11 %
6	C	7.02 % / 62.34 %	20	A	14.01 % / 65.25 %	34	D	10.96 % / 70.62 %	48	D	6.0 % / 68.48 %	62	E	11.67 % / 72.13 %	76	C	0.06 % / 99.9 %
7	A	12.03 % / 62.46 %	21	D	9.94 % / 65.33 %	35	C	11.01 % / 70.45 %	49	D	8.34 % / 68.93 %	63	C	15.13 % / 72.66 %	77	B	0.02 % / 99.9 %
8	E	9.74 % / 62.75 %	22	C	11.13 % / 67.44 %	36	D	1.1 % / 96.76 %	50	D	1.82 % / 69.2 %	64	E	11.61 % / 72.93 %	78	C	0.06 % / 99.9 %
9	B	17.29 % / 64.46 %	23	A	10.91 % / 67.96 %	37	B	1.14 % / 97.04 %	51	D	1.34 % / 69.0 %	65	C	12.39 % / 73.37 %	79	D	0.05 % / 99.9 %
10	E	10.2 % / 64.96 %	24	D	9.32 % / 67.88 %	38	A	1.13 % / 97.1 %	52	B	5.09 % / 69.64 %	66	C	5.09 % / 73.66 %	80	D	0.02 % / 99.91 %
11	B	16.29 % / 64.72 %	25	C	9.94 % / 67.48 %	39	B	1.28 % / 97.12 %	53	D	7.21 % / 69.79 %	67	C	2.3 % / 74.46 %			
12	D	16.92 % / 64.64 %	26	C	20.69 % / 66.87 %	40	B	1.16 % / 97.14 %	54	A	7.33 % / 70.08 %	68	D	9.61 % / 74.58 %			
13	C	10.79 % / 64.29 %	27	C	20.73 % / 67.17 %	41	C	19.73 % / 65.34 %	55	A	3.52 % / 69.98 %	69	E	10.19 % / 75.42 %			
14	A	28.56 % / 64.22 %	28	E	12.22 % / 67.4 %	42	C	18.07 % / 65.67 %	56	D	14.11 % / 69.81 %	70	C	2.74 % / 76.12 %			

Reasoning

Ques (1-5):Direction: Study the following information carefully and answer the question given below.

Eight friends - Divya, Riya, Ridhima, Prerana, Ishaan, Suman, Nandini and Monika likes different colours - Red, Brown, Green, Yellow, Pink, Orange, Black and White but not necessarily in the same order. They also like a different bird namely, Sparrow, Crow, Parrot, Pigeon, Owl, Eagle, Goose, and Duck but not necessarily in the same order.

Ishaan likes Brown colour and Crow is his favourite bird. Riya does not like the Orange colour. Suman's favourite colour is White and the one who likes White colour do not like Eagle. Ridhima likes Green colour but does not like Ducks. Nandini likes Owl and her favourite colour is Yellow. Monika likes Pigeon and Prerana likes only Red colour. The one who likes Pigeon likes Pink colour. Riya likes Goose. The one who likes Red does not like Sparrow. Neither Prerana nor Suman likes Parrots. The one who likes the Orange colour likes Sparrow.

Q.1 Which of the following is the correct combination?
A.   Monika - Pink - Pigeon
B.   Suman - Black - Pigeon
C.   Riya - Black - Crow
D.   Divya - Orange - Duck
E.   Prerana - Pink - Eagle

Q.2 Which of the following is true in reference to Divya?
A.   She likes Black colour
B.   She likes Pink colour
C.   She likes Eagle
D.   She does not like Sparrow.
E.   She likes Orange colour

Q.3 Which of the following likes Eagle?
A. Ridhima   **B.** Riya   **C.** Nandini   **D.** Monika
E. Prerana

Q.4 Who amongst the following likes Orange colour?
A. Riya   **B.** Ishaan   **C.** Prerana   **D.** Monika
E. Divya

Q.5 Who among the following like ducks?
A. Monika   **B.** Nandini   **C.** Suman   **D.** Riya
E. Divya

Q.6 How many pairs of letters are there in the word "ACCUBATION" that has as many letters between them in the word as in the alphabet?
A. One   **B.** Two   **C.** Four   **D.** Seven
E. Five

Q.7 How many meaningful six letter English words can be formed, starting with M and ending with R, using each letter only once from the word MEGA and KEEPER?
A. None   **B.** One
C. Two   **D.** Three
E. More than three

Ques (8-10):Direction: Study the following information carefully and answer the question given below.

A person starts from point A and goes 6 km towards the east direction to reach point B. He then turns right and goes for 4 km to reach point C and then turns to his left and go 2 km to reach point D. After reaching point D he again takes a left turn and walks for 1 km to reach point E and then once again he takes a left turn to reach point F which is 8 km far from point E. He again takes a left turn and walks for 8 km to reach point G.

Q.8 What is the shortest between G and the point which is 3 km to the south of B?
A. 5 km   **B.** 6 km   **C.** 10 km   **D.** 7 km
E. 17 km

Q.9 What is the shortest distance between A and G?
A. 3 km   **B.** 8 km   **C.** 10 km   **D.** 11 km
E. 5 km

Q.10 What is the direction of D with respect to B?
A. North   **B.** South
C. North-East   **D.** South-East
E. South-West

Ques (11-12):Direction: Study the following information carefully and answer the questions that follow.

(i) A × B means 'A is the mother of B'.

(ii) A + B means 'A is the sister of B'.

(iii) A ÷ B means 'A is the father of B'.

(iv) A - B means 'A is the brother of B'.

Q.11 Which of the following means 'O is the niece of P'?
A. O - U ÷ J - P   **B.** P ÷ O - K
C. K - U ÷ O - P   **D.** P + U ÷ O + K
E. None of these

Q.12 Which of the following means 'H is the maternal grandfather of V'?
A. V ÷ T ÷ H   **B.** H ÷ T × V
C. H × T × V   **D.** H × T ÷ V
E. None of these

Ques (13-17):Direction: Study the following information and answer the questions that follow.

Seven people, namely P, Q, R, S, T, U, and V like seven different colours namely Red, Blue, Green, Yellow, Black, Pink, and Orange but not necessarily in the same order. Each people also works in the same office but at a different department on the basis of experience namely DTP, HR, Finance, Content, Marketing, Quality, and Administration.

Note: Each person has been allocated to a department as per increasing order of experience with the one in DTP being the least experienced whilst the one in Administration being the most experienced.

Only one person has less experience than U. The one who has less experience than U likes Yellow. Only one person has more experience than P. The one in Quality likes Black. Only two people have more experience than the one who likes Red. V likes Orange and has more experience than the one who likes Red. S has less experience than the one in Content, but more experience than the one who likes Green. T neither has the least experience nor he works in Marketing. Q does not work in Marketing. The one who likes Blue does not work in Content.

Q.13 As per the given arrangement, DTP is related to Yellow and Administration is related to Orange in a certain way. To which of the following is Finance related in the same way?

A. Green   **B.** Red   **C.** Pink   **D.** Black
E. Blue

Q.14 Which of the following pairs of people who have more experience than S but less experience than P?

A. V, R   **B.** Q, U   **C.** R, V   **D.** T, R
E. R, U

Q.15 Which combination represents the department that R works in and the colour he likes?

A. Marketing – Red   **B.** Content – Green
C. Marketing – Pink   **D.** Finance – Yellow
E. DTP – Yellow

Q.16 Who among the following works in DTP?

A. S   **B.** R
C. P   **D.** Q
E. None of these

Q.17 Which of the following colors does S like?

A. Green   **B.** Pink   **C.** Red   **D.** Yellow
E. Blue

Ques (18-20):Direction: In the following question, the symbols >, <, ≥, ≤, = are used with the following meanings as illustrated below-

'A > B' means 'A is either B or less than B'

'A < B' means 'A is neither greater than nor smaller than B'

'A ≥ B' means 'A is less than B'

'A ≤ B' means 'A greater than B'

'A = B' means 'A is equal to B'

Assuming the statements to be true, find which of the conclusion(s) given below follow(s)?

Q.18 Statement:

A = B; B ≥ C; D > C; D ≤ E
Conclusion:

I. D ≥ B

II. B > D

A. Both Conclusions I and II are true

B. Only Conclusion II is true

C. Only Conclusion I is true

D. Neither Conclusion I nor II is true

E. Either Conclusion I or II is true

Q.19 Statement-

M ≥ N = P < O ≥ Q

Conclusions-

I. N ≥ Q

II. M ≤ Q

A. Only conclusion I follows

B. Only conclusion II follows

C. Both conclusions I and II follow

D. Either conclusion I or II follows

E. Neither conclusion I nor II follows

Q.20 Statement:

B ≥ C = D ≥ X; E ≤ X; Z ≥ D

Conclusion:

I. B > E

II. Z ≥ B

A. Either Conclusion I or II is true

B. Neither Conclusion I nor II is true

C. Both Conclusions I and II are true

D. Only Conclusion I is true

E. Only Conclusion II is true

Ques (21-25):Direction: Study the following information carefully to answer the given questions:

Eight friends: A, B, C, D, E, F, G, and H - are sitting around two concentric tables. A, B, C, and D are seating on the inner square table(which was inside the circular table) along the corner, and E, F, G, and H are sitting on the outer circular table. People sitting at the circular tables are facing towards the center while those in the square tables are facing away from the center. Each person sitting at the inner square table is facing a person in the outer circle. 1, 2, 3, 4, 6, 7, 8, and 9 are a lucky number of these eight friends but not necessarily in the same order.

On the inner table, A sits at the diagonally opposite corner of B opposite to whom F sits on the outer table. All three of them have an even-numbered lucky number and among them, B has the smallest lucky number and F have the largest. C sits on the immediate right of B. C's lucky number is one-sixth of the lucky number of D. H sits opposite D having a lucky number which is half of D's lucky number. E cannot sit opposite A. E's lucky number is the largest of all.

Q.21 Whose lucky number is 7?

A. A   **B.** B   **C.** F   **D.** G
E. H

Q.22 Who sits opposite to A in the outer circular table?

A. B   **B.** E   **C.** F   **D.** G
E. H

Q.23 What is the lucky number of A?
A. 1   **B.** 2   **C.** 4   **D.** 6
E. 8

Q.24 What is the lucky number of D?
A. 1   **B.** 2   **C.** 4   **D.** 6
E. 8

Q.25 Who sits is to the immediate left of F?
A. E   **B.** G   **C.** H   **D.** B
E. C

Ques (26-30):Direction: Study the following information carefully and answer the questions given below:

L, M, N, O, P, Q, R, and D are sitting in a straight line equidistant from each other (but not necessarily in the same order). Some of them are facing south while some are facing north. (Note: Facing the same direction means, if one is facing north then the other is also facing north and if one is facing south then the other is also facing south. Facing the opposite directions means, if one is facing north then the other is facing south and vice versa.) L faces north. Only two persons sit to the right of L. M sits third to the left of L. Only one person sits between M and Q. Q sits on the immediate right of P. Only one person sits between P and D. Both the immediate neighbors of M face the same direction. N sits third to the left of Q. M faces the opposite directions of L. R does not sit at any of the extreme ends of the line. O faces the same direction as P. Both R and N face the opposite direction of D.

Q.26 How many persons in the given arrangement are facing south?
A. Two   **B.** Three
C. One   **D.** Four
E. More than four

Q.27 Four of the following five are alike in a certain way, and so form a group. Which of the following does not belong to the group?
A. O, M   **B.** Q, P   **C.** R, L   **D.** N, D
E. P, L

Q.28 What is the position of Q with respect to D?
A. Second to the right   **B.** Second to the left
C. Third to the right   **D.** Immediate right
E. Immediate left

Q.29 Who is sitting second to the right of M?
A. Q   **B.** P   **C.** O   **D.** D
E. L

Q.30 Who among the following sits exactly between D and P?
A. M   **B.** R   **C.** N   **D.** Q
E. D

Ques (31-35):Direction: These questions are based on the following information.

8 people: A, B, C, D, E, F, G, and H participated in a contest and secured ranks from 1 to 8. They work in different companies: Edugorilla, Google, BHEL, Wipro, Microsoft, HP, Infosys, and Wolfram.

D does not work at Google or HP and B does not work at Google. A person with a rank of 7 works at Wipro and a person with a rank of 6 at BHEL. The sum of ranks of G and H is 11 and the rank of H is more than that of G. C's rank is 3 and works at Infosys. G works at Microsoft. The rank of B is the sum of ranks of C and E. Rank of D is the sum of ranks of B and C. A works at Edugorilla. E's rank is 2.

Q.31 Who works at Wolfram?
A. A   **B.** B   **C.** C   **D.** D
E. E

Q.32 Where does B works?
A. Edugorilla   **B.** Wipro
C. Infosys   **D.** HP
E. None of these

Q.33 Who works at BHEL?
A. A   **B.** C   **C.** D   **D.** E
E. F

Q.34 What is the sum of ranks of A and H?
A. 4   **B.** 6
C. 8   **D.** 3
E. None of these

Q.35 Where does E work?
A. HP   **B.** BHEL   **C.** Google   **D.** Wipro
E. Wolfram

Ques (36-40):Direction: Study the following information carefully and answer the questions given below.

Eight students Kajal, Fatima, Deesha, Madhu, Rukhsar, Parul, Ira, and Prachi are going for the IBPS SO exam in a particular Exam Center on different shifts, on different days of April viz. 5th, 6th, 7th, and 8th but not necessarily in the same order. On each day, they will attend the exam at 10 am or at 12 pm. Only one student will attend the exam on these given shifts.

Two students will attend the exam between Kajal and Parul. Deesha will attend the exam after Madhu. Two students will attend the exam between Rukhsar and Ira. Only one student will attend the exam between Parul and Fatima. Four students will attend the exam between Rukhsar and Prachi. Fatima will attend the exam on the 7th. There is no one between Fatima and Ira. Rukhsar will attend the exam at 12 pm on any of the given days but before Ira.

Q.36 How many students will attend the exam between Madhu and Ira?
A. Two   **B.** Ihree   **C.** Four   **D.** Five
E. One

Q.37 Who among the following will attend the exam on 5th April?
A. Deesha   **B.** Madhu   **C.** Parul   **D.** Ira
E. Kajal

Q.38 Who among following will attend the exam on 10 am of 8th April?
A. Prachi   **B.** Madhu   **C.** Deesha   **D.** Fatima

E. Parul

Q.39 How many students will attend the exam after Deesha?

A. One   **B.** Two   **C.** Three   **D.** No one
E. Four

Q.40 Madhu attends the exam on which of the following schedule?

A. 10 am; 6ᵗʰ April   **B.** 10 am; 7ᵗʰ April
C. 12 pm; 7ᵗʰ April   **D.** 12 pm; 8ᵗʰ April
E. None of these

Quantitative Aptitude

Ques (41-45):Direction: The pie charts given below show the number of officers in Scale I and in Scale II in five different cities. Study the charts carefully and answer the question that follows-

Scale I Officers - 250

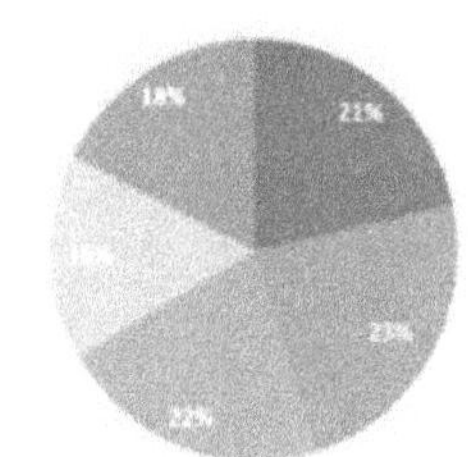

Scale II Officers - 120

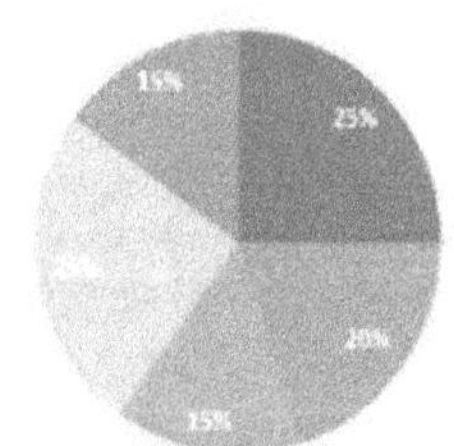

Q.41 Scale I officers in Mumbai and Kolkata together is what percent more than scale II officers in Odisha, Chennai, and Assam together?

A. 75%   **B.** 50%   **C.** $33\frac{1}{3}$ **D.** 32%
E. 125%

Q.42 Find the ratio of Scale I officers in Mumbai and Assam together to Scale II officers in Kolkata and Chennai together?

A. 7 : 5   **B.** 5 : 3   **C.** 8 : 5   **D.** 9 : 5
E. 9 : 4

Q.43 An average number of scale I officer in Odisha, Kolkata, and Chennai together is how much more than an average number of scale II officers in Odisha, Kolkata, and Mumbai together?

A. 22   **B.** 24   **C.** 26   **D.** 28
E. 30

Q.44 In Kolkata, HR officers and Management officers under scale I are in the ratio 5 : 3 while it is 2 : 3 under scale II. Find the total number of HR officers in Kolkata if only two types of officers are working under Scale I and Scale II.

A. 21   **B.** 18   **C.** 30   **D.** 24
E. 37

Q.45 In the Manipur scale, I officers and scale II officers are in the ratio 5 : 6. If scale I officers in Manipur in 25% more than scale II officers in Odisha, then find the total number of scale I and scale II officers in Manipur

A. 60   **B.** 66   **C.** 72   **D.** 78
E. 86

Q.46 An amount was divided among three brothers - Neel, Nitin, and Mukesh. The ratio of Neel's share to that of Mukesh's share is _______. Mukesh got half as much as Neel and Nitin together got. Neel got $\frac{1}{3}$rd of what Nitin and Mukesh together got.

A. 4 : 5   **B.** 5 : 6
C. 6 : 5   **D.** 3 : 4
E. None of these

Q.47 Find the compound interest on rupees 12000 at 16% per annum for 9 months compounded quarterly.

A. Rs. 1342.425   **B.** Rs. 1252.256
C. Rs. 1562. 45   **D.** Rs. 1498.368
E. Rs. 1542.425

Q.48 There are 3 mixtures A, B, and C of Alcohol and water. The ratios of Alcohol and Water in these mixtures are 5 : 3, 2 : 3, and 7 : 3. These mixtures are taken in the ratio of capacities 2 : 4 : 3 and stored in a vessel then find the ratio of alcohol and water in it.

A. 7 : 3   **B.** 13 : 7   **C.** 3 : 1   **D.** 11 : 9
E. 7 : 13

Q.49 In what time will rupees 8000 become rupees 9261 at 5% per annum compounded annually.

A. 2 years   **B.** 3 years
C. 4 years   **D.** 5 years
E. None of these

Q.50 The product of two numbers is 4107 if the HCF of the numbers is 37, the greatest number is

A. 185   **B.** 111   **C.** 107   **D.** 101
E. 100

Q.51 LCM of two numbers is 2079 and their HCF is 27. If one of the numbers is 189, the other number is:

A. 297   **B.** 584   **C.** 189   **D.** 216
E. 210

Ques (52-55):Direction: In the following question, two equations numbered I and II are given. You have to solve both the equation and the given answer.

Q.52 I. $21x^2 - 23x + 6 = 0$

II. $28y^2 - 41y + 15 = 0$

A. If x > y

B. If x < y
C. If x ≥ y
D. If x ≤ y
E. If x = y or no relation can be established.

Q.53 I. $6x^2 - 47x + 77 = 0$
II. $18y^2 - 81y + 91 = 0$
A. If x > y
B. If x < y
C. If x ≥ y
D. If x ≤ y
E. If x = y or no relation can be established.

Q.54 I. $x^2 - 5(\sqrt{3} + 2\sqrt{2})x + 50\sqrt{6} = 0$
II. $y^2 - (3\sqrt{5} + 2\sqrt{7})y + 6\sqrt{35} = 0$
A. If x > y
B. If x < y
C. If x ≥ y
D. If x ≤ y
E. If x = y or no relation can be established.

Q.55 I. $\sqrt{(x + 153)} - 6 = 7$
II. $\sqrt{(y - 12)} = \sqrt{1156} - \sqrt{1024}$
A. If x > y
B. If x < y
C. If x ≥ y
D. If x ≤ y
E. If x = y or no relation can be established.

Ques (56-57):Direction: Read the following paragraph and answer the following question based on the data given:

James is a manufacturer of TV sets and refrigerators. He sells his products to a wholesaler Paul and Paul then sells them to a retailer Antony. The customer purchases goods from the retailer. The cost of manufacturing a TV set is Rs. 10,000 and a refrigerator is Rs. 20,000. Each of James, Paul, and Antony makes a profit of 10% on each TV set and refrigerator sold.

A customer buys 2 TV sets and 3 refrigerators from Antony and then resells them. He makes a loss of 5% on selling the 2 TV sets and a profit of 5% on selling 3 refrigerators.

Q.56 Find his total profit/loss percentage?
A. 2.5% profit
B. 2.5% loss
C. 5% loss
D. 5% profit
E. Neither profit nor loss

Q.57 If the cost of manufacturing a TV set goes up by 2% and that of a refrigerator goes up by 5% and the percentage of profit made by James, Paul and Antony remain unchanged. Find the total amount that a customer needs to pay to buy 1 TV set and 1 refrigerator? (Ignore the decimal part)
A. Rs. 41277
B. Rs. 41227
C. Rs. 41557
D. Rs. 41727
E. Rs. 41527

Q.58 The LCM of two numbers is 1820 and their HCF is 26. If one number is 130, then the other number is:

[MP Sub Inspector (MPSI), 2017]

A. 70
B. 1690
C. 364
D. 1264
E. 1000

Q.59 In a class of 60 students, 30% are girls. In a class test, the class average was 17 out of 30 marks. 50% of the girls went for an inter-school basketball match and could not take the test. Initially, the teacher assumed them to be absent and gave them 0 marks. If the teacher has to award each of the 20 marks, find the new class average.
A. 18
B. 21
C. 20
D. 17
E. 19

Q.60 What is $\dfrac{5+\sqrt{10}}{5\sqrt{5}-2\sqrt{20}-\sqrt{32}+\sqrt{50}}$ equal to?
A. 5
B. $5\sqrt{2}$
C. $5\sqrt{5}$
D. $\sqrt{5}$
E. 10

Q.61 What is the value of $\dfrac{(443+547)^2+(443-547)^2}{443\times443+547\times547}$?
A. 0
B. 1
C. 2
D. 3
E. 4

Q.62 What will come in the place of the question mark '?' in the following question?

$$1\tfrac{1}{2} + 11\tfrac{1}{2} + 111\tfrac{1}{2} + 1111\tfrac{1}{2} + 11111\tfrac{1}{2} = ?$$

A. $12347\tfrac{1}{2}$
B. $12346\tfrac{1}{2}$
C. $12345\tfrac{1}{2}$
D. $\tfrac{1}{2}$
E. None of these

Q.63 A started a business with a capital of Rs. 1,00,000. One year later, B joined him with a capital of Rs. 2,00,000. At the end of 3 years from the start of the business, the profit earned was 84,000. The share of B in the profit exceeded the share of A by
A. Rs. 18,000
B. Rs. 14,000
C. Rs. 12,000
D. Rs. 16,000
E. None of these

Q.64 Atul started a business with investing Rs. 8000 and after some months, Balu joined with investing Rs. 6000. At the end of one year, the total profit was Rs. 4375 and the share of Atul is Rs. 2800. For how many months did Balu joined the business?
A. 4
B. 9
C. 5
D. 2
E. None of these

Q.65 A and B started a business in partnership by investing Rs. 10,000 and Rs. 4000 respectively. The condition of partnership is that B will get Rs. 1200 from the annual profit for the management of the business. A and B also paid 5% interest for their capital from their profit amount. The remaining annual profit is distributed between them in the ratio of their investment. Find the total share of A in the total annual profit of Rs. 4000.
A. Rs. 3000
B. Rs. 2500
C. Rs. 1500
D. Rs. 2000

E. None of these

Ques (66-70):Direction: What should come in place of the question mark '?' in the following number series?

Q.66 6, 15, 42, ? , 366
A. 320   B. 190   C. 220   D. 123
E. 198

Q.67 11, 31, 71, 151, ?, 631
A. 332   B. 190   C. 420   D. 311
E. 320

Q.68 7, 28, 70, 154, ?, 558
A. 320   B. 280   C. 322   D. 205
E. 220

Q.69 4, 14, 44, 134, ?
A. 234   B. 404   C. 224   D. 334
E. 444

Q.70 44, 59, 76, 95, ?
A. 109   B. 116   C. 121   D. 106
E. 220

Q.71 The amount of water (in ml) that should be added to convert 9 ml lotion, containing 50% alcohol, to a lotion containing 30% alcohol is?
A. 6 ml   B. 11 ml
C. 15 ml   D. 9 ml
E. None of these

Q.72 A jar was full with honey. A person used to draw out 20% of the honey from the jar and replaced it with sugar solution. He has repeated the same process a total of 4 times and thus there was only 512 gm of honey left in the jar, the rest part of the jar was filled with the sugar solution. The initial amount of honey in the jar was filled with the sugar solution. The initial amount of honey in the jar was:
A. 1.25 kg   B. 1 kg
C. 1.5 kg   D. 2.5 kg
E. None of these

Q.73 A container contains 50 liters of milk. From that 8 liters of milk was taken out and replaced by water. This process was repeated further two times. How much milk is now contained by the container?
A. 24.52 liters   B. 29.63 liters
C. 28.21 liters   D. 25.14 liters
E. 30.14 liters

Q.74 Which of the following rational numbers is the largest?
A. $\frac{1}{3}$ B. $\frac{2}{5}$ C. $\frac{4}{7}$ D. $\frac{5}{9}$
E. $\frac{1}{2}$

Q.75 Cube root of 4096 is:
A. 24   B. 14   C. 16   D. 12
E. 15

Q.76 Direction: Given below are two quantities named A and B. Based on the given information, you have to determine the relationship between the two quantities. You should use the given data and your knowledge of Mathematics to choose between the possible answers.

Quantity A: x where $4x^2 - 5x + 1 = 0$
Quantity B: y where $y^2 - 3y + 2 = 0$
A. Quantity A > Quantity B
B. Quantity A < Quantity B
C. Quantity A ≥ Quantity B
D. Quantity A ≤ Quantity B
E. Quantity A = Quantity B OR relationship cannot be determined

Q.77 Find HCF and LCM of 28 & 42.
A. 84, 14   B. 14, 42   C. 14, 84   D. 42, 14
E. 84, 14

Q.78 Which of the following is not a perfect cube?
A. 27   B. 64
C. 216   D. 432
E. None of these

Ques (79-80):Direction: Given below are two quantities named A and B. Based on the given information, you have to determine the relation between the two quantities. You should use the given data and your knowledge of Mathematics to choose between the possible answers.

Q.79 Quantity A: x where $x^3 - 4x^2 + 3x = 0$
Quantity B: y where $7y^3 - 23y^2 + 6y = 0$
A. Quantity A > Quantity B
B. Quantity A < Quantity B
C. Quantity A ≥ Quantity B
D. Quantity A ≤ Quantity B
E. Quantity A = Quantity B OR relationship cannot be determined

Q.80 N is a natural number
Quantity A: Sum of cubes of first N odd natural numbers
Quantity B: Sum of cubes of first (N - 1) even natural numbers
A. Quantity A > Quantity B
B. Quantity A < Quantity B
C. Quantity A ≥ Quantity B
D. Quantity A ≤ Quantity B
E. Quantity A = Quantity B OR relationship cannot be determined

// Smart Answer Sheet //

Correct	Percentage of students who answered correctly.	Skipped	Percentage of students who skipped.

Q.	Ans.	Correct / Skipped	Q.	Ans.	Correct / Skipped	Q.	Ans.	Correct / Skipped	Q.	Ans.	Correct / Skipped	Q.	Ans.	Correct / Skipped	Q.	Ans.	Correct / Skipped	Q.	Ans.	Correct / Skipped
1	A	65.81 % / 12.21 %	15	A	17.39 % / 39.57 %	29	C	27.94 % / 37.91 %	43	C	14.98 % / 43.91 %	57	E	0.95 % / 52.96 %	71	A	4.66 % / 57.87 %
2	E	61.38 % / 16.25 %	16	D	19.49 % / 38.81 %	30	A	30.91 % / 37.23 %	44	E	10.32 % / 47.47 %	58	C	36.17 % / 39.64 %	72	A	3.91 % / 61.35 %
3	E	55.3 % / 17.59 %	17	E	16.68 % / 37.75 %	31	D	30.83 % / 34.47 %	45	B	8.77 % / 48.15 %	59	C	6.92 % / 51.14 %	73	B	4.7 % / 62.45 %
4	E	62.29 % / 17.55 %	18	E	14.82 % / 27.2 %	32	D	39.09 % / 35.42 %	46	D	8.22 % / 43.87 %	60	D	30.4 % / 42.52 %	74	C	3.44 % / 62.84 %
5	C	61.54 % / 17.87 %	19	A	8.26 % / 27.67 %	33	E	33.32 % / 36.4 %	47	D	25.18 % / 36.76 %	61	C	9.25 % / 49.33 %	75	C	3.68 % / 61.97 %
6	C	52.21 % / 14.15 %	20	B	29.05 % / 29.33 %	34	C	35.45 % / 37.0 %	48	D	7.51 % / 46.56 %	62	A	6.4 % / 52.73 %	76	D	15.61 % / 50.87 %
7	C	7.19 % / 32.45 %	21	D	13.64 % / 39.88 %	35	C	34.86 % / 36.76 %	49	B	20.36 % / 41.97 %	63	C	5.77 % / 54.43 %	77	C	3.0 % / 55.22 %
8	C	38.26 % / 21.7 %	22	D	12.25 % / 43.72 %	36	E	9.25 % / 46.17 %	50	B	6.4 % / 47.63 %	64	B	9.8 % / 53.88 %	78	D	7.11 % / 59.1 %
9	D	38.34 % / 20.51 %	23	C	14.86 % / 44.67 %	37	E	9.25 % / 52.33 %	51	A	5.18 % / 43.91 %	65	D	7.15 % / 53.8 %	79	E	8.66 % / 57.23 %
10	D	56.4 % / 18.98 %	24	D	14.15 % / 44.82 %	38	A	11.34 % / 53.92 %	52	B	23.0 % / 38.98 %	66	D	39.05 % / 39.8 %	80	A	6.6 % / 60.2 %
11	D	37.91 % / 22.17 %	25	A	10.87 % / 43.52 %	39	D	11.3 % / 54.04 %	53	C	12.21 % / 43.13 %	67	D	44.35 % / 39.68 %			
12	B	38.02 % / 23.84 %	26	D	25.93 % / 35.06 %	40	A	9.8 % / 53.28 %	54	A	4.43 % / 49.17 %	68	C	30.83 % / 43.6 %			
13	E	15.14 % / 35.93 %	27	E	20.79 % / 38.38 %	41	D	14.31 % / 36.24 %	55	E	10.32 % / 46.52 %	69	B	37.55 % / 42.09 %			
14	D	19.37 % / 38.26 %	28	C	31.23 % / 37.94 %	42	B	21.58 % / 41.11 %	56	A	3.28 % / 50.36 %	70	B	40.91 % / 42.73 %			

Reasoning

Q.1 Four options have been given out of which three are alike in some manner, while one is different. Choose the odd one.

A. 97   **B.** 135   **C.** 167   **D.** 199
E. 200

Q.2 In a certain code 'LIGHT' is written as 'JMTUI', then how will 'VALUE' be written in the same language?

A. BWMFV   **B.** WBOVF
C. BWOFV   **D.** WBMVF
E. BWPVF

Ques (3-5):Direction: In a certain code language, "break the old rule" is written as "te od ul re", "follow the tough rule" is written as "gu lw te ul", "rule is always tough" is written as "wa mn ul gu".

Q.3 What is the code for 'rule?

A. te   **B.** ul   **C.** gu   **D.** lw
E. re

Q.4 What is the code for 'break'?

A. od   **B.** re
C. te   **D.** Either 'od' or 're'
E. Either 're' or 'te'

Q.5 What is the code for 'always follow'?

A. lw wa   **B.** mn te
C. mn lw   **D.** Either (A) or (B)
E. Either (A) or (C)

Ques (6-10):Direction: Read the following information carefully and answer the question asked below.

There are seven friends Tanu, Deepak, Jyoti, Vijay, Indu, Laxmi and Jeetu are going for the exam in a week starting from Monday to Sunday (of the same week) but not necessarily in the same order. Only one person goes for an exam on each day.

Deepak goes for the exam on Thursday. Deepak does not go immediately before or immediately after Indu. Only one friend goes for the exam between Tanu and Deepak. Only one person goes for the exam between Deepak and Jyoti. Jyoti does not go for the exam before Tanu. Only one friend goes for the exam between Indu and Laxmi. Vijay goes for the exam either immediately before or immediately after Jyoti. Vijay goes for the exam one of the days after Jeetu.

Q.6 On which day Indu goes for the exam?

A. Monday   **B.** Wednesday
C. Friday   **D.** Saturday
E. Sunday

Q.7 Who among the following goes for the exam on Sunday?

A. Indu   **B.** Jeetu   **C.** Vijay   **D.** Laxmi
E. Jyoti

Q.8 Who goes for the exam immediate before Deepak?

A. Jeetu   **B.** Laxmi   **C.** Indu   **D.** Vijay
E. Jyoti

Q.9 Which of the following combination is false?

A. Deepak – Thursday   **B.** Tanu – Tuesday
C. Jyoti – Saturday   **D.** Vijay – Friday
E. Indu – Monday

Q.10 How many friends give exam in between Indu and Jeetu?

A. None   **B.** One   **C.** Two   **D.** Three
E. Four

Q.11 Which of the following symbols should replace the sign (&) and (#) in the expression 'M > P ≥ D & E < R ≤ A = C # Q ≥ T' in order to make the expressions C > D and A ≥ T definitely true?

A. ≥, >   **B.** ≤, ≤
C. <, =   **D.** =, ≥
E. Both (C) and (D)

Ques (12-14):Direction: In the question below are given two statements followed by two conclusions numbered I and II. You have to take the given statements to be true even if they seem to be at variance with commonly known facts. Read all the conclusions and then decide which of the given conclusions logically follows from the given statements disregarding commonly known facts.

Q.12 Statement:

Only fruits are apples.

Some apples are green.

Conclusion:

I. Some fruits are green.

II. No fruit is green.

A.   Only I follows
B.   Only II follows
C.   Either I or II follows
D.   Neither I nor II follows
E.   Both I and II follow

Q.13 Statement:

All candle is wax.

No wax is light.

Conclusion:

I. Some candle being light is a possibility.

II. Some wax is not light.

A.   Only I follows
B.   Only II follows
C.   Either I or II follows
D.   Neither I nor II follows
E.   Both I and II follow

Q.14 Statement:

All heart is good.

Very few good is excellent.

Conclusion:

I. Very few hearts are excellent.

II. No heart is excellent.

A. Only I follows

B. Only II follows

C. Either I or II follows

D. Neither I nor II follows

E. Both I and II follow.

Ques (15-16):Direction: In the following question assuming the given statement to be true. Find which of the following conclusion(s) among given conclusions is/are definitely true then give your answer accordingly.

Q.15 Statement: Z < M ≥ Y, Y ≥ N > L

Conclusion:

I. Z < L

II. M > L

A. None is true

B. Only II is true

C. Both I and II are true

D. Only I is true

E. Either I or II is true

Q.16 Statement: 1 > 2 ≥ 3 = 4, 5 < 6 ≤ 7 < 4

Conclusion:

I. 1 > 7

II. 2 ≥ 6

A. Only I is true

B. Only II is true

C. Both I and II are true

D. None is true

E. Either I or II is true.

Ques (17-21):Direction: Read the information carefully and answer the question asked below.

Eight persons Mohit, Lalita, Harsh, Trikesh, Bala, Ekta, Kajal and sunil are sitting around circular table but not necessarily in the same order. Some of them are facing the centre while others are facing outside the centre. Lalita is sitting third left to Sunil, who is facing towards the centre. Ekta is sitting second to the right of Lalita. Mohit and Trikesh sit opposite to each other. Trikesh is not the immediate neighbour of lalita. Bala sits second to the left of Mohit. Kajal sits second to the left Ekta. Immediate neighbours of lalita are facing opposite direction. Trikesh faces outside of the centre. Harsh sits immediate to the left Trikesh. Kajal and Hrash are facing the same direction as that of ekta.

Q.17 Who among the following are immediate neighbors of Trikesh?

A. Kajal, Ekta

B. Harsh, Kajal

C. Ekta, Bala

D. Bala, Harsh

E. Mohit, Kajal

Q.18 What is the position of Ekta with respect to Sunil?

A. Immediate to the right

B. Second to the right

C. Immediate to the left

D. Third to the right

E. Second to the left

Q.19 Which of the following is true about Bala?

A. Bala sits immediate right of Harsh

B. Bala sits second to the right of Mohit

C. Two people sit between Bala and Sunil

D. Lalita and Harsh are immediate neighbors of Bala

E. All are true

Q.20 How many persons sit between Kajal and Mohit when counted anticlockwise from Mohit?

A. One   B. Two   C. Three   D. Four

E. None

Q.21 Four are the same in a certain way out of five. Which of the following is different from others?

A. Ekta   B. Kajal   C. Harsh   D. Bala

E. Mohit

Q.22 Given below is a question and two statements numbered I and II given below it. You have to decide whether the data provided in the statements is sufficient to answer the question. You should use the given data and your knowledge of Mathematics to choose between the possible answers.

What will be the day of week on 26th March this year?

I. This year is a leap year.

II. The first day of last year was a Sunday.

A. The data in statement I alone is sufficient to answer the question, while the data in statement II alone is not sufficient to answer the question.

B. The data in statement II alone is sufficient to answer the question, while the data in statement I alone is not sufficient to answer the question.

C. The data in statement I alone or in statement II alone is sufficient to answer the question.

D. The data in both the statements I and II is not sufficient to answer the question.

E. The data in both the statements I and II together is necessary to answer the question.

Q.23 Directions: The question below consists of a question and two statements I and II given below it. You have to decide whether the data provided in the statements are sufficient to answer the question. Read both the statements and give answer.

How many daughter does Y have?

I. E and Q are the only daughters of N.

II. D is the only brother of E and son of Y.

A. Data in statement I alone are sufficient to answer the question, while the data in statement II alone are not sufficient to answer the question.

B. Data in statement II alone are sufficient to answer the question, while the data in statement I alone are not sufficient to answer the question.

C. Data either in statement I alone or in statement II alone are sufficient to answer the question.

D. Data given in both the statements I and II together are not sufficient to answer the question.

E. Data in both the statements I and II together are necessary to answer the question.

Q.24 Directions: The question below consists of a question and two statements numbered I and II given below it. You have to decide whether the data provided in the statements are sufficient to answer the question. Read both the statements and give answer.

Among P, Q, R, S and T sitting in a straight line, facing North, who sits exactly in the middle of the line?

I. P sits third to left of S. T is an immediate neighbor of P as well as R.

II. T sits second to left of S. Q is not an immediate neighbor of either T or S.

A. Data in statements I alone are sufficient to answer the question, while the data in Statement II alone are not sufficient to answer the question.

B. Data in statement II alone are sufficient to answer the question, while the data in Statement I alone are not sufficient to answer the question.

C. Data in either Statement I alone or in Statement II alone are sufficient to answer the question.

D. Data in neither Statement I alone or in Statement II alone are sufficient to answer the question.

E. Data in both the Statement I and II together are necessary to answer the question.

Q.25 Directions: The question below consists of a question and two statements I and II given below it. You have to decide whether the data provided in the statements are sufficient to answer the question. Read both the statements and give answer.

Who is tallest among A, B, C and D?

I. A is taller than D, who is taller than B.

II. C is shorter than B.

A. Data in Statements I alone are sufficient to answer the question, while the data in Statement II alone are not sufficient to answer the question.

B. Data in Statement II alone are sufficient to answer the question, while the data in Statement I alone are not sufficient to answer the question.

C. Data in Statement I alone or in Statement II alone are sufficient to answer the question.

D. Data in both the Statements I and II are not sufficient to answer the question.

E. Data in both the Statements I and II together are necessary to answer the question.

Ques (26-30):Direction: Study the following series carefully and answer the question given below.

Q.26 A @ D 1 5 % K & 6 I 9 # V 8 E 3 ¥ 7 M L 2 U € F S © 9 1 X Z

How many such letters are there in the series each of which is immediately preceded by a symbol and followed by cube number?

A. One   **B.** Two   **C.** Three   **D.** Four

E. None

Q.27 A @ D 1 5 % K & 6 I 9 # V 8 E 3 ¥ 7 M L 2 U € F S © 9 1 X Z

If all the numbers in the above arrangement are deleted then which among the following element is ninth form the right end?

A. ¥   **B.** U   **C.** M   **D.** V

E. #

Q.28 A @ D 1 5 % K & 6 I 9 # V 8 E 3 ¥ 7 M L 2 U € F S © 9 1 X Z

If '@' is related to 'X', '5' is related to '©' in a certain way then 'K' is related to which of the following in the same way?

A. €   **B.** F   **C.** ¥   **D.** S

E. 8

Q.29 A @ D 1 5 % K & 6 I 9 # V 8 E 3 ¥ 7 M L 2 U € F S © 9 1 X Z

Which among the following element is second to the left of the tenth element from the left end?

A. 2   **B.** €   **C.** I   **D.** #

E. &

Q.30 A @ D 1 5 % K & 6 I 9 # V 8 E 3 ¥ 7 M L 2 U € F S © 9 1 X Z

Four of the five given in the options are same in a certain way. Choose the option which is different from others.

A. M7L   **B.** %5K   **C.** V#8   **D.** U2€

E. I96

Ques (31-33):Direction: Read the information carefully and answer the questions asked below.

Q.31 K is the aunt of R, who is the son of M. M is the spouse of N. N is the daughter-in-law of L, who is the father of K.

How N is related to R?

A. Daughter   **B.** Mother

C. Son   **D.** Cousin

E. Niece

Q.32 K is the aunt of R, who is the son of M. M is the spouse of N. N is the daughter-in-law of L, who is the father of K.

If K is married to J. How J is related to M?

A. Son-in-law   **B.** Father-in-law

C. Brother-in-law   **D.** Sister-in-law

E. None of these

Q.33 K is the aunt of R, who is the son of M. M is the spouse of N. N is the daughter-in-law of L, who is the father of K.

If O is the only child of K. How O is related to L?

A. Grandfather

B. Grandmother

C. Grandson

D. Granddaughter

E. Cannot be determined

Ques (34-35):Direction: Read the information carefully and answer the questions asked below.

Q.34 Point O is 16 m north of point C. Point L is 10 m east of point O. Point C is 6 m west of point D, which is 8 m south of point A.

What is the distance between point C and point A?

A. 8 m   **B.** 6 m   **C.** 10 m   **D.** 12 m
E. 15 m

Q.35 Point O is 16 m north of point C. Point L is 10 m east of point O. Point C is 6 m west of point D, which is 8 m south of point A.

Point A is in which direction with respect to O?

A. North - East   **B.** South - East
C. South – West   **D.** South
E. North - West

Ques (36-38):Direction: Read the following information carefully and answer the question that follows:

Darshana moved 1 km South to reach point P. She turns 60° to her left and goes 7 km to point Q. She takes a 150° turn to her right and goes 12 km to reach point R. Now she turns 120° to her right and goes 9 km to reach S.

Q.36 Starting Pointis in which direction with respect to R?

A. Northeast   **B.** Northwest
C. Southeast   **D.** East
E. Southwest

Q.37 Point S is in which direction with respect to point Q?

A. Northwest   **B.** Southeast
C. Northeast   **D.** East
E. Southwest

Q.38 What is the total distance covered by Darshana when she reaches point S?

A. 25 km   **B.** 49 km   **C.** 30 km   **D.** 29 km
E. 20 km

Ques (39-40):Directions: The critical reasoning question given below consists of passage followed by two questions involving three statements. You must read the passage and statements carefully and choose the correct answer from the alternatives given below.

We must inculcate good manners in children from childhood itself. Words like "Sorry" and "Thank You" must become part of our daily vocabulary so that together we can build a civilised society. We must also teach them to be kind and understanding towards fellow human beings. They must learn to empathise with others. These things, if done effectively, can greatly curtail the intolerance that is prevalent in our nation today. Tomorrow, at least, will be brighter.

Q.39 Which of the following can be inferred from the passage above?

A. The present generation was not taught good manners at all.

B. Saying "Sorry" and "Thank You" wherever required are part of good manners.

C. Civilized societies elsewhere have successfully proved that improving empathy and civic sense will eliminate intolerance.

D. Both (A) and (B)
E. None of the above

Q.40 Which of the above incidents, if true, best repudiates the argument put forward by the passage?

A. Mr. A was born to a rich family, was taught good manners and empathy effectively, but was convicted for mob-lynching.

B. Mr. B was born to a poor family, behaved rudely in general, but rescued a person who was being mob lynched.

C. Mr. C was an alcoholic and drug addict but still had good manners.

D. Both (A) and (B)
E. None of the above

Quantitative Aptitude

Q.41 What should come in place of question Mark '?' in the following number series?

9, 5, 6, 10.5, 23, ?

A. 50   **B.** 65   **C.** 70   **D.** 55
E. 60

Q.42 What should come in place of question mark '?' in the following number series?

34, 10, 50, 18, ?

A. 28   **B.** 58   **C.** 68   **D.** 42
E. 8

Q.43 What should come in place of question mark '?' in the following number series?

$$\frac{-1}{2}, 1, \frac{7}{2}, ?, \frac{23}{2}$$

A. $\frac{17}{2}$ **B.** $\frac{15}{2}$ **C.** 9   **D.** 7
E. 6

Q.44 What should come in place of question Mark '?' in the following number series?

50, 45, 36, ? , 15.12, 7.56

A. 25.12   **B.** 27.56   **C.** 25.2   **D.** 30
E. 25

Ques (45-50): In the following question, two equations numbered I and II are given. Solve both the equations and give an answer.

Q.45 I. $2x^2 - 17x + 36 = 0$

II. $3y^2 - 4y - 32 = 0$

A. x > y
B. x < y
C. x ≥ y
D. x ≤ y
E. x = y or no relationship could be established.

Q.46 (I). $3x + 5y = 18$

(II). $7x + 8y = 42$

A. if $x < y$
B. If $x \geq y$
C. If $x \leq y$

D. If $x > y$
E. If $x = y$ or no relationship can be established

Q.47 I. $15x^2 - 19x + 6 = 0$
II. $45y^2 - 47y + 12 = 0$
A. $x < y$
B. $x \le y$
C. $x > y$
D. $x \ge y$
E. $x = y$ or no relationship can be obtained

Q.48 I. $(625)^{\frac{1}{4}}x + \sqrt{1225} = 155$
II. $\sqrt{196y} + 13 = 279$
A. If x > y
B. If x < y
C. If x ≥ y
D. If x ≤ y
E. If x = y or relation cannot be established.

Q.49 I. $12x^2 + 11x - 56 = 0$
II. $4y^2 - 15y + 14 = 0$
A. x > y
B. x < y
C. x ≥ y
D. x ≤ y
E. x = y or relation cannot be established

Q.50 I. $7x + 4y = 3$
II. $5x + 3y = 3$
A. x > y
B. x < y
C. x ≥ y
D. x ≤ y
E. x = y or relation cannot be established

Ques (51-54):Direction: Study the table and answer the questions. The number of 5 types of cycles manufactured by a company over the years is given below:

Years	Types of cycles (in 1000)				
	A	B	C	D	E
1997	200	150	78	90	65
1998	150	180	100	105	70
1999	180	175	92	110	85
2000	195	160	120	125	75
2001	220	185	130	135	80

Q.51 What was the approximate percentage decrease in production of 'D' type of the cycle from 2000 to 1998?
A. 10   **B.** 19   **C.** 15   **D.** 17
E. 16

Q.52 In the case of which type of cycles was total production of the given 5 years was the maximum?
A. A   **B.** B   **C.** C   **D.** D
E. E

Q.53 What was the percentage drop in production of A type cycle from 1997 to 1999?

A. 10   **B.** 25   **C.** 20   **D.** 15
E. 30

Q.54 The production of E type of cycle in 2001 was what percent of production of B type in 2000?
A. 40   **B.** 50   **C.** 45   **D.** 25
E. 35

Q.55 The average temperature in the first three days of a week is 45 degrees and average for the second, third and fourth day is 46 degrees. The temperature on the first day is $93\frac{3}{4}$% of the temperature on the fourth day. Find the average temperature on the first and fourth day of the week.
A. 31.0 degrees   **B.** 42.5 degrees
C. 46.5 degrees   **D.** 48.5 degrees
E. 47.5 degrees

Q.56 A, B and C are working together to complete a piece of work for Rs. 15000. A and B together are supposed to do 60% of the work and B and C together $\frac{2}{3}$ of the work. Then, wages of A is what percent of wages of C?
A. 83.33%   **B.** 80%   **C.** 39.76%   **D.** 12%
E. 66.67%

Q.57 In a mixture of 50 liters, ratio of sucrose solution to glucose solution is 3 : 1. What amount of glucose solution must be added in the mixture so that new sucrose to glucose solution will be 1 : 3?
A. 50 liters   **B.** 75 liters
C. 86 liters   **D.** 95 liters
E. 100 liters

Q.58 A vessel is full of Petrol. $\frac{1}{4}$th of the Petrol is taken out and replaced with kerosene oil. If the process is repeated 3 more time, 81 litres of Petrol is finally left in the vessel. Find the capacity of vessel.
A. 144 L   **B.** 256 L   **C.** 625 L   **D.** 512 L
E. 324 L

Q.59 A sum of money was invested for 2 years at the rate of 10% compounded annually. After that, the received amount is invested for another 3 years at rate of 15% simple interest. Finally, the amount becomes Rs. 1, 75, 450. _____ is the initial sum of money that was invested?

[SBI Clerk, 2019]

A. 110000   **B.** 100000   **C.** 140000   **D.** 160000
E. 130000

Q.60 Ram gave 50% of his total saving Rs. 1682 to his wife and distributed the reaming amount between his two sons Rahul and Ravi. The age of Rahul and Ravi at that time was 18 years and 16 years respectively. He divides the money in such a way that each son when they attain the age of 21 years, would receive the same amount at 5% interest compounded annually. What was the amount given to Ravi?
A. Rs. 541   **B.** Rs. 841   **C.** Rs. 441   **D.** Rs. 400
E. Rs. 141

Q.61 Mohit can go on a motorboat at a speed of 15 km/hour in still water to a certain upstream point and comes back to the starting point in a river which flows at a speed of 5 km/hour. Find the average speed of the motorboat for the whole journey.

A. $11\frac{2}{3}$ km/h

B. $11\frac{1}{3}$ km/h

C. $13\frac{1}{3}$ km/h

D. $13\frac{2}{3}$ km/h

E. None of these

Q.62 A train overtakes two persons who are walking in the same direction in which the train is going at the rate of 3 km/hr and 6 km/hr and passes them completely in 36 sec and 60 sec respectively. Find the length of train (in m).

A. 82 m   **B.** 70 m   **C.** 72.5 m   **D.** 65 m

E. 75 m

Q.63 Ram alone can complete a job in 30 days. Shyam alone can complete the same job in 20 days. Ram works for 18 days and then the remaining job is completed by Shyam. How many days will it take Shyam to complete the remaining job alone?

A. 10 days   **B.** 4 days   **C.** 6 days   **D.** 8 days

E. 12 days

Q.64 The area of the trapezium is 504 cm². If the ratio of value of parallel side of trapezium is in the ratio of 4 : 5 and the height is 16 cm. The multiplication of parallel side is _______ m.

A. 98

B. 0.98

C. 0.098

D. 980

E. None of the above

Q.65 If the compound ratio of $x^2 : y$ and $y^2 : z$ is $z : y$, then which of the following is true?

A. x = yz

B. y = xz

C. z = xy

D. xyz = 1

E. None of the above

Q.66 Manoj earns a profit of 30% by selling books. What would be the approximate percent change in the profit, if he had paid 20% less and sold at 20% more?

A. 165%

B. 251%

C. 195%

D. 217%

E. None of these

Q.67 A man bought a car at Rs. 700000 and if he gives car on rent then his probability to earn profit is $\frac{2}{5}$ then find selling price if he may earn profit of Rs. 50000?

A. 825000   **B.** 750000   **C.** 748000   **D.** 720000

E. 752000

Q.68 A salesman purchases an article for _______ and sells it a loss of 20%. Had he paid 15% less for buying the article and sold it at Rs. 50 more, he would have made a profit of 30%. (Calculate approximate value).

A. Rs. 130   **B.** Rs. 164   **C.** Rs. 125   **D.** Rs. 148

E. Rs. 145

Q.69 Two integers are selected from the 1ˢᵗ 10 natural numbers. If the sum is even find the probability that both numbers are odd.

A. $\frac{1}{2}$

B. $\frac{3}{5}$

C. $\frac{2}{5}$

D. $\frac{1}{5}$

E. None of these

Q.70 A bag contains 20 yellow balls, 10 green balls, 5 white balls, 8 black balls, and 1 red ball. How many minimum balls one should pick out so that to make sure the he gets at least 2 balls of same color.

A. 7 balls   **B.** 4 balls   **C.** 8 balls   **D.** 6 balls

E. 9 balls

Q.71 Two letters are chosen randomly from English alphabet. What is the probability that none of them is a vowel and they are consecutive letters?

A. $\frac{8}{325}$

B. $\frac{12}{325}$

C. $\frac{16}{325}$

D. $\frac{4}{325}$

E. $\frac{9}{325}$

Q.72 A number is 50% less than the third number and another number is 54% less than the third number. By how much percent is the second number less than the first number?

A. 13

B. 11

C. 9

D. 15

E. None of these

Q.73 As Jio entered into market, other telecom sectors have to struggle alot in order to remain in the market. The effect is also seen on the share price of the companies. A survey is being conducted for share price fluctuation of Airtel. It has been observed that share price of Airtel rose by 10% from July to August. Then, it has been dropped 20% from August to September and again rose by 50% from September to October. What was the percentage increase for the whole quarter in 2017?

A. 31%   **B.** 24%   **C.** 26%   **D.** 32%

E. 23%

Q.74 A is five time as Large as B. The Percent that B is less than A is:

A. 20%   **B.** 80%   **C.** 60%   **D.** 46%

E. 50%

Q.75 Two pipes A and B can fill a cistern in 24 hours and 32 hours respectively. If both pipes are opened simultaneously, find out when the pipe A must be turned off so that the cistern can be filled in exactly 16 hours?

A. 14 hr

B. 8 hr

C. 6 hr

D. 10 hr

E. None of these

Q.76 Three pipes A, B and C can fill a cistern in 10, 12, and 15 hours respectively, when working alone. If all the three pipes are opened together, then the times taken to fill the cistern will be?

A. 4 hours

B. 6 hours

C. 7 hours

D. 5 hours

E. None of these

Q.77 The average weight of a group of 75 girls was calculated as 48 kg. It was later discovered that the weight of one of the girls was read as 44 kg, whereas her actual weight was 26 kg.

What is the actual average weight of the group of 75 girls? (Rounded off to two digits after decimal)?

A. 46.73 kg

B. 48.76 kg

C. 45.76 kg

D. 45.85 kg

E. None of these

Q.78 If twice the perimeter of a square is 5.8 cm less than 3 times the sum of its diagonals, then find the side of the square.

A. 8 cm

B. 10 cm

C. 12 cm

D. 15 cm

E. 16 cm

Q.79 Rs. 68,000 is divided among $A, B,$ and C in the ratio of $1/2 : 1/4 : 5/16$. The difference between the greatest part and the smallest part is:

A. Rs. 8000

B. Rs. 32000

C. Rs. 9000

D. Rs. 12000

E. None of these

Q.80 The ratio of capacity of buckets P and Q is 3 : 4. Both are filled to half their capacity with water. From bucket P, 15 liters of water is taken and poured into bucket Q. Now, the ratio of water in buckets P and Q becomes 3 : 11. Find the capacity of bucket Q (in liters).

A. 40

B. 60

C. 75

D. 80

E. 150

// Smart Answer Sheet //

| Correct | Percentage of students who answered correctly. | Skipped | Percentage of students who skipped. |

Q.	Ans.	Correct / Skipped	Q.	Ans.	Correct / Skipped	Q.	Ans.	Correct / Skipped	Q.	Ans.	Correct / Skipped	Q.	Ans.	Correct / Skipped	Q.	Ans.	Correct / Skipped	Q.	Ans.	Correct / Skipped
1	B	21.58 % / 18.35 %	15	B	66.55 % / 24.1 %	29	E	52.52 % / 32.73 %	43	D	17.27 % / 52.51 %	57	E	10.43 % / 70.15 %	71	C	0 % / 100 %
2	C	28.42 % / 39.21 %	16	A	53.96 % / 24.82 %	30	E	48.56 % / 34.53 %	44	C	4.68 % / 58.27 %	58	B	4.32 % / 73.02 %	72	E	0.36 % / 92.09 %
3	B	72.3 % / 21.58 %	17	B	36.33 % / 38.13 %	31	B	42.45 % / 41.36 %	45	C	31.29 % / 46.41 %	59	B	3.6 % / 74.46 %	73	D	0.72 % / 92.09 %
4	D	67.63 % / 22.66 %	18	C	33.09 % / 40.29 %	32	C	36.33 % / 42.81 %	46	D	9.71 % / 58.64 %	60	D	0.36 % / 76.98 %	74	B	3.6 % / 92.08 %
5	E	53.96 % / 23.74 %	19	D	28.78 % / 42.44 %	33	E	34.53 % / 43.89 %	47	D	17.63 % / 57.19 %	61	B	2.88 % / 75.18 %	75	E	0.36 % / 92.09 %
6	A	56.12 % / 26.97 %	20	B	22.66 % / 41.73 %	34	C	44.6 % / 42.45 %	48	A	21.22 % / 56.84 %	62	E	0.36 % / 78.06 %	76	A	2.52 % / 92.44 %
7	C	53.96 % / 28.41 %	21	E	25.18 % / 42.45 %	35	B	34.53 % / 41.73 %	49	D	11.15 % / 63.67 %	63	D	11.51 % / 74.1 %	77	E	1.44 % / 92.44 %
8	B	53.24 % / 27.7 %	22	E	23.02 % / 44.25 %	36	A	15.47 % / 57.19 %	50	B	24.46 % / 57.19 %	64	C	1.08 % / 79.5 %	78	C	0.36 % / 92.45 %
9	D	54.68 % / 28.77 %	23	E	37.77 % / 36.33 %	37	A	14.75 % / 60.07 %	51	E	17.27 % / 59.71 %	65	C	0.36 % / 90.65 %	79	E	0 % / 100 %
10	D	52.16 % / 28.78 %	24	E	23.38 % / 38.49 %	38	D	17.63 % / 61.15 %	52	A	27.7 % / 59.35 %	66	D	0 % / 100 %	80	D	0.36 % / 99.28 %
11	E	29.86 % / 31.65 %	25	E	44.24 % / 38.49 %	39	B	15.47 % / 61.87 %	53	A	25.18 % / 60.79 %	67	A	0.36 % / 92.09 %			
12	A	25.18 % / 24.82 %	26	B	24.82 % / 34.17 %	40	A	11.87 % / 61.51 %	54	B	29.5 % / 60.07 %	68	B	0.72 % / 92.45 %			
13	B	37.77 % / 23.74 %	27	C	55.76 % / 33.45 %	41	E	29.5 % / 44.96 %	55	C	3.96 % / 71.94 %	69	A	0.36 % / 92.45 %			
14	C	43.53 % / 27.69 %	28	B	52.88 % / 34.53 %	42	B	16.19 % / 46.4 %	56	A	2.88 % / 72.66 %	70	D	0.36 % / 92.45 %			

Reasoning

Ques (1-5):Direction: Study the following information carefully and answer the given question.

i) Twelve people are sitting in two parallel rows containing six people in each such that they are equidistant from each other. In row 1: M, N, O, P, Q and R are sitting facing south. In row 2: G, H, I, J, K and L are sitting facing north but not necessarily in the same order.

ii) Therefore in the given seating arrangement each member sitting in a row faces another member of the other row.

iii) Three persons sit between O and P. Either O or P sits at an extreme end of the line. The one who faces P sits third to the left of I. J faces the one who sits third to the left of M and he cannot sit adjacent to I. The immediate neighbour of H faces the immediate neighbour of M.

iv) Only one person sits between G and K, who is facing the one sitting on the immediate right of Q. Neither Q nor R faces I. L and H cannot sit adjacent to each other.

Q.1 Which of the following faces N?

A. G **B.** H **C.** K **D.** I
E. J

Q.2 Which of the following sit at the extreme ends of the row?

A. P, H **B.** K, R **C.** Q, J **D.** N, K
E. R, H

Q.3 If Q is related to G in the same way as O is related to J, then which of the following is M related to, following the same pattern?

A. L
B. I
C. H
D. K
E. Cannot be determined

Q.4 Which of the following sit at the extreme ends of the row?

A. None **B.** One **C.** Two **D.** Three
E. Four

Q.5 Which of the following faces N?

A. G - P **B.** H - R **C.** H - M **D.** J - N
E. I - Q

Ques (6-8):Direction: Study the information given carefully and answer the question given below.

In a certain code language,

"fasting relax digestive system" is coded as "G49 E81 X25 M36".

"boosts brain function efficiency" is coded as "Y100 N64 S36 N25".

"increases energy daily body" is coded as "Y36 Y16 S81 Y25".

"fasting cures life threatening" is coded as "E16 G49 S25 G121".

Q.6 What will be the code for the word "percentage" in this coded language?

A. E81 **B.** G100 **C.** E64 **D.** P100
E. E100

Q.7 The code for "S36 G49 S81 X25" represents?

A. Life energy digestive brain
B. Increases boosts fasting relax
C. Threatening body efficiency relax
D. Cures life energy function system
E. Relax energy digestive body

Q.8 Which of the following may represent "get well suffer"?

A. L9 T16 R25 **B.** T9 R36 L16
C. G9 S36 W16 **D.** T16 L25 R9
E. T25 R9 W16

Q.9 How many such pairs of letters are there in the word 'DEMEANOR', each of which has as many letters between them in the word (both forward and backward direction) as they have between them in the English Alphabet?

A. None **B.** One **C.** Two **D.** Three
E. Four

Q.10 In a certain code 'REPUBLIC' is written as 'SGSYGRPK', then how will 'COMPUTER' be written in the same language?

A. DQPTZZMZ **B.** DQTPZZLZ
C. DQPTZZLZ **D.** DPQTZZMZ
E. DPQPZZMZ

Ques (11-12):Direction: Read the following information carefully and answer the question asked below.

P is the mother of two children M and N, who are of different genders. O is M's spouse. R is of the same gender as N. R and P are a married couple. S is a child of M and gender of S is the same as O.

Q.11 How many male members are there in the family?

[RBI Assistant, 2019]

A. One
B. Two
C. Three
D. Four
E. Cannot be determined

Q.12 If Q is married to N, then how Q is related to S?

A. Uncle **B.** Aunt **C.** Sister **D.** Niece
E. Nephew

Ques (13-15):Direction: Question below consists of a question and two statements numbered I and II given below it. You have to decide whether the data provided in the statements are sufficient to answer the question.

Q.13 There are seven friends M, N, O, P, Q, R and S are sitting in a row. All are facing towards the north direction. Who sits in the middle of the row?

I. Three friends sit between O and N. None of them sits at the extreme ends.

II. N sits second to the left of S. Q sits third to the right of S.

A. Data in statement I alone sufficient to answer the question, while the data in statement II alone are not sufficient to answer the question.

B. Data in statement II alone are sufficient to answer the question, while the data in statement I alone are not sufficient to answer the question.

C. Data either in statement I alone or in statement II alone are sufficient to answer the question.

D. Data in both the statements I and II together are not sufficient to answer the question.

E. Data in both the statements I and II together are necessary to answer the question.

Q.14 Six boys Amrit, Ankit, Abhinav, Abhay, Ashu and Anirudh are sitting around a circular table. All are facing towards the center. Who among the following sits immediate right of Abhinav?

I. Abhay sits third to the right of Abhinav. Amrit is second to the left of Abhay.

II. Ashu sits third to the right of Anirudh, who sits to the immediate right of Amrit.

A. Data in statement I alone sufficient to answer the question, while the data in statement II alone are not sufficient to answer the question.

B. Data in statement II alone are sufficient to answer the question, while the data in statement I alone are not sufficient to answer the question.

C. Data either in statement I alone or in statement II alone are sufficient to answer the question.

D. Data in both the statements I and II together are not sufficient to answer the question.

E. Data in both the statements I and II together are necessary to answer the question.

Q.15 Find the total number of persons in the row.

I. Rahul is 9th from the left end and there are two persons sit between Rahul and Ravi.

II. Ravi is 12th from the left end and 13th from the right end.

A. Data in statement I alone sufficient to answer the question, while the data in statement II alone are not sufficient to answer the question.

B. Data in statement II alone are sufficient to answer the question, while the data in statement I alone are not sufficient to answer the question.

C. Data either in statement I alone or in statement II alone are sufficient to answer the question.

D. Data in both the statements I and II together are not sufficient to answer the question.

E. Data in both the statements I and II together are necessary to answer the question.

Ques (16-18):Direction: Read the information carefully and answer the questions asked below.

M, N, O, P, Q, and R are six villages located at a certain distance from one another. O is 17 km to the North-East of M and 8 km to the East of N. R is 10 km to the North of O. Q is 8 km to the West of R. P is 7 km to the South of Q. Q, N and M are on a straight line.

Q.16 What is the distance between village P and village N?

A. 8 km   **B.** 10 km   **C.** 5 km   **D.** 3 km
E. 12 km

Q.17 Village Q is located in which direction with respect to village O?

A. South-West   **B.** North-West
C. North   **D.** South-East
E. South

Q.18 What is the distance between N and M?

A. 12 km
B. 14 km
C. 10 km
D. 15 km
E. Cannot be determined

Ques (19-23):Direction: Study the following information carefully and answer the question given below.

ICA1, ICA2, ICA3, ICA4, ICA5, ICA6, and ICA7 not in the same order are the seven internet connections in an organization. These internet connections are provided on seven days of the week (starting from Monday), with one internet connection per day.

ICA7 is not scheduled for Tuesday. ICA5 is scheduled to be provided either on Monday or Saturday. ICA6 is scheduled to be provided before ICA3. ICA1 is not scheduled for Tuesday and Thursday. ICA7 is not scheduled for Wednesday. At least four connections are scheduled between ICA5 and ICA3. ICA6 is not scheduled for Tuesday. ICA1 is immediately preceded by ICA4. The connection ICA3 is not scheduled for Saturday. ICA4 is not provided on Thursday and Wednesday.

Q.19 The internet connection provided on Thursday is______.

A. ICA1   **B.** ICA4
C. ICA7   **D.** ICA5
E. None of these

Q.20 The internet connection ICA2 is provided on ______.

A. Monday   **B.** Wednesday
C. Sunday   **D.** Tuesday
E. Friday

Q.21 Which internet connection is provided exactly between Tuesday and Saturday?

A. ICA1   **B.** ICA7   **C.** ICA4   **D.** ICA3
E. ICA6

Q.22 Which internet connection is exactly in the middle of ICA6 and ICA3?

A. ICA4   **B.** ICA7   **C.** ICA6   **D.** ICA1

E. ICA2

Q.23 Identify the incorrect statement.
A. ICA5 is scheduled for Monday.
B. ICA2 is scheduled between ICA5 and ICA6.
C. ICA7 is preceded by ICA4.
D. ICA3 is scheduled on the last day of the week.
E. ICA6 is scheduled for Wednesday.

Ques (24-26):Direction: Study the following information carefully and answer the question given below.

In a class, 8 toppers are listed A, B, C, D, E, F, G & H but not in the same manner.

The rank of E is greater than B's.

The rank of A is greater than C & D's rank.

The rank of D is greater than F but less than C.

The rank of G lies between the ranks of B and E.

The rank of G is greater than A's.

The rank of B is less than the rank of G but greater than A.

The rank of H is greater than all of the students.

Q.24 What is the position of C in the class?
A. 2nd   **B.** 3rd   **C.** 4th   **D.** 6th
E. 8th

Q.25 What is the name of the person whose rank is 4th?
A. C   **B.** F   **C.** A   **D.** B
E. G

Q.26 What is the position of E in the class?
A. 2nd   **B.** 3rd   **C.** 4th   **D.** 6th
E. 7th

Q.27 How many meaningful words of 5 letters can be made with the alphabets K, E, D, H, I each being used only once in each word?
A. One   **B.** Two
C. Three   **D.** More than three
E. None

Ques (28-31):Direction: In the question below are given some statements followed by some conclusions. You have to take the given statements to be true even if they seem to be at variance with commonly known facts. Read all the conclusions and then decide which of the given conclusions logically follows from the given statements disregarding commonly known facts.

Q.28 Statements:
All vegetables are fruit
No fruit are drink
Some drink are honey.
Conclusions:
I. Some honey is not fruit.
II. No vegetables are drink.
A. Only conclusion II is true
B. Only conclusion I is true
C. Both conclusions I and II are true
D. Either conclusion I or II is true
E. Neither conclusion I nor II is true

Q.29 Statement I: All µ are £
Statement II: All € are µ
Conclusion I: Some € are £
Conclusion II: Some µ are €
A. Only conclusion I follow
B. Only conclusion II follows
C. Both conclusions I and II follow
D. Either conclusion I or conclusion II follows
E. Neither I nor II follows

Q.30 Statements:
All mats are golfs.
No golfs are crickets.
Some crickets are cans.
All bugs are beetles.
No cans are beetles.
Conclusions:
I. Some cans are bugs.
II. All mats are crickets.
III. No cans are golfs.
IV. Some beetles are bugs.
A. Only IV follows
B. All follows
C. Only III follows
D. Only II and III follow
E. None follows

Q.31 Statements:
Some Oil are Wax.
All Gases are Oil.
Some Fuel are Gases.
Conclusions:
I. No Fuel is an Oil.
II. No Gases is a Fuel.
III. Some Oil are Fuel.
A. Either I or II follows
B. Only I follows
C. Only III follows
D. None follows
E. All Follow

Q.32 In which of the following expressions either 'Z < V' or 'V = Z' is definitely true?
A. S > Z ≥ X = U < N ≤ V
B. X > S = V ≤ P = U < Z
C. S ≥ V = U ≥ N = X ≥ Z
D. X > S = Z ≤ P = U ≥ V
E. None of these

Ques (33-35):Direction: In each of the following questions assuming the given statements to be true, find which of the

following conclusion I and II given below is/are definitely true and given your answer accordingly.

Q.33 Statements:

C ≥ L, L > U, U = G, I < G

Conclusions:

I. C > U

II. C < U

A. Only I is true

B. Only II is true

C. Either I or II is true

D. Neither I nor II is true

E. Both I and II are true

Q.34 Statements:

P ≥ R > Q = T ≥ S; R = U > Y = Z ≥ X

Conclusions:

I. P ≥ Q

II. P > X

III. Q ≥ S

A. Only I is true

B. Only I and II are true

C. Only II and III are true

D. Only III is true

E. All are true

Q.35 Statements: Y ≤ L < B = T; B < C < N; I ≥ B < Q

Conclusions:

I. I > C

II. Y < Q

A. Only I is true

B. Only II is true

C. Either I or II true

D. Neither I nor II is true

E. Both I and II are true.

Ques (36-40):Direction: Read the information carefully and answer the question given below.

Eight people M, N, O, P, Q, R, S and T are sitting around a circular table. All are facing towards the center but not necessarily in the same order.

M sits second to the left of R. Only two people sit between R and T. O sits second to the right of T. P and N are immediate neighbors of each other. Neither P nor N is an immediate neighbor of either T or R. Q sits second to the right of N.

Q.36 Who among the following sits exactly opposite to O?

A. N   B. M   C. P   D. Q

E. S

Q.37 What is the position of N with respect to R?

A. Third to the left

B. Third to the right

C. Second to the left

D. Second to the right

E. Cannot be determined

Q.38 How many persons sit between R and Q?

A. Four   B. Three   C. Two   D. One

E. None

Q.39 Which of the following statement/statements is/are true about M?

A. M is an immediate neighbor of Q

B. M sits third to the right of S

C. M sits opposite to N

D. M sits third to the left of P

E. All the given statements are true.

Q.40 Four among the five are alike in a certain way. Find the one that does not belong to that group.?

A. TQ   B. RO   C. NS   D. PQ

E. OP

Quantitative Aptitude

Ques (41-45):Direction: What should come in place of the question mark '?' in the following number series?

Q.41 824, 408, 200, 96, 44, 18, ?

A. 11   B. 5   C. 26   D. 14

E. 13

Q.42 -4, 1, 18, ?, 112

A. 51   B. 39   C. 28   D. 53

E. 32

Q.43 84, 24, 15, ?, 33.5

A. 7   B. 18.5   C. 15   D. 25.5

E. 14.5

Q.44 14, 63, 196, 1183, ?

A. 2789   B. 5654   C. 4542   D. 3556

E. 2351

Q.45 0.5, 1.5, 5, ?, 76, 385

A. 28   B. 21   C. 18   D. 15

E. 12

Ques (46-50):Direction: Read the given information and answer the question given below.

A leading pizza store sells two different types of pizzas during different months of the year. Each pizza comes in two different sizes. The following table shows the number of the different types of pizza sold during these months and gives the ratio of different sizes of pizza sold.

Month	Cheese-burst	Farmhouse	Cheese-burst Regular : Large	Farmhouse Regular : Large
January	1000	880	2 : 3	3 : 5
February	1500	760	1 : 2	1 : 3
March	1200	960	7 : 5	9 : 7
April	1100	950	5 : 6	9 : 10
May	1300	840	7 : 6	3 : 2
June	1400	920	3 : 4	12 : 11

Q.46 Find the average number of cheese-burst PIZZAS sold in the months of March and April and the number of farmhouse pizzas in the month of January and June.

A. 1000   **B.** 1025   **C.** 1050   **D.** 1075
E. 1100

Q.47 The number of large-size farmhouse pizzas sold in May is what percentage of regular cheese-burst pizzas sold in February?

A. 69.33%   **B.** 72%   **C.** 66.33%   **D.** 66.66%
E. 67.2%

Q.48 Find the ratio of cheese-burst pizzas sold to farmhouse pizzas sold during all 6 months.

A. 250 : 171   **B.** 177 : 250
C. 250 : 177   **D.** 173 : 250
E. 250 : 173

Q.49 What is the difference between large cheese-burst pizzas sold in May and regular farmhouse pizzas in February?

A. 130   **B.** 30
C. 510   **D.** 410
E. None of these

Q.50 What is the sum of all regular pizzas sold in April and all large pizzas sold in May?

A. 1886   **B.** 1866   **C.** 1686   **D.** 1688
E. 1888

Ques (51-55):Direction: The following question has two statements. Study the question and the statements and decide which of the statement(s) is/are necessary to answer the question.

Q.51 The amount was invested for 3 years. What is the rate of interest?

I. The compound interest obtained from sum of amount Rs. 48, 000 was Rs. 7566.

II. With a sum of Rs. 48,000, the difference between compound interest and simple interest was Rs. 366 for the same rate.

A. If the data given in the statement I alone is sufficient to answer the question whereas the data given in statement II alone are not sufficient to answer the question.

B. If the data given in the statement II alone is sufficient to answer the question whereas the data given in statement I alone are not sufficient to answer the question.

C. If the data given in either statement I or in statement II alone is sufficient to answer the question.

D. If the data given in both statement I and II is not sufficient to answer the question.

E. If the data given in both statement I and II is necessary to answer the question.

Q.52 Calculate the net profit percentage?

I) Ashwin marks price of 1 kg packet of wheat by 50% and offers a discount of 20% on it.

II) Faulty weight used by Ashwin, measures 1000 gm for 700 gm.

A. Only I   **B.** Only II
C. Both I and II   **D.** Either I or II
E. None of the above

Q.53 The height of a right circular cone is 'h' and radius is 'r'. A small cone is cut-off at the top by a plane parallel to the base. At what height above the base, the section has been made?

I) Height of cone (h) = 40 cm

II) Volume of smaller cone : volume of larger cone = 1 : 30

A. Only I   **B.** Only II
C. Both I and II   **D.** Either I or II
E. None of the above

Q.54 What is the value of a 3-digit number?

I. Two-third of that number is less by 50 of that number.

II. The sum of the digits is 6.

A. Statement (1) ALONE is sufficient, but statement (2) alone is not sufficient to answer the question asked

B. Statement (2) ALONE is sufficient, but statement (1) alone is not sufficient to answer the question asked

C. BOTH statements (1) and (2) TOGETHER are sufficient to answer the question asked, but NEITHER statement ALONE is sufficient

D. EACH statement ALONE is sufficient to answer the question asked

E. Statements (1) and (2) TOGETHER are NOT sufficient to answer the question asked, and additional data are needed

Q.55 The average age of P, Q, R and S is 60 years. How old is R?

I. The sum of ages of P and R is 30 years.

II. S is 10 years younger than R.

A. Only I   **B.** Only II
C. Both I and II   **D.** Either I or II
E. Neither I nor II

Ques (56-60):Direction: In the given question, two equations numbered I and II are given. You have to solve both the equations and mark the appropriate answer.

Q.56 I. $x^2 - 60x + 900 = 0$

II. $y^2 - 24y + 143 = 0$

A. $x > y$
B. $x \geq y$
C. $x < y$
D. $x \leq y$
E. $x = y$ or the relationship cannot be established

Q.57 I. $4x^2 - 8x + 3 = 0$

II. $2y^2 - 7y + 6 = 0$

A. $x > y$
B. $x < y$
C. $x \geq y$
D. $x \leq y$
E. $x = y$ or no relationship could be established

Q.58 I. $2x^2 - 15x + 25 = 0$

II. $3y^2 + 4y - 4 = 0$

A. If $x > y$
B. If $x \geq y$
C. If $x < y$
D. If $x \leq y$

E. If x = y or relationship between x and y cannot be established

Q.59 I. 7x - 3y = 13

II. 5x + 4y = 40

A. x > y

B. x < y

C. x ≥ y

D. x ≤ y

E. x = y or relation cannot be established

Q.60 I. $6x^2 - 19x + 15 = 0$

II. $10y^2 - 29y + 21 = 0$

A. x > y

B. x < y

C. x ≥ y

D. x ≤ y

E. x = y or relation cannot be established

Ques (61-63):Direction: What approximate will come in the place of the question mark '?' in the following question?

Q.61 $121.22 + 89.88 - 81.20 = 1.91 \times ?$

A. 40   **B.** 65   **C.** 80   **D.** 45

E. 30

Q.62 $(77.88 \times 9.60) \div 38.77 = ? \times 4.82 + 4.71$

A. 3   **B.** 5   **C.** 2   **D.** 8

E. 10

Q.63 $931.45 + (113.67 - 84.95 \div 5.20) = 67.11 + ?^2$

A. 45   **B.** 28   **C.** 31   **D.** 25

E. 15

Q.64 Simplify:

$$\frac{1}{8}\left\{\left(x + \frac{1}{y}\right)^2 - \left(x - \frac{1}{y}\right)^2\right\}$$

A. $\frac{x}{2y}$ **B.** $\frac{x}{y}$ **C.** $\frac{4x}{y}$ **D.** $\frac{2x}{y}$

E. $\frac{3x}{2y}$

Q.65 Find the value of x:

$$\sqrt{169} \div 13 + \sqrt{196} = 3 \times x$$

A. 2   **B.** 3   **C.** 4   **D.** 5

E. 10

Q.66 The average weight of 4 friends Utkarsh, Ashu, Kamal & Himanshu is 100. If the average weight of Ashu & Kamal is 60, and that of Ashu & Himanshu is 72.5, then find the weight of Utkarsh if the weight of Kamal is 55?

A. 150   **B.** 125

C. 175   **D.** 200

E. Can't be determined

Q.67 A shopkeeper sold five old items of a cost price Rs. 500, Rs. 1200, Rs. 1500, Rs. 900 and Rs. 700 at 15% gain, 8% loss, 16% loss, 25% gain and 8% loss respectively. His overall profit or loss is:

A. Profit 8%   **B.** Loss 8%

C. Profit $1\frac{11}{12}\%$ **D.** Loss $1\frac{11}{12}\%$

E. None of these

Q.68 A mixture contains 148 litres of milk & water. If we add 6 litres of milk and 6 litres of water more, then the ratio becomes 2 : 3 in the mixture respectively. Find the initial quantity of milk.

A. 64 litre   **B.** 58 litre

C. 90 litre   **D.** 84 litre

E. None of these

Q.69 The difference between the simple and compound interest on a certain sum for 3 years at 10% p.a. is Rs. 1,395. What is the compound interest on the sum for 2 years at 6% p.a.?

A. Rs. 5,652   **B.** Rs. 5,564

C. Rs. 5,654   **D.** Rs. 5,546

E. None of these

Q.70 Ram employed as I.T. officer in Bank of Baroda bank, From the salary of May 2020 he gives 15% to his wife, 40% of remaining on household expenditure and donate 21% of his salary to Prime minister relief fund, then he has only Rs.18,000 with him, What was the salary of Ram on May 2020.

A. Rs.59,750   **B.** Rs.60,000

C. Rs.61,100   **D.** Rs.60,100

E. None of these

Q.71 A car has to cover a distance of 180 km in 30 hours. If it covers half of the journey in $\frac{2}{5}$th of the time, the speed to cover the remaining distance in the time left has to be?

A. 5 kmph   **B.** 15 kmph

C. 12 kmph   **D.** 7.5 kmph

E. 30 kmph

Q.72 A train running at a speed of 90 km/hr. crossed a platform in 11 seconds. If the length of the train is 83.33% of the length of the platform, find the length of the train.

A. 100 m   **B.** 110 m   **C.** 125 m   **D.** 145 m

E. 160 m

Q.73 A and B can together do a work in $7\frac{1}{2}$ days. Their time ratio is in the ratio of 3 : 5 respectively. Find the how many days A alone can do a same work?

A. 18 days   **B.** 20 days   **C.** 15 days   **D.** 12 days

E. 24 days

Q.74 If the length and breadth of rectangle A is $\frac{4}{5}$ and $\frac{1}{2}$ of the length and breadth of rectangle B respectively, then the area of rectangle A is what percentage of the area of rectangle B?

A. 10%   **B.** 20%   **C.** 30%   **D.** 40%

E. 50%

Ques (75-79):Directions: The following bar graph shows the monthly expenditure(in Rs.) of a family over the period of five months during three different years.

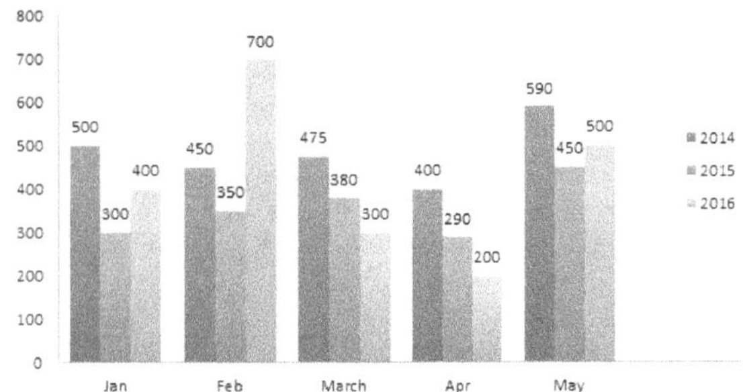

Q.75 Find the average monthly expenditure in the year 2016.

A. 420   **B.** 400   **C.** 300   **D.** 350

E. 677

Q.76 Find the percentage increase in expenditure in Feb 2016 as compared to Feb 2015.

A. 45%   **B.** 200%   **C.** 100%   **D.** 300%

E. 150%

Q.77 Which of the following statements is correct?

A. In 2014, Jan was the month during which the expenditure was maximum for the year.

B. In 2016, Feb was the month during which the expenditure was maximum for the year.

C. In 2015 Jan was the month during which the expenditure was minimum for the year.

D. In 2014, Jan was the month during which the expenditure was minimum for the year.

E. None of these

Q.78 For how many months of the given years has the expenditure been consistently increasing or decreasing?

A. 2   **B.** 4

C. 1   **D.** 3

E. None of these

Q.79 Which of the following month given in the options accounts for the maximum combined expenditure for three years?

A. Jan   **B.** Feb   **C.** March   **D.** April

E. May

Q.80 Three friends A, B and C started a business by investing a sum of money in the ratio of 5 : 7 : 6 After 6 months C withdraws half of his capital. If the sum invested by. 'A' is Rs. 40,000, out of total annual profit of Rs. 33,000, C's share will be

A. Rs. 10,000   **B.** Rs. 12,000

C. Rs. 11,000   **D.** Rs. 9,000

E. None of these

// Smart Answer Sheet //

Correct Percentage of students who answered correctly. **Skipped** Percentage of students who skipped.

Q.	Ans.	Correct / Skipped	Q.	Ans.	Correct / Skipped	Q.	Ans.	Correct / Skipped	Q.	Ans.	Correct / Skipped	Q.	Ans.	Correct / Skipped	Q.	Ans.	Correct / Skipped
1	D	19.7 % / 21.68 %	15	B	21.67 % / 50.74 %	29	C	25.62 % / 55.17 %	43	B	4.93 % / 64.04 %	57	D	26.11 % / 55.66 %	71	A	5.42 % / 77.34 %
2	B	10.84 % / 55.66 %	16	D	30.54 % / 49.76 %	30	A	33.0 % / 54.19 %	44	D	5.91 % / 65.52 %	58	A	33.0 % / 58.13 %	72	C	3.45 % / 78.32 %
3	B	11.33 % / 60.1 %	17	B	35.47 % / 50.24 %	31	C	36.45 % / 53.21 %	45	C	7.88 % / 60.59 %	59	B	17.73 % / 62.07 %	73	D	3.45 % / 78.82 %
4	D	13.3 % / 59.11 %	18	D	22.66 % / 53.2 %	32	C	33.99 % / 54.19 %	46	B	13.3 % / 60.1 %	60	C	14.78 % / 63.55 %	74	D	0.99 % / 80.29 %
5	B	11.82 % / 59.12 %	19	C	14.78 % / 55.17 %	33	A	45.81 % / 51.23 %	47	E	8.87 % / 64.04 %	61	B	15.76 % / 68.97 %	75	A	8.37 % / 79.81 %
6	E	18.72 % / 50.25 %	20	D	16.26 % / 58.12 %	34	C	35.47 % / 51.72 %	48	C	11.33 % / 63.55 %	62	A	8.37 % / 74.88 %	76	C	6.9 % / 81.77 %
7	B	26.11 % / 49.26 %	21	B	13.79 % / 58.13 %	35	B	36.45 % / 54.19 %	49	D	11.33 % / 65.02 %	63	C	9.85 % / 74.39 %	77	B	5.42 % / 83.74 %
8	B	19.7 % / 52.22 %	22	A	8.87 % / 59.6 %	36	C	25.62 % / 58.62 %	50	A	10.34 % / 66.01 %	64	A	3.45 % / 76.35 %	78	C	1.97 % / 84.73 %
9	D	35.47 % / 43.84 %	23	C	7.88 % / 66.01 %	37	D	28.57 % / 61.58 %	51	C	11.33 % / 65.52 %	65	D	9.85 % / 75.86 %	79	E	5.42 % / 83.74 %
10	C	34.98 % / 45.81 %	24	D	12.32 % / 66.99 %	38	B	30.05 % / 62.07 %	52	C	9.36 % / 65.52 %	66	D	13.3 % / 69.46 %	80	D	0 % / 100 %
11	D	35.47 % / 40.88 %	25	D	9.85 % / 67.98 %	39	C	25.12 % / 62.56 %	53	C	8.37 % / 67.49 %	67	D	3.94 % / 71.92 %			
12	B	34.48 % / 44.34 %	26	A	10.34 % / 69.46 %	40	E	24.63 % / 60.59 %	54	A	7.88 % / 65.52 %	68	B	6.9 % / 74.38 %			
13	E	27.09 % / 46.8 %	27	A	4.93 % / 67.98 %	41	B	43.35 % / 48.28 %	55	E	9.85 % / 62.56 %	69	E	1.48 % / 77.83 %			
14	A	26.11 % / 49.75 %	28	C	32.02 % / 50.25 %	42	D	5.42 % / 62.07 %	56	A	25.12 % / 59.61 %	70	B	2.96 % / 76.35 %			

Reasoning

Ques (1-3):Direction: Study the following information carefully and answer the given questions:

A word and number arrangement device when given an input line of words and numbers rearranges them following a particular pattern in each step. The following is an illustration of input and rearrangement (All the numbers are two-digit numbers).

Input: can now 18 16 27 all done 36 insert 49

Step I: 16 18 can now 27 all done 36 insert 49

Step II: 16 18 all can now 27 done 36 insert 49

Step III: 16 18 all can 27 36 now done insert 49

Step IV: 16 18 all can 27 36 done insert now 49

Step V: 16 18 all can 27 36 done insert 49 now

And Step V is the last step of the above input

As per the pattern followed in the above steps, find out in each of the following questions the appropriate step for the given input.

Input: 57 19 professor male 28 correct 36 38 47 female doctor 51 study

Q.1 Which element is third to the right of 'female' in Step V?

A. 38

B. Professor

C. Study

D. 51

E. male

Q.2 Which of the following is the third element from the left end of Step III?

A. 38   **B.** 57   **C.** Correct   **D.** Doctor

E. female

Q.3 Which step number is the following output?

19 28 correct doctor 36 38 female-male 47 51 57 professor study

A. Step V

B. Step VI

C. Step IV

D. Step III

E. There is no such step

Q.4 How many 3 letter meaningful words starting with R and S respectively can be made from all the letters of "WORDS"?

A. 1, 3   **B.** 3, 1   **C.** 2, 3   **D.** 3, 2

E. 2, 2

Q.5 How many letters are there which has a vowel second to its left and third to its right, in the word which is formed by concatenating the words 'QUEUEING' and 'GATE'?

A. One   **B.** Two

C. None   **D.** Three

E. More than three

Ques (6-7):Direction: In the question below there are three statements followed by three conclusions I, II, and III. You have to take the three given statements to be true even if they seem to be at variance from commonly known facts and then decide which of the given conclusions logically follows from the three statements disregarding commonly known facts.

Q.6 Statements:

I. Only cricket are football.

II. Some cricket are baseball.

III. Only a few baseballs are golf.

Conclusions:

I. A few cricket can be golf.

II. Some golf are football.

III. Some baseball are football.

A. Both conclusion I and conclusion II follow

B. Only conclusion I follows

C. Only conclusion III follows

D. None of the conclusions follows

E. Either Conclusion I or Conclusion II follows

Q.7 Statements:

I. No thermal is tidal.

II. Some winds are tidal.

III. All winds are energy.

Conclusions:

I. Some energy being thermal is a possibility.

II. Some winds are not thermal.

A. Only conclusion I follows

B. Both the conclusions I and II follow

C. Neither conclusion I nor II follow

D. Only conclusion II follows

E. Either conclusion I or II follows

Q.8 Direction: Read the following information carefully and answer the question which follows:

Point B is 3m to the west of point A. Point C is 4m north of point B. Point G is exactly midway between point B and point C. Point H is 6m south of point C. Point D is 3m to the west of point C and point F is 4m south of point D. Point E is 3m to the west of point H.

What is the shortest distance between C and A is?

A. 3 m

B. 4 m

C. 5 m

D. 6 m

E. Cannot be determined

Q.9 A man walks 1 km to East and then he turns to South and walks 5 km. Again he turns to East and walks 2 km. After this, he turns to North and walks 9 km. Now, how far is he from his starting point?

A. 3 km
B. 4 km
C. 5 km
D. 6 km
E. None of the above

Q.10 Find the one that does not belong to the group.

A. LO
B. HS
C. DW
D. JR
E. None of these

Q.11 Find the odd one out

[CLAT UG, 2018]

A. Police station
B. Railway station
C. Supermarket
D. Airport
E. None of these

Q.12 Find the next group of alphabets

CFI, DHL, ILO, LPT, _____?

[CLAT UG, 2018]

A. ORU
B. RUW
C. OQT
D. OSV
E. None of these

Q.13 Select the term that will come next in the following series.

HM, EJ, BG, ?

A. YD
B. SC
C. TE
D. YC
E. None of the above

Ques (14-17):Direction: In the question below are given four statements followed by four conclusions numbered I, II, III and IV. You have to take the given statements to be true even if they seem to be at variance with commonly known facts. Read all the conclusions and then decide which of the given conclusions logically follows from the given statements disregarding commonly known facts.

Q.14 Statements:

Some fathers are brothers.
All brothers are uncles.
No uncle is a husband.
Some husbands are the son.

Conclusions:

I. Some sons are uncle.
II. No father is a husband.
III. Some uncles are fathers.
IV. Some husbands are brothers.

A. Only conclusion I follows
B. Only conclusion II follows
C. Only conclusion I, II, and III follow
D. Only conclusion III follows
E. None follows

Q.15 Statements:

Some men are singers.
All singers are actors.
No actor is a teacher.
Some teachers are artists.

Conclusions:

I. Some artists are actors.
II. Some men are teachers.
III. Some actors are men.
IV. No singer is a teacher.

A. None follows
B. Either I or III follows
C. Only III & IV follow
D. Only II & III follow
E. All conclusions follow

Q.16 Statements:

Some planets are stars.
Some stars are the moon.
All moon are sun.
Some earth are moon.

Conclusions:

I. Some planets are sun.
II. Some earth are star.
III. No sun is an earth.
IV. Some suns are not Earth.

A. All conclusions follow
B. Either I or IV follows
C. Only III & IV follow
D. Only I, II & III follow
E. None follows

Q.17 Statements:

All sea are oceans.
Some lakes are rivers.
All rivers are ponds.
Some ponds are sea.

Conclusions:

I. Some ocean are river.
II. Some lakes are ponds.
III. Some sea are lakes.
IV. Some ocean being river is possible.

A. Only conclusion I follows
B. Only conclusion II and III follow
C. Only conclusion I, II, and III follow
D. Only conclusion II and IV follow
E. All follow

Q.18 Direction: In the question below are given four statements followed by four conclusions numbered I, II, and III. You have to take the given statements to be true even if they seem to be at variance with commonly known facts. Read all the conclusions and then decide which of the given conclusions logically follows from the given statements disregarding commonly known facts.

Statements:

Some L are R.

All R are A.

All A are F.

No F is a D.

Conclusions:

I. All D are L.

II. Some D are A.

III. No R is a D.

A.   Only conclusion I follow

B.   Only conclusion II and III follow

C.   Only conclusion I and II follow

D.   Only conclusion II and III follow

E.   Only conclusion III follows

Ques (19-21):Direction: Study the following information and answer the below-given questions.

In a family, there are six members Ajay, Kavya, Vivek, Omkar, Shruti, and Kajal. Ajay and Kavya are a married couple, Ajay being a male member. Omkar is the only son of Vivek, who is the brother of Ajay. Shruti is the sister of Omkar. Kavya is the daughter-in-law of Kajal, whose husband has died.

Q.19 How is Kajal related to Kavya?

A. Mother

B. Mother-in-law

C. Sister-in-law

D. Sister

E. Aunt

Q.20 How many female members are there in the family?

A. One

B. Two

C. Three

D. Four

E. Can't be determined

Q.21 How is Kajal related to Shruti?

A.   Maternal grandmother

B.   Paternal grandmother

C.   Aunt

D.   Mother-in-law

E.   Can't be determined

Ques (22-26):Direction: Study the following information carefully and answer the questions follows:

There are eight different restaurants A, B, C, D, E, F, G, and H. Each restaurant has its own special dish: D1, D2, D3, D4, D5, D6, D7, and D8 not necessarily in the same order. These restaurants are at a distance of 4, 6, 7, 9, 11, 12, 13, and 15 km, but not necessarily in the same order.

Dish D6 is served in the restaurant which is the farthest. Restaurant E serves dish D3 and it is 3 km farther than restaurant F. Restaurant B serves the D8 dish and it is half the distance as compared to the restaurant which serves the D1 dish. Dish D4 is served in restaurant G and it is 4 km less far than restaurant D. The distance of restaurant D is the multiple of 3. Restaurant A neither serves the dish D5 nor it is 12 km far. Restaurant H serves dish D7 and it is 4 km farther than restaurant A.

Q.22 Which dish is served in Restaurant A?

A. D1

B. D6

C. D2

D. D3

E. None of these

Q.23 What is the distance of Restaurant C?

A. 11 km

B. 13 km

C. 7 km

D. 12 km

E. 9 km

Q.24 Which of the following combinations is correct?

A. A – D8 – 6 km

B. F – D2 – 4 km

C. B – D8 – 7 km

D. H – D7 – 13 km

E. None of these

Q.25 How far is the restaurant in which Dish D5 is served?

A. 7 km

B. 4 km

C. 9 km

D. 11 km

E. 13 km

Q.26 Which of the following is not true?

A.   Restaurant D is 15 km away

B.   Dish D5 is servedin Restaurant F

C.   Restaurant H is 11 km away

D.   Restaurant B is 6 km away

E.   All are true

Ques (27-28):Direction: The following question consists of three statements numbered I, II and III. Decide if the data given in the statements are sufficient to answer the question below.

Q.27 A, B, C, D, and E study in the same school, where playing one sport is mandatory out of the five sports i.e. Cricket, Volleyball, Basketball, Hockey, and Kabaddi. No two students play the same sport in this case. What sport does A play?

I. B and C play Kabaddi and Basketball but not necessarily in the same order.

II. D plays either Cricket or Volleyball.

III. A does not play volleyball and E does not play Hockey.

A.   All the statements are needed

B.   Only I and II are sufficient

C.   Only II and III are sufficient

D.   Only I and III are sufficient

E.   Insufficient data

Q.28 L, M, N, O, P, and Q are six friends whose heights are different. How many people are taller than P?

I. P is shorter N, who is shorter than at least three people.

II. Two people are taller than M but shorter than L, P is one of them.

III. At least 2 people are shorter than Q.

A.   All the statements are needed

B.   Only I and II are sufficient

C.   Only II and III are sufficient

D.   Only I and III are sufficient

E.   Insufficient data

Q.29 Direction: In the question below consists of a question and two statements numbered I and II given below it. You have to decide whether the data provided in the statements are sufficient to answer the question. Read both the statements and give the answer.

In a row of five buildings - A, B, C, D, and E which building is in the middle?

Statements:

I. Buildings D and B are at the two extreme ends of the row.

II. Building E is to the right of building C.

A. I alone is sufficient while II alone is not sufficient

B. II alone is sufficient while I alone is not sufficient

C. Either I or II is sufficient

D. Neither I nor II is sufficient

E. Both I and II are sufficient

Q.30 Direction: In the following question, assuming the given statements to be true, find which of the conclusion(s) among given conclusions is/are definitely true and then give your answers accordingly.

Statements:

N = C > O ≤ A; A = M < B; N < L = B

Conclusions:

I. O < A

II. C < L

III. M = O

IV. N > B

A. Only I follows

B. Either I or II follows

C. Only IV follows

D. Only II and either I or III follows

E. None follows

Q.31 Which of the following symbols should be placed in the blank spaces respectively (in the same order from left to right) in order to complete the given expression in such a manner that 'M > I' definitely holds true?

I _ L _ K _ J _ M

A. =, >, ≤, <

B. =, ≤, =, <

C. ≥, >, =, >

D. ≥, <, =, >

E. None of these

Ques (32-34):Direction: In the following question assuming the given statements to be true, find which of the conclusion(s) among given conclusions is/are definitely true and then give your answers accordingly.

Q.32 Statements:

A ≥ B > C; A < D; F = B; G < H < F

Conclusions:

I. G < C

II. F > C

III. B < G

IV. D > C

A. None is true

B. Only I is true

C. Only I and III are true

D. Only II and IV are true

E. Only IV is true

Q.33 Statements:

A > Z; Z > D = B; B ≥ F = H; P < H

Conclusions:

I. Z ≤ P

II. A < B

III. P < D

A. Only III is true

B. Only I and II are true

C. Only I is true

D. Only II is true

E. Only II and III are true

Q.34 Statements:

R = B > C ≥ D; P > Q ≥ R = S < H

Conclusions:

I. D ≤ R

II. P < B

III. Q < H

A. Only III is true

B. Both I and II are true

C. Only I is true

D. None is true

E. Both II and III are true

Ques (35-39):Direction: Study the given information carefully and answer the following questions below.

Seven boxes P, Q, R, S, T, U, and V were kept in a showroom which contains shoes of different brands which are Nike, Adidas, Puma, Skechers, Hush-puppies, Reebok, and Clarks but not necessarily in the same order. Each box contains shoes of different colors viz Blue, White, Black, Pink, Brown, Neon, and Grey but not necessarily in the same order. The cost of each pair of shoes is different.

Box R does not contain shoes of either Hush-puppies or Adidas. Box U contains grey-colored shoes. Box T contains either Nike or Puma shoes. The cost of Puma shoes is Rs. 2200 less than the cost of shoes in box R. Shoes of Skechers are of Neon color. The cost of shoes for Hush-puppies is Rs. 2300. The cost of shoes in box U is Rs. 1800 more than the cost of shoes in box S but Rs. 800 more than that of shoes in box Q. Box V contains neither brown nor blue shoes. The color of Adidas shoes is not white. The cost of shoes of Skechers is the highest and the cost of shoes of Nike is 2nd highest. Box Q does not contain either white or brown shoes. The cost of shoes in box T is Rs. 700 more than the shoes in box V but Rs. 2200 more than the shoes in box Q. Cost of Adidas shoes is a multiple of 11. Box Q contains either Hush-puppies or Reebok and the cost is $\frac{8}{11}$ of the cost of shoes of box V. The cost of black shoes is Rs. 2300 and the cost of white shoes is in a multiple of 3.

Q.35 Which box contains shoes of brown color?

A. U

B. P

C. T

D. Q

E. None of these

Q.36 What is the color of the costliest shoes?

A. Brown

B. Pink

C. Neon

D. Grey

E. None of these

Q.37 If all the boxes are rearranged according to the cost of shoes in increasing order from top to bottom, the position of which box will remain unchanged?

A. Box containing brown shoes
B. Box containing black shoes
C. Box containing white shoes
D. Box containing Neon shoes
E. None of these

Q.38 What is the difference between the cost of shoes of Clarks and Adidas?

A. 2400
B. 3000
C. 2300
D. 2500
E. None of these

Q.39 Which of the following combination is not true?

A. R - Skechers - 7000
B. T - Nike - 6200
C. V - Adidas - 4800
D. P - Hush-puppies - 2300
E. None of these

Q.40 A man starts from Point A, walks 15 km West, then turns to left and walks 20 km, again he turns to left and walks 25 km, again he turns to left and walks 20 km. How far and in which direction is he from the starting point?

A. 12 km - East
B. 10 km - East
C. 15 km - East
D. 14 km - West
E. 20 km - West

Quantitative Aptitude

Ques (41-45):Directions: Answer the questions on the basis of the information given below.

Six employees - Abhishek, Babu, Chinki, Dinesh, Eshan, and Farooq - are working at different positions in Geosis Technology. The first pie - chart shows the break - up of gross salary and the second pie - chart shows the distribution of the percentage of gross salary deducted as tax of these six employees.

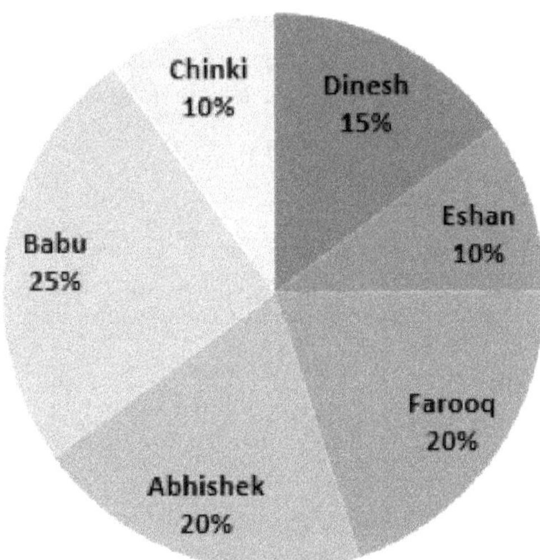

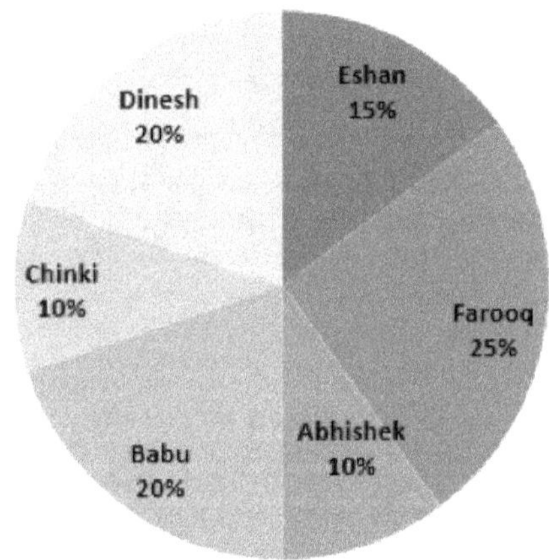

Net salary = Gross salary – Tax deducted

Q.41 What is the gross salary of Abhishek, if Farooq pays Rs. 2,000 as tax?

A. Rs. 5000
B. Rs. 10000
C. Rs. 6000
D. Rs. 8000
E. None of these

Q.42 What is the ratio of the total gross salary of all six employees to that of their total net salary?

A. 41 : 32
B. 8 : 5
C. 40 : 33
D. Cannot be determined
E. None of these

Q.43 What is the ratio of tax paid by Abhishek, Babu, and Chinki put together to that by Dinesh, Eshan and Farooq put together?

A. 19 : 17
B. 17 : 19

C. 19 : 16   **D.** 16 : 19
E. None of these

Q.44 The difference in net salary is minimum for which of the following pairs?
A.   Chinki and Babu
B.   Farooq and Babu
C.   Farooq and Dinesh
D.   Farooq and Eshan
E.   Dinesh and Abhishek

Q.45 What is the percentage of Babu's net salary as a percentage of the total net salary of all employees?
A. 24.24%   **B.** 46.25%   **C.** 61.3%   **D.** 26%
E. 40%

Ques (46-48): What approximate value should come in place of the question mark (?) in the following question? (You do not have to calculate the exact value.)

Q.46 $(27.89)^2 - (21.78)^2 + (2345.68 + 154.23) \div ? = 350$
A. 36   **B.** 45   **C.** 50   **D.** 65
E. 55

Q.47 $\{(16.99)^2 + (23.01)^2\} \div ? = 2.01$
A.   409   **B.**   41
C.   19   **D.**   10
E.   None of these

Q.48 $\left\{ \sqrt[3]{(274.9 + 66.01)} \times (9.02)^2 \right\} \div 3.1 = ?$
A.   21   **B.**   189
C.   217   **D.**   45
E.   None of these

Q.49 25, 28, 31, 34, _________then find which term is equal to 142?
A. 41   **B.** 43   **C.** 40   **D.** 50
E. 60

Q.50 At the end of a business conference, all the ten people present all shake hands with each other once. How many handshakes will there be together?
A. 20   **B.** 45   **C.** 55   **D.** 90
E. 60

Q.51 In how many ways can a panel of 3 judges be formed from a group of 5 judges?
A. 12   **B.** 15   **C.** 24   **D.** 10
E. 84

Q.52 To complete a work, A takes 50% more time than B. If together they take 18 days to complete the work, how much time shall B take to do it?
A.   30 days   **B.**   35 days
C.   40 days   **D.**   45 days
E.   None of these

Q.53 If 10 men or 20 boys can make 260 mats in 20 days, then how many mats will be made by 8 men and 4 boys in 20 days?
A. 260   **B.** 240   **C.** 280   **D.** 520

E. 652

Ques (54-58): What should come in place of the question mark '?' in the following series?

Q.54 11, 20, 29, 38, ?
A. 45   **B.** 49   **C.** 47   **D.** 41
E. 53

Q.55 3, 7, 16, 36, 78, 144, 222, ?
A.   272   **B.**   312
C.   322   **D.**   324
E.   None of these

Q.56 2, 4, 10, 28, 82, 244, ?
A.   580   **B.**   680
C.   730   **D.**   880
E.   None of these

Q.57 0, 2, 15, 92, ?
A. 235   **B.** 698   **C.** 595   **D.** 453
E. 150

Q.58 100, 50.5, 51.5, 78.75, ?
A. 205.5   **B.** 95.5   **C.** 125.675   **D.** 159.5
E. 180.75

Q.59 Neha can complete a project in 25 days and Sunita can complete it in 30 days. Neha, Sunita and Priya together can complete the same project in $\dfrac{600}{59}$ days. If the total amount paid for the project by the company is Rs. 70,800 and this amount is shared by them in the proportion to their work, then Sunita's share (in Rs.) is-
A.   24,000   **B.**   20,000
C.   28,000   **D.**   18,000
E.   None of these

Q.60 If the diameter of the circle is 56 cm, then what is the area (in cm²) of the circle?
A. 1484   **B.** 2484   **C.** 2464   **D.** 2684
E. 2685

Q.61 If the circumference of the circle is 176 cm, then what is the radius (in cm) of the circle?
A.   24
B.   28
C.   32
D.   36
E.   Cannot be determined

Q.62 If the total compound interest on the same principle at the rate of interest of 15% per annum for 2 years and at a rate of interest of 40% per annum for a year is Rs. 28900, then find the total principal amount including both transactions. (Interest calculated annually)
A.   Rs. 65000   **B.**   Rs. 90000
C.   Rs. 80000   **D.**   Rs. 45000
E.   Rs. 50000

Q.63 A shopkeeper makes a profit of 25% in the first year, he suffers the loss of 20% and 10% in the second year and the third year respectively. What is the difference between the total amount he gets after three years and the amount of money he invested initially if the amount of money he invested initially is Rs. 50000?

A. Rs. 4000
B. Rs. 4500
C. Rs. 5000
D. Rs. 8500
E. None of these

Q.64 Direction: Given below are quantities named A and B. Based on the given information, you have to determine the relationship between the two quantities. You should use the given data and your knowledge of mathematics to choose among the possible answer.

Odin divided Rs.1301 between his two sons Thor and Loki. He divided so that the amount of Thor after 7 years is equal to the amount of Loki after 9 years at the rate of 4% per annum compounded annually.

Quantity A: Share of Thor

Quantity B: Share of Loki

A. Quantity A ≥ Quantity B
B. Quantity A ≤ Quantity B
C. Quantity A > Quantity B
D. Quantity A < Quantity B
E. Quantity A = Quantity B

Q.65 15% of the age of A is equal to 25% of the age of B. Present Age of C is two-thirds the age of B. After 5 years, the ratio of the ages of A and B will be 10 : 7. What is the ratio of ages of B and C, 6 years from now?

A. 4 : 3
B. 8 : 7
C. 7 : 6
D. 6 : 5
E. 5 : 4

Q.66 30 litres of spirit was mixed with 150 litres of whisky, 30 litres of this mixture was sold and some more quantity of whisky and spirit was added in the respective ratio of 5 : 6. If the final quantity of whisky was 500% of the initial quantity of spirit, what was the quantity of spirit that was added?

A. 30 litres
B. 34 litres
C. 28 litres
D. 52 litres
E. None of these

Q.67 The value of a car decreases at the rate of 3.2% per annum. Its present value is Rs. 735000. If the car was launched 5 years ago, what was its original value?

A. Rs. 750000
B. Rs. 895000
C. Rs. 775000
D. Rs. 875000
E. Rs. 633620

Q.68 Pure sugar costs Rs. 100 per kg. After adulterating it with salt costing Rs. 50 per kg, a shopkeeper sells the mixture at the rate of Rs. 96 per kg, thereby making a profit of 20%. In what ratio does he mix the two?

A. 2 : 3
B. 3 : 2
C. 1 : 2
D. 1 : 3
E. 3 : 5

Q.69 A man bought a number of clips at 3 for a rupee and an equal number at 2 for a rupee. At what price per dozen should he sell them to make a profit of 20%?

A. Rs. 4
B. Rs. 5
C. Rs. 6
D. Rs. 7

E. Rs. 8

Q.70 A sum of Rs. 250000 is deposited for 3 years compounded annually at 4%, 5% and 6% for the first, second and third year respectively. What will be the amount at the end of the three years?

A. Rs. 301,400
B. Rs. 256,590
C. Rs. 325,680
D. Rs. 289,380
E. None of these

Q.71 When Pankaj finishes a certain work, he gets a total wage of Rs. 90. When Kamal finishes the same work, he gets a total wage of Rs. 105. The daily wages of Pankaj and Kamal are Rs. 4.5 and Rs. 3.5 respectively. If both of them do it together, what is the cost of work?

A. Rs. 120
B. Rs. 84
C. Rs. 108
D. Rs. 96
E. None of these

Q.72 A box contains 50 marbles of different colors i.e. purple, pink, and blue. Find the number of pink marbles in the box, if the probability of picking purple marble is $\frac{3}{5}$ and that of either purple or pink marble is $\frac{4}{5}$.

A. 6
B. 8
C. 5
D. 10
E. None of these

Q.73 A 450 m long train moving with an average speed of 118.8 km/h crosses a platform in 20 seconds. A man crosses the same platform in 15 seconds. What is the speed of the man?

A. 15 m/s
B. 16 m/s
C. 17 m/s
D. Cannot be determined
E. None of these

Ques (74-76):Direction: The bar chart given below shows the sales (in lacs) of 2 companies X and Y from year 2011 to 2015.

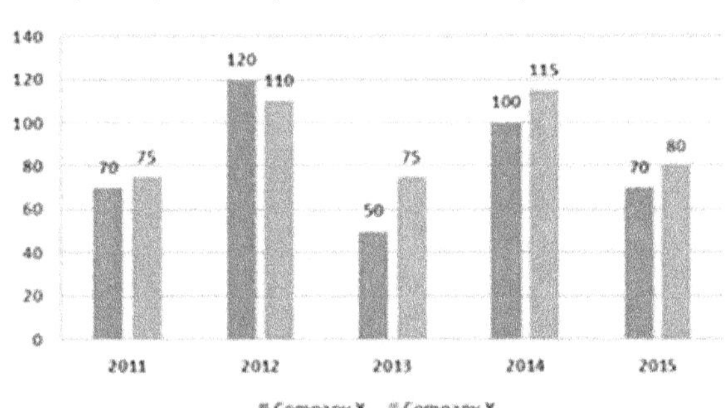

Q.74 In how many years was the sale of company X more than that of company Y?

A. 2
B. 5
C. 1
D. 3
E. 8

Q.75 What was the percentage change in the sale of company X from the year 2013 to 2015?

A. 30
B. 80
C. 40
D. 60
E. 50

Q.76 What was the average sale (in lacs) of company Y from 2011 to 2015?

A. 104   **B.** 0.125   **C.** 170.5   **D.** 140

E. 91

Q.77 Tickets numbered 1 to 20 are mixed up and then a ticket is drawn at random. What is the probability that the ticket drawn has a number which is a multiple of 3 or 5?

A. $\dfrac{1}{2}$ **B.** $\dfrac{2}{5}$

C. $\dfrac{8}{15}$ **D.** $\dfrac{9}{20}$

E. None of these

Q.78 In a box, there are 8 red, 7 blue and 6 green balls. One ball is picked up randomly. What is the probability that it is neither red nor green?

A. $\dfrac{1}{3}$ **B.** $\dfrac{3}{4}$ **C.** $\dfrac{7}{19}$ **D.** $\dfrac{8}{21}$

E. $\dfrac{9}{21}$

Q.79 HCF and LCM of two fractions is $\dfrac{1}{35}$ and $\dfrac{15}{1}$, if one fraction is $\dfrac{3}{5}$, then the second fraction is:

A. $\dfrac{3}{7}$ **B.** $\dfrac{7}{3}$

C. $\dfrac{5}{7}$ **D.** $\dfrac{7}{5}$

E. None of these

Q.80 $X = \dfrac{\left(1^2 - 2^2 + 3^2 - 4^2 \ldots\ldots + 19^2 - 20^2\right)}{\left(1^3 - 2^3 + 3^3 - 4^3 \ldots\ldots + 19^3 - 20^3\right)}$. Find the value of X?

A. $\dfrac{11}{230}$ **B.** $\dfrac{84}{430}$ **C.** $\dfrac{10}{830}$ **D.** $\dfrac{21}{430}$

E. $\dfrac{12}{230}$

// Smart Answer Sheet //

Correct — Percentage of students who answered correctly. **Skipped** — Percentage of students who skipped.

Q.	Ans.	Correct / Skipped	Q.	Ans.	Correct / Skipped	Q.	Ans.	Correct / Skipped	Q.	Ans.	Correct / Skipped	Q.	Ans.	Correct / Skipped	Q.	Ans.	Correct / Skipped
1	D	24.62 % / 69.84 %	15	C	47.03 % / 32.1 %	29	D	43.33 % / 37.3 %	43	D	64.41 % / 32.33 %	57	C	51.75 % / 41.31 %	71	D	56.01 % / 34.59 %
2	C	23.68 % / 74.96 %	16	E	59.2 % / 31.5 %	30	D	46.58 % / 31.72 %	44	C	65.63 % / 30.35 %	58	D	64.31 % / 34.53 %	72	D	42.23 % / 33.55 %
3	A	13.15 % / 74.45 %	17	D	47.58 % / 42.71 %	31	B	68.99 % / 30.34 %	45	A	58.04 % / 34.91 %	59	A	40.41 % / 52.3 %	73	E	48.84 % / 33.77 %
4	E	57.46 % / 34.64 %	18	E	57.32 % / 38.46 %	32	D	46.71 % / 45.32 %	46	C	68.63 % / 30.97 %	60	C	78.5 % / 15.02 %	74	C	59.68 % / 36.47 %
5	A	61.23 % / 30.59 %	19	B	52.51 % / 41.56 %	33	A	48.44 % / 35.01 %	47	A	59.64 % / 39.65 %	61	B	80.16 % / 14.55 %	75	C	57.7 % / 37.82 %
6	B	62.48 % / 31.94 %	20	C	67.46 % / 30.16 %	34	D	42.76 % / 42.16 %	48	B	47.62 % / 42.83 %	62	C	25.03 % / 73.01 %	76	E	64.64 % / 35.15 %
7	B	46.99 % / 36.29 %	21	B	40.7 % / 56.47 %	35	C	46.52 % / 31.84 %	49	C	49.25 % / 38.49 %	63	C	26.78 % / 73.0 %	77	D	61.17 % / 32.25 %
8	C	64.88 % / 34.59 %	22	C	25.76 % / 69.97 %	36	C	42.32 % / 38.15 %	50	B	42.04 % / 50.99 %	64	C	18.69 % / 72.16 %	78	A	44.59 % / 38.27 %
9	C	54.67 % / 31.76 %	23	D	27.57 % / 68.21 %	37	B	51.74 % / 45.67 %	51	D	47.23 % / 32.19 %	65	E	43.7 % / 38.84 %	79	C	45.06 % / 46.11 %
10	D	68.03 % / 31.24 %	24	D	60.29 % / 32.51 %	38	D	58.61 % / 40.65 %	52	A	46.6 % / 43.85 %	66	A	47.58 % / 41.2 %	80	D	42.09 % / 52.69 %
11	A	48.66 % / 39.01 %	25	B	22.29 % / 69.16 %	39	C	59.5 % / 33.05 %	53	A	56.2 % / 30.66 %	67	D	57.54 % / 40.15 %			
12	A	42.76 % / 43.85 %	26	C	24.34 % / 73.12 %	40	B	63.35 % / 34.74 %	54	C	61.07 % / 30.98 %	68	B	46.14 % / 41.75 %			
13	A	44.64 % / 40.59 %	27	A	56.24 % / 37.49 %	41	D	58.19 % / 30.5 %	55	D	56.84 % / 42.86 %	69	C	56.23 % / 34.04 %			
14	D	47.25 % / 52.06 %	28	B	44.38 % / 37.14 %	42	C	58.1 % / 39.96 %	56	C	57.6 % / 41.31 %	70	D	66.6 % / 31.24 %			

Reasoning

Ques (1-4):Direction: In the question below are given three statements followed by three conclusions numbered I, II, and III. You have to take the given statements to be true even if they seem to be at variance with commonly known facts. Read all the conclusions and then decide which of the given conclusions logically follows from the given statements disregarding commonly known facts.

Q.1 Statements:

I: All apple are chickoo.

II: Only orange are chickoo.

III: No apple is kiwi.

Conclusions:

I. No orange is kiwi.

II. All orange are chickoo is a possibility.

III. Some oranges are chickoo.

A. Only I and III follow

B. Only II and III follow

C. Only I and II follow

D. All follow

E. None of these

Q.2 Statements:

I. All Watch are Digital.

II. All Digital are Camera.

III. No Camera is anAutomatic.

Conclusions:

I. All Watch are Camera.

II. No Digital is an Automatic.

III. No Watch is an Automatic.

A. Only I follows

B. Only II follows

C. Only III follows

D. Both II and III follow

E. All follow

Q.3 Statements:

I. No Bag is a Box.

II. Some Box are Square.

III. All Square are Circle.

Conclusions:

I. Some Circle are Box.

II. No Box is a Square.

III. Some Square being a Bag is a possibility.

A. Only I follows

B. Both I and II follow

C. Both I and III follow

D. Both II and III follow

E. All follow

Q.4 Statements:

I: All TV are fridges.

II: Some computers are TV

III: All AC are computers.

Conclusions:

I. Some AC are fridges.

II. Some fridges are computers.

III. All TV are computers.

A. Only I follows

B. Only II follows

C. Only III follows

D. Both I and II follow

E. Both II and III follow

Q.5 How many pairs of letters are there in the word "CREDIBILITY" that has as many letters between them in the word as in the alphabet?

A. One

B. Two

C. Three

D. Four

E. More than five

Ques (6-10):Direction: Study the following information carefully and answer the questions given below.

Toukir visited seven different places in seven different months of a year i.e. January, February, April, June, September, October, and November. He visited only one place in a month. He visited more than one place between Victoria Memorial and India Gate. He visited Lal Qila immediately before his visit to Lotus temple but in the month which has not less than 30 days. He went to Char Minar in the month which has 31 days. He visited Qutub Minar immediately after the Char Minar. He visited Victoria Memorial in the month which has 31 days. He visited the Taj Mahal before Char Minar.

Q.6 Toukir visited which among the following places in the month of June?

A. Qutub Minar

B. India Gate

C. Lotus temple

D. Char Minar

E. Taj Mahal

Q.7 In which month did he visit India Gate?

A. September

B. November

C. April

D. January

E. October

Q.8 How many places did he visit after he visited Lal Qila?

A. Two

B. Three

C. Four

D. Five

E. One

Q.9 In the month of February, he visited ______.

A. India Gate

B. Victoria Memorial

C. Qutub Minar

D. Char Minar

E. None of the above

Q.10 Which among the following is not true?

A. He visited Taj Mahal after he visited Lotus temple.

B. He visited Qutub Minar in the month which has less than 30 days.

C. He visited India Gate in the month of June.

D. He visited Victoria Memorial after he visited India Gate.

E. All of the above

Q.11 Direction: In the following question, select the one which is different from the other three responses.

A. GED **B.** TRQ
C. QPO **D.** VTS
E. None of these

Ques (12-15):Direction: In the following question assuming the given statements to be true, find which of the conclusion among given conclusions is/are definitely true and then give your answers accordingly.

Q.12 Statements:

Q = X < R < G; G ≥ T < Y; O > X

Conclusions:

I. O > Q

II. O > G

III. Q = Y

A. Only III is true

B. Only I is true

C. Only I and II are true

D. Either I or III is true

E. Only II is true

Q.13 Statements:

A > T, E ≤ M, F ≤ T, E < A

Conclusions:

I. A > M

II. F < E

A. Only conclusion I is true

B. Only conclusion II is true

C. Either conclusion I or II is true

D. Neither conclusion I nor II is true

E. Both conclusions I and II are true

Q.14 Statements:

W ≥ Z, E > O, O < Z, E ≤ M

Conclusions:

I. W > E

II. O < W

A. Only conclusion I is true

B. Only conclusion II is true

C. Either conclusion I or II is true

D. Neither conclusion I nor II is true

E. Both conclusions I and II are true

Q.15 Statements: M > A ≥ N = L ≥ U > T; Q = N < S

Conclusions:

I. M > Q

II. U ≤ A

III. T < S

A. Only III is true

B. Only I is true

C. Both II and III are true

D. Both I and III are true

E. All are true

Ques (16-18):Direction: Study the following information carefully and answer the given questions.

In a certain code language:

'very large risk associated ' is written as 'nu ta ro gl',

'risk is very low' is written as 'gl se nu mi',

'is that also associated' is written as 'ta mi po fu' and

'inherent risk also damaging' is written as 'fu nu di yu'.

Q.16 What would be the code for 'inherent large risk'?

A. fu gl nu **B.** ta di nu **C.** ro fu nu **D.** ro nu di
E. yu ro di

Q.17 Which of the following codes is used for 'associated' in the code language?

A. ta **B.** mi **C.** se **D.** ro
E. gl

Q.18 What would be the code for 'that damaging'?

A. po mi **B.** yu di
C. di po **D.** yu po
E. Either (C) or (D)

Ques (19-20):Direction: Study the given information carefully and answer the given questions.

M is the mother of N. N is the sister of O. P is the son of O. Q is the brother of P. R is the mother of Q. S is the granddaughter of M. T has only two children N and O.

Q.19 Who is the mother of S?

A. O **B.** N
C. R **D.** Either N or R
E. Either O or R

Q.20 How is O related to Q?

A. Father **B.** Son
C. Mother **D.** Cousin Brother
E. Can't be determined

Q.21 Direction: The question consists of two statements, an assertion and a reason. The student must determine whether each statement is true and then whether the reason holds true to the assertion.

Assertion(A): Over a period of time rust accumulates on iron.

Reason(R): When iron is exposed to oxygen and moisture for a length of time, it forms rust.

A. Both A and R are true and R is the correct explanation of A

B. Both A and R are true and R is not the correct explanation of A.

C. A is true but R is false.

D. A is false but R is true.
E. Both A and R are false.

Ques (22-25):Direction: Study the following information carefully and answer the question given below.

Eight people A, B, C, D, E, F, G, H are sitting around a circular table and all of them are facing outside. Each of them is wearing different coloured shirts viz. White, Black, Red, Purple, Yellow, Indigo, Brown and Blue but not necessarily in the same order. G who is wearing neither Blue nor Brown is sitting opposite to E. A is sitting second to the right of B, who is not an immediate neighbour of C and G. The person wearing Red colour shirt is sitting to the immediate left of A, who is wearing a yellow shirt. Only three people are sitting between the persons who are wearing White and Blue colour shirts. The person wearing Black is sitting between the person wearing White and G. Only one person is sitting between A and D who is not wearing blue. E sits third to the right of C, who is wearing an indigo colour shirt. Only two people sit between H and the person who is wearing a Brown colour shirt.

Q.22 Who is wearing the brown shirt?
A. B
B. G
C. D
D. E
E. None of these

Q.23 Who sits 2nd to the right of the person who wears red shirt?
A. G
B. C
C. B
D. H
E. A

Q.24 How many persons are sitting between C and F when counting from C in anticlockwise direction?
A. No one
B. 4
C. 6
D. 5
E. None of these

Q.25 Who is sitting opposite to B?
A. E
B. D
C. the person who is wearing black colour
D. the person who is wearing blue colour
E. Both (B) and (C)

Ques (26-27):Direction: Study the following alphabet series and answer the question that follow.

A B C D E F G H I J K L M N O P Q R S T U V W X Y Z

Q.26 In the above alphabet series, if each letter from F onwards, is represented by the months of the year starting from January, then what is the position of first occurring June from the right?
A. 4th
B. 6th
C. 7th
D. 5th
E. None of these

Q.27 Four of the following five are alike in a certain way and so from a group. Which one does not belong to the group?
A. BAB
B. FCD
C. JEF
D. DBD
E. HDE

Ques (28-30):Direction: Study the information given below carefully and answer the questions that follow.

Shaan starts from point P, walks 4 km East, and reaches point Q. At point Q, he turns left and reaches point R after going 4 km. After reaching point R, he turns right and walks 4 km to reach point S. Further, he goes 7 km after taking a right turn and reaches point T. He further takes a left turn, covers 4 km to reach point U. Finally, he covers a distance of 5 km after taking a left turn and reaches point V.

Q.28 What is the direction of the final position of Shaan with respect to his initial position?
A. North
B. North-West
C. South-West
D. North-East
E. South-East

Q.29 What is the shortest distance between point Q and T?
A. 3 km
B. 5 km
C. 15 km
D. 4 km
E. 8 km

Q.30 What is the total distance covered by Shaan?
A. 17 km
B. 19 km
C. 38 km
D. 28 km
E. 10 km

Ques (31-35):Direction: Study the following information carefully to answer the given questions.

Seven students P, Q, R, S, T, U, and V are sitting in a row. All of them are facing the South. The distance between any of the two students is the same. Each of them has different ages viz. 9 years, 11 years, 16 years, 17 years, 18 years, 19 years, and 20 years.

The age difference between the neighbors of U is 9 years. The youngest one sits at one of the extreme ends of the row. V is not an immediate neighbor of the one who is 17 years old. V is elder than S and Q but not the eldest one. Q sits fourth to the left of V. P sits between R and S. R is older than only U and T.

Q.31 Who among the following sits at one of the extreme ends of the row?
A. R
B. U
C. V
D. P
E. None of these

Q.32 How many persons are there between P and U?
A. One
B. Two
C. Four
D. More than Four
E. Three

Q.33 If the distance between V and S is 12 meters, then find out the distance between R and Q?
A. 16 meters
B. 8 meters
C. 12 meters
D. 4 meters
E. None of these

Q.34 How many seats are there between the third youngest among them and Q?
A. One
B. Two
C. Three
D. None
E. Can't say

Q.35 Who among following sits third to the right of the one who is 17 years old?

A. V

B. P

C. Q

D. T

E. None of these

Ques (36-40):Direction: Study the following information carefully to answer the given question:

Eight persons from different bank viz. UCO bank, Syndicate bank, Canara bank, PNB, Dena Bank, Oriental Bank of Commerce, Indian bank and Bank of Maharashtra are sitting in two parallel rows containing four people each, in such a way that there is an equal distance between adjacent persons. In row 1: A, B, C and D are seated and all of them are facing south. In row 2: P, Q, R and S are seated and all of them are facing north. Therefore, in the given seating arrangements each member seated in a row faces another member of the other row. (All the information given above does not necessarily represent the order of seating as in the final arrangement).

- C sits second to right of the person from Bank of Maharashtra. R is an immediate neighbor of the person who faces the person from Bank of Maharashtra.

- Only one person sits between R and the person for PNB. Immediate neighbour of the person from PNB faces the person from Canara Bank.

- The person from UCO bank faces the person from Oriental Bank of Commerce. R is not from Oriental Bank of Commerce. P is not from PNB. P does not face the person form Bank of Maharashtra

- Q faces the person from Dena Bank. The one who faces S sits to the immediate left of A.

- B does not sit at any of the extreme ends of the line. The person from Bank of Maharashtra does not face the person from Syndicate Bank.

Q.36 Four of the following five are alike in a certain way based on the given seating arrangement and thus from a group, which is the one that does not belong to that group?

A. Canara bank

B. R

C. Syndicate bank

D. Q

E. Oriental Bank of Commerce

Q.37 P is related to Dena Bank in the same way as B is related to PNB based on the given arrangement. To who amongst the following is D related to following the same pattern?

A. Syndicate bank=

B. Canara bank

C. Bank of Maharashtra

D. Indian Bank

E. Oriental Bank of Commerce

Q.38 Who amongst the following sit at extreme ends of the rows?

A. D and the person from PNB

B. The person from Indian bank and UCO bank

C. The person from Dena bank and P

D. The person form Syndicate bank and D

E. C, Q

Q.39 Who is seated between R and the person from PNB?

A. The person from Oriental Bank of Commerce

B. P

C. Q

D. The person from Syndicate bank

E. S

Q.40 Which of the following is true regarding A?

A. The person from UCO bank faces A

B. The person from Bank of Maharashtra is an immediate neighbor of A

C. A faces the Person who sits second to right of R

D. A is from Oriental Bank of Commerce

E. A sits at one of the extreme ends of the line

Quantitative Aptitude

Ques (41-45):Direction: The pie chart shows the percentage of total flights of different airlines from an airport. The total number of flights from the airport in a month is 2500. Study the chart carefully and answer the questions.

Perentage of total flights

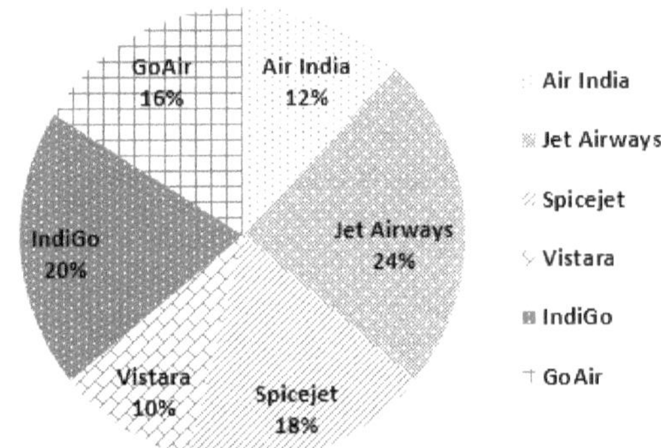

Q.41 30% of the flights of Vistara are International flights and 60% of the flights of Jet Airways are Domestic flights then find the total number of Domestic flights of Vistara and Jet Airways.

A. 485 **B.** 475 **C.** 535 **D.** 510

E. 525

Q.42 Find the difference in the number of flights of Air India and Go Air together and the number of flights of IndiGo and Spice jet together.

A. 250 **B.** 500 **C.** 375 **D.** 175

E. 400

Q.43 If IndiGo stops its services at that Airport then what would be the changed percentage of Go Air flights out of total flights?

A. 18% **B.** 30% **C.** 25% **D.** 20%

E. 22.5%

Q.44 If 15% of the flights of Air India and 10% of the flights of Spice jet are International flights. Find the ratio of international flights of Air India and Spice jet.

A. 1 : 2 **B.** 1 : 1 **C.** 2 : 3 **D.** 3 : 4
E. 4 : 5

Q.45 By what percentage the number of flights of Jet Airways are more than the number of flights of Go Air?
A. 40% **B.** 100% **C.** 33.34% **D.** 66.67%
E. 50%

Ques (46-50):Direction: What should come in place of question mark '?' in the following number series?

Q.46 1, 5, 14, 39, 88, ?
A. 169 **B.** 209 **C.** 224 **D.** 175
E. 189

Q.47 6, 40, 84, 143, 222, ?
A. 234 **B.** 315 **C.** 326 **D.** 290
E. 345

Q.48 154, 54, 254, -146, ?
A. 456 **B.** 946 **C.** 654 **D.** 564
E. -946

Q.49 23, ?, 38, 53, 73, 98

[SBI Apprentice, 2021]

A. 30 **B.** 28
C. 25 **D.** 32
E. None of these

Q.50 13, 14, 30, ?, 376, 1885
A. 93 **B.** 75 **C.** 15 **D.** 55
E. 65

Ques (51-55):Direction: The table below shows the Distance (In kms) traveled by five friends on six different days of a week. Study the data carefully and answer the questions.

	A	B	C	D	E
Monday	180	150	200	160	240
Tuesday	240	200	160	240	320
Wednesday	300	250	180	320	300
Thursday	320	180	220	180	200
Friday	160	220	140	280	150
Saturday	120	150	150	260	180

Q.51 If the speed of C on Tuesday was 20% more than the speed of D on Thursday then find the ratio of time taken by C to travel on Tuesday and D on Thursday.
A. 20 : 27 **B.** 14 : 13 **C.** 3 : 2 **D.** 6 : 5
E. 10 : 9

Q.52 What is the average distance traveled by B in all the six days together?
A. 166.67 km **B.** 206.67 km
C. 187.5 km **D.** 191.67 km
E. 195 km

Q.53 If the average speed of A on Wednesday was 37.5 km/hr and the average speed of C on Friday was 35 km/hr then find the difference of time taken by A on Wednesday and C on Friday.
A. 3 hours **B.** 4 hours

C. 4.5 hors **D.** 5 hours
E. 2.5 hours

Q.54 If the ratio of time taken by E to travel the respective distances on Monday and Tuesday is 5 : 8 then find the difference of speeds of E on Monday and Tuesday.
A. 10 **B.** 8
C. 12 **D.** 6
E. Can't be determined

Q.55 If D took 6.5 hours on Saturday and the speed of E on Wednesday was 25% more than the speed of D on Saturday then find the time taken by E to travel the distance on Wednesday.
A. 5 hours **B.** 4.5 hours
C. 6 hours **D.** 8 hours
E. 4 hours

Ques (56-60):Direction: In the following questions, two equations numbered are given in variables x and y. You have to solve both the equations and find out the relationship between x and y. Then give an answer accordingly.

Q.56 I. $3x^2 + 8x - 35 = 0$
II. $3y^2 - 23y + 42 = 0$
A. x > y
B. x < y
C. x ≥ y
D. x ≤ y
E. x = y or relationship cannot be determined

Q.57 I. $3x^2 - 10x + 8 = 0$
II. $3y^2 - 22y + 35 = 0$
A. If x > y
B. If x < y
C. If x ≥ y
D. If x ≤ y
E. If x = y or relation cannot be established

Q.58 I. $2x^2 - 13x + 18 = 0$
II. $2y^2 + 3y - 9 = 0$
A. If x > y
B. If x < y
C. If x ≥ y
D. If x ≤ y
E. If x = y or relation cannot be established

Q.59 I. $x^2 - 41x + 148 = 0$
II. $y^2 - y - 132 = 0$
A. If x > y
B. If x < y
C. If x ≥ y
D. If x ≤ y
E. If x = y or relation cannot be established

Q.60 I. $2x^2 - 15x + 27 = 0$
II. $3y^2 - 11y + 6 = 0$
A. If x > y
B. If x < y

C. If x ≥ y
D. If x ≤ y
E. If x = y or relation cannot be established

Ques (61-65):Direction: In a school, there is a total of 20 teachers of 5 different subjects viz. Math, English, Science, Hindi, History. The line graph below shows the number of teaches in each subject. Study the data carefully and answer the question.

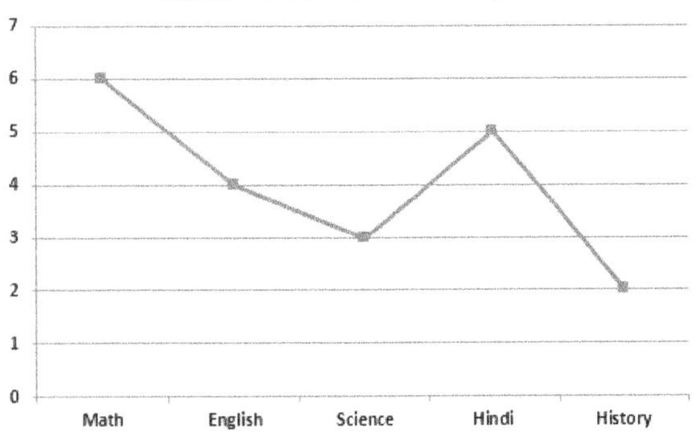

Q.61 In how many ways, 4 teachers can be selected to teach either Hindi or English such that out of 4 selected, one particular English teacher is fixed and at least one teacher should be there of each subject.

A. 60　　**B.** 80　　**C.** 120　　**D.** 50
E. 40

Q.62 A committee of 6 teachers is to be formed from Maths and Science teachers. In how many ways it can be done if the committee should have at least 4 math teachers.

A. 64　　**B.** 48　　**C.** 63　　**D.** 49
E. 60

Q.63 In how many ways the teachers can be seated in a row so that same subject teachers remain together.

A.　6! × 4! × 3! × 5! × 2! × 4!
B.　6! × 4! × 3! × 5! × 2! × 5!
C.　6! × 4! × 3! × 5! × 2!
D.　6! × 4! × 3! × 5! × 2! × 6!
E.　None of these

Q.64 If a committee of 5 teachers is to be formed so that it must have 1 teacher of each subject. In how many ways it can be done?

A. 360　　**B.** 840　　**C.** 120　　**D.** 720
E. 600

Q.65 If Science and Hindi teachers are to be seated in a row of seats (numbered 1 – 8), then in how many ways they can be seated if Science teachers occupy an even-numbered seat only.

A.　3! × 5!　　　　**B.**　$^4C2 × 3! × 5!$
C.　$^4C_3 × 3!$　　　**D.**　3! × 5! × 2!
E.　$^4C_3 × 3! × 5!$

Q.66 What is the average of the first four numbers in a Geometric Progression having a common ratio of 5 and the first number of series is 1.5?

A. 58.5　　**B.** 25　　**C.** 96.5　　**D.** 93.6
E. 48.6

Q.67 The number of Males & Females in a town is 150 & 100 respectively. The percentage of child included in Male & Female both is x%. Find the total number of adult females if the total number of child is 30.

A. 88　　**B.** 78　　**C.** 82　　**D.** 94
E. 76

Q.68 The ratio of incomes of P, Q and R is 3 : 7 : 4 and the ratio of their expenditures is 4 : 3 : 5. If P saves $14\frac{2}{7}\%$ of his income, then find the ratio of the saving done by P, Q and R.

A.　4 : 5 : 1　　　　**B.**　6 : 71 : 11
C.　8 : 61 : 13　　　**D.**　7 : 45 : 12
E.　None of these

Q.69 3 years ago, the ratio of age of A and B is 1 : 3 and the ratio of the present age of B and C is 2: 7. Find the C's age after 3 years if the sum of the present age of A and B is 34 years.

A. 81 years　**B.** 87 years　**C.** 78 years　**D.** 89 years
E. 85 years

Q.70 A invest Rs.3000 and B invest x amount in a partnership. After 6 months, C replaced B with some amount in his hand. If A's share in profit at the end of the year is Rs.2000, find the amount that B invested.

A.　Rs. 2000
B.　Rs. 2500
C.　Rs. 3500
D.　Rs. 4000
E.　Cannot be determined

Q.71 If the selling price of a chair is 5 times the discount offered, and the discount percentage is equal to the profit percentage then find the ratio of discount offered to the cost price of the chair.

A. 6 : 30　　**B.** 7 : 30　　**C.** 7 : 35　　**D.** 6 : 35
E. 5 : 25

Q.72 The length of the first train is 300 meters and its speed is 25 km/h and the length of the second train is 200 meters and both the trains are running towards each other. If a higher speed train crosses the lower speed train in 45 seconds, then find the speed of the second train in km/h.

A. 12 km/h　**B.** 10 km/h　**C.** 15 km/h　**D.** 22 km/h
E. 18 km/h

Q.73 A boat covers 36 km downstream in 4 hours and 18 km upstream in 6 hours. Find the speed of the boat.

A. 12 km/hr　**B.** 9 km/hr　**C.** 6 km/hr　**D.** 5 km/hr
E. 3 km/hr

Q.74 A can do a work in 20 days. After completing $\frac{1}{4}$ of the work A calls B and the remaining work is completed in 9 days. B alone can-do work in:

A.　24　　　　　　**B.**　27
C.　32　　　　　　**D.**　35
E.　None of these

Q.75 A cylinder of diameter 14 cm has a volume of 2310 cm³.
What is the curved surface area of the cylinder?

A. 330 cm² **B.** 440 cm² **C.** 550 cm² **D.** 660 cm²
E. 770 cm²

Ques (76-80):Direction: What should come in place of the question mark (?) in the following question?

Q.76 $\sqrt{6084} \div \sqrt{169} \times 24^2 + (66 \div 3)^2 =?$

A. 3940 **B.** 9144
C. 7844 **D.** 8644
E. None of these

Q.77 383 ÷ 255 × 25.5 + 12 = ?

A. 50.3 **B.** 222.14
C. 68.30 **D.** 124.24
E. None of these

Q.78 $15^2 + 24^2 \div (3 \times 2^2) + 98 \div 14 = ?$

A. 250 **B.** 360 **C.** 420 **D.** 280
E. 160

Q.79 18% of 27 + 2% of 207 = $(?)^2$

A. 3 **B.** 5
C. 7 **D.** 6
E. None of these

Q.80 4003 × 77 – 22175 = ? × 116

A. 2477 **B.** 2478
C. 2467 **D.** 2466
E. None of these

// Smart Answer Sheet //

Correct Percentage of students who answered correctly.   **Skipped** Percentage of students who skipped.

Q.	Ans.	Correct / Skipped	Q.	Ans.	Correct / Skipped	Q.	Ans.	Correct / Skipped	Q.	Ans.	Correct / Skipped	Q.	Ans.	Correct / Skipped	Q.	Ans.	Correct / Skipped
1	B	41.38 % / 2.3 %	15	E	51.15 % / 36.78 %	29	B	23.56 % / 61.5 %	43	D	10.34 % / 61.5 %	57	B	29.89 % / 56.89 %	71	B	1.72 % / 78.17 %
2	E	54.02 % / 33.34 %	16	D	40.8 % / 40.81 %	30	D	20.69 % / 63.79 %	44	B	20.69 % / 59.77 %	58	A	29.31 % / 57.47 %	72	C	2.87 % / 78.74 %
3	C	46.55 % / 34.48 %	17	A	53.45 % / 41.38 %	31	C	2.3 % / 69.54 %	45	E	20.69 % / 61.49 %	59	E	21.26 % / 59.2 %	73	C	5.17 % / 76.44 %
4	B	39.66 % / 35.05 %	18	E	40.23 % / 42.53 %	32	B	4.6 % / 75.29 %	46	B	17.24 % / 55.17 %	60	C	22.99 % / 60.92 %	74	E	4.02 % / 76.44 %
5	E	46.55 % / 36.21 %	19	D	33.33 % / 43.68 %	33	C	3.45 % / 77.01 %	47	C	20.11 % / 59.78 %	61	B	1.72 % / 72.42 %	75	D	3.45 % / 78.16 %
6	C	21.84 % / 47.7 %	20	A	41.95 % / 45.41 %	34	B	2.3 % / 78.16 %	48	C	12.64 % / 60.92 %	62	A	1.72 % / 73.57 %	76	A	18.39 % / 72.41 %
7	A	25.29 % / 52.3 %	21	A	9.77 % / 64.94 %	35	A	1.72 % / 75.87 %	49	B	18.97 % / 62.64 %	63	B	1.15 % / 73.56 %	77	A	16.67 % / 74.13 %
8	C	19.54 % / 52.3 %	22	A	4.6 % / 68.39 %	36	D	0.57 % / 96.56 %	50	A	12.07 % / 63.22 %	64	D	1.15 % / 76.44 %	78	D	10.92 % / 77.59 %
9	E	28.74 % / 51.72 %	23	D	2.87 % / 74.72 %	37	D	0.57 % / 97.13 %	51	A	5.75 % / 63.79 %	65	E	1.72 % / 76.44 %	79	A	14.94 % / 77.01 %
10	E	17.82 % / 52.87 %	24	C	2.87 % / 72.99 %	38	D	0.57 % / 97.71 %	52	D	22.41 % / 62.07 %	66	A	4.6 % / 71.26 %	80	D	8.05 % / 77.01 %
11	C	47.7 % / 40.23 %	25	E	3.45 % / 70.11 %	39	E	0.57 % / 98.28 %	53	B	8.05 % / 67.24 %	67	A	5.75 % / 72.99 %			
12	B	53.45 % / 37.35 %	26	A	7.47 % / 64.94 %	40	B	1.15 % / 97.13 %	54	E	4.02 % / 67.24 %	68	B	2.87 % / 74.14 %			
13	D	48.85 % / 36.78 %	27	D	21.84 % / 60.92 %	41	C	18.97 % / 60.34 %	55	C	4.6 % / 68.39 %	69	B	2.3 % / 75.29 %			
14	B	54.02 % / 36.78 %	28	D	18.39 % / 62.64 %	42	A	26.44 % / 58.04 %	56	B	22.41 % / 55.18 %	70	E	2.3 % / 77.01 %			

Reasoning

Ques (1-5):Direction: Study the following information carefully and answer the given question.

A word and number arrangement machine when given an input line of words and numbers rearranges them following a particular hide in each step. The following is an illustration of input and rearrangement. (All the numbers are two digit numbers).

Input: 76 toy high 12 wish 98 10 flag link dig 54 87 58

Step I: dig 76 toy high 12 wish 98 flag link 54 87 58 10

Step II: flag dig 76 toy high wish 98 link 54 87 58 12 10

Step III: high flag dig 76 toy wish 98 link 87 58 54 12 10

Step IV: link high flag dig toy wish 98 87 76 58 54 12 10

Step V: toy link high flag dig wish 98 87 76 58 54 12 10

Step VI: wish toy link high flag dig 98 87 76 58 54 12 10

And Step VI is the last step of the above input, as the desired arrangement is obtained.

As per the hides followed in the above steps, find out in the question, the appropriate step for the given input. (All the numbers are two-digit numbers).

Input: height math 23 98 11 ugly and 54 owl 20 67 queen fish 32

Q.1 What is the position of "height" in step V?
A. Fourth from the right
B. Third from the right
C. Twelfth from right
D. Tenth from right
E. None of above

Q.2 Which is the last step after all arrangements?
A. V   **B.** VII   **C.** IX   **D.** VIII
E. IV

Q.3 What will be position of 98 in third step?
A. Fifth from the left
B. Fifth from the right
C. Seventh from the right
D. Eighth from left
E. None of above

Q.4 Which would be IV step?
A. math height fish and 98 ugly owl 67 queen 54 32 23 20 11
B. queen owl math height fish and ugly 98 67 54 32 23 20 11
C. ugly queen owl math height fish and 98 67 54 32 23 20 11
D. height fish and math 98 ugly 54 owl 67 queen 32 23 20 11
E. owl math height fish and 98 ugly queen 67 54 32 23 20 11

Q.5 What is the position of "fish" in last step?
A. Eighth from right   **B.** Fifth from left
C. Sixth from left   **D.** Seventh from right
E. None of above

Ques (6-9):Direction: Study the given information and answer the questions that follow.

8 members in a family - Sudha, Ravi, Shardul, Sakshi, Teju, Ramu, Deepak and Ramya went to Shimla to beat their summer heat. Family consists of 2 couples. Ramu has four children. Out of them, only one is married. The married son of Ramu has a daughter named Sakshi. Sudha is grandmother of Sakshi. Sakshi's mother is the wife of Shardul who has an only sister named Ramya. Ravi is the younger brother of Shardul, who is not eldest. Teju is the wife of the brother of Ravi. Ramu is a male.

Q.6 Who is the wife of Ramu?
A. Teju   **B.** Sudha
C. Ramya   **D.** Sakshi
E. Data insufficient

Q.7 How Sakshi is related to Ravi?
A. Sister   **B.** Daughter
C. Sister in law   **D.** Niece
E. Wife

Q.8 Who is Teju in this family?
A.   Ravi's sister
B.   Sudha's Mother in law
C.   Deepak's wife
D.   Shardul's daughter
E.   Ravi's sister in law

Q.9 Who is the elder brother of Shardul?
A.   Ramu
B.   Ravi
C.   Deepak
D.   Cannot be determined
E.   None of the above

Q.10 How many pairs of digits in the number 689324 have as many numbers between them as in the series of natural numbers both in backward and forward directions?
A. Five   **B.** Four
C. Three   **D.** More than five
E. None of these

Q.11 Directions: In the following question, assuming the given statements to be true, find which of the conclusion(s)among given conclusions is /are definitely true and then give your answers accordingly.

Statements:

$C \leq I > B = S;\ C \geq L = E;\ K = R > E$

Conclusions:

I. I > L

II. E = I

III. K ≥ L

IV. R > S

A. Either I or II follows

B. II and IV follows

C. Only IV follows

D. II and III follows

E. Either I or III follows

Q.12 Which of the following symbols should be placed in the blank spaces respectively (in the same order from left to right) in order to complete the given expression in such a manner that 'R > T' definitely holds false?

R _ S _ Q _ P _ T

A. >, =, >, ≥

B. <, >, =, ≥

C. <, ≤, =, <

D. =, <, =, >

E. None of these

Q.13 Directions: In the following question, assuming the given statements to be true, find which of the conclusion(s)among given conclusions is /are definitely true, and then give your answers accordingly.

Statements:

q < P ≤ R = T; Q ≤ p = T; t > r < Q

Conclusions:

I. q > Q

II. P ≥ p

III. R > r

IV. T < t

A. Only I and IV is true

B. Either II or III is true

C. Only III is true

D. Only I and either II or III is true

E. None of these

Ques (14-18):Direction: Read the following information carefully and answer the questions that follow.

Six people visit a building on six different days of a single week other than Sunday for six different jobs. A, B, C, D, E, and F are the six people who perform Cleaning of the floor, Delivery of package, Washing of windows, Collecting garbage, Repairing ducts, and Checking for technological faults not necessarily in the same order. B visits on one of the first three days of the week and does not deliver packages. Cleaning of the floor is performed by A and visits either on Monday or Thursday. There are two people visiting between C and D. Washing of windows is done on any day after Thursday. D does repair on Friday. F doesn't visit either on Thursday or Saturday and collects garbage. Checking for technological faults is done on Monday.

Q.14 Which job is performed by B?

A. Cleaning of floor

B. Delivery of package

C. Checking for technological faults

D. Repairing of ducts

E. Collecting of garbage

Q.15 Who delivers the packages?

A. A   **B.** B   **C.** C   **D.** E

E. F

Q.16 Who visits on the last working day?

A. A   **B.** B   **C.** E   **D.** F

E. C

Q.17 Which combination of "Day-People" is not true?

A. Monday-B   **B.** Thursday-A

C. Friday-D   **D.** Wednesday-F

E. Tuesday-E

Q.18 Which job is performed after A leaves and before E enters the building?

A. Cleaning of floor

B. Delivery of package

C. Checking for technological faults

D. Repairing of ducts

E. Collecting of garbage

Ques (19-21):Direction: Study the following information carefully and answer the given questions.

A # B means A is the father of B.

A + B means A is the mother of B.

A – B means A is the brother of B.

A * B means A is the sister of B.

Q.19 If U – V * X # Z, then U is Z's?

A. Sister

B. Aunt

C. Grandmother

D. Uncle

E. Cannot be determined

Q.20 Which of the following shows that A is the Grandmother of E?

A. A – B + C # D * E   **B.** A * B # C * D – E

C. A # B * C + D – E   **D.** A + B – C * D # E

E. A + B * C – D * E

Q.21 If W + X * Y # Z, how is Z related to W?

A. Daughter

B. Granddaughter

C. Son

D. Grandson

E. Cannot be determined

Ques (22-26):Direction: Read the following information carefully and answer the questions that follow.

Eight friends H, I, J, K, L, M, N and O are sitting in a row facing north. All of them like different colours – Red, Pink, Orange, Green, Yellow, Black, Violet and Blue.

- There is only 1 person between J and one who likes Violet. N is neither an immediate neighbour of J nor he likes Green.H sits fourth to the left of the one who

likes Violet but she does not like pink. The person who likes Black is sits third to the right of the onw who likes Green and sits on the immediate right of H.

- The one who likes Green sits at one of the extreme ends of the row. I does not like Green. M is an immediate neighbour of both N and J. O sits at one of the extreme end of the row but he does not like green.The one who likes Blue sits second to the right of the one who likes Orange. The one who likes Black and Pink are immediate neighbours. L sits third to the left of J and likes Yellow. There is only one person sitting between the one who likes yellow and black.

Q.22 How many persons are there between I and N?
A. One
B. Two
C. Three
D. Four
E. None of these

Q.23 Who among the following sits third to the right of the person who likes Pink?
A. One who like Blue
B. One who likes Black
C. One who likes Red
D. One who likes Green
E. None of these

Q.24 Who among the following likes Orange?
A. O
B. N
C. M
D. L
E. None of these

Q.25 N likes which of the following color?
A. Red
B. Black
C. Green
D. Violet
E. None of these

Q.26 Who are the immediate neighbors of the person who likes Red color?
A. L and I
B. L and N
C. J and H
D. L and K
E. None of these

Ques (27-31):Direction: Study the following information carefully and answer the questions given below.

M4, L6, U4 is written as "tell your name"

E8, K8, R2 is written as "marks are obtained"

U4, E8, V4 is written as "give your number"

H4, E8, S10 is written as "she secured highest".

Q.27 "Tell your number" is coded as ____
A. L6, V4, E10
B. U4, E8, L6
C. E8, V4, L4
D. V4, E10, L6
E. None of the above

Q.28 What is the code for "highest marks secured"?
A. E8, K6, S12
B. K8, E6, S10
C. E8, K8, S10
D. S8, K6, E8
E. None of the above

Q.29 Decode the sentence "All are intelligent".
A. L2, R4, N12
B. R4, L6, N10
C. N8, L6, R8
D. N14, R2, L4
E. None of these

Q.30 What is the code for "obtained"?
A. E10
B. B6
C. E8
D. B10
E. None of the above

Q.31 "M4, N4, E8" is written as ____.
A. Name or Place
B. Number and Place
C. Name and Number
D. Place and Name
E. None of the above

Ques (32-35):Direction: Study the following information carefully and answer the questions given below.

P, Q, R, S, T, U, V, and W are eight members of a family. The members belong to three different generations. Three of the 8 members are married couples. All members are seated around a circular table facing the center, but not in the same order.

1. S and U are married couples. U's wife S, is second to the left of her husband
2. R and P are children of S. P is not an immediate neighbor of his mother
3. Only one person sits between R and his niece V, but that person is not the father of V
4. T sits third to the right of his uncle P, but neither to the contrary nor to the immediate left of his father
5. V is not an immediate neighbor of his aunt. No three women sit together
6. R and his sister-in-law are immediate neighbors.

Q.32 Who among the following is V's father?
A. U
B. P
C. W
D. Q
E. Can't be determined

Q.33 Calculate the number of females in the family?
A. One
B. Three
C. Five
D. Can't be determined
E. None of these

Q.34 What is S's position in relation to his granddaughter?
A. Second to right
B. Fourth left
C. Third on the right
D. Second left
E. None of these

Q.35 Who among the following is sitting opposite his wife?
A. U
B. R
C. P
D. T
E. None

Q.36 Direction: One statement is given followed by two conclusions, I and II. You have to consider the statement to be true, even if it seems to be at variance from commonly known facts. You are to decide which of the given conclusions can definitely be drawn from the given statement.
Statement:

People nowadays make sure that their kids know classical music and dance.

Conclusions:

I) Kids are the pillars of a strong future.

II) Our rich traditional and cultural roots will be alive.

A. Only Conclusion I follows

B. Only Conclusion II follows

C. Both Conclusions I and II follow

D. Neither Conclusion I nor II follows

E. None of the above

Q.37 In the question, a statement is given, followed by two arguments, I and II. You have to consider the statement to be true even if it seems to be at variance from commonly known facts. You have to decide which of the given arguments, if any, is a strong argument.

Statement:

Is pen mightier than a sword?

Arguments:

I. Yes. Writers can influence the thinking of people which a sword can't do.

II. No. With a sword, a person can win any battle and conquer anything.

A. Only argument I is strong

B. Only argument II is strong

C. Either argument I or argument II is strong

D. Both arguments are strong

E. Neither argument is strong

Q.38 Direction: There are two statements marked as Assertion (A) and Reason (R). Read both the statements carefully and choose the correct option

Assertion (A): We should prefer conventional sources of energy as much as possible.

Reason (R): Conventional sources will last for 50-60 years.

A. Both A and R are true and R is the correct explanation of A

B. Both A and R are true but R is not the correct explanation of A

C. A is true but R is false

D. A is false but R is true

E. Both A and R are false

Ques (39-40):Direction: In the following question, a given question is followed by information in three statements. You have to decide the data in which statement (s) is sufficient to answer the question and mark your answer accordingly.

Q.39 Who is to the immediate left of P among six people P, Q, R, S, T, and U facing north?

I. R is fourth to the left of Q and Q is not at any of the extreme ends.

II. Q is exactly between P and U, who is at the extreme right end. T is the immediate right of R.

A. The data in statement I alone are sufficient to answer the question, while the data in statement II are not sufficient to answer the question

B. The data in statement II alone are sufficient to answer the question, while the data in statement I are not sufficient to answer the question

C. The data in statement I alone or data in statement II are sufficient to answer the question

D. The data in both statements I and II together are necessary to answer the question

E. The data even in both statements I and II together are not sufficient to answer the question

Q.40 What is the position of O with respect to P?

I. M is south to N.

II. N is east to O and P is west to M.

III. Q is south west to O.

A. All the statements are required

B. Only I and II are sufficient

C. Only II and III are sufficient

D. Only I and III are sufficient

E. Insufficient data

Quantitative Aptitude

Ques (41-45):Direction: The line graph provides the data of electricity consumption, in KW, by different houses in a month, whereas the Table gives data of costs charged on a different means from the houses. Read the questions related to the graph and answer them.

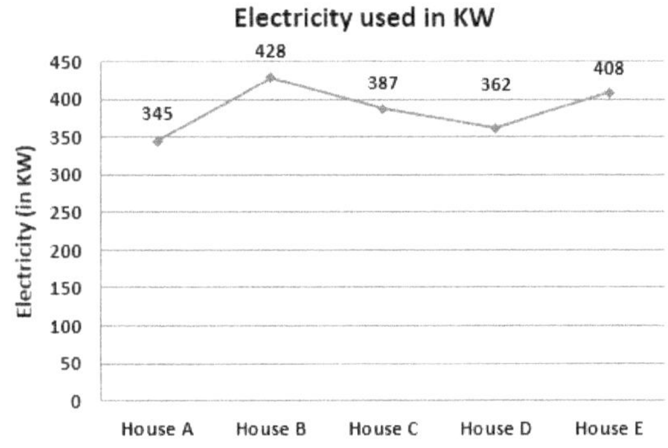

	Rent (Rs)	Internet	Food	Miscellaneous
House A	20,000	6000	12,500	15,000
House B	22,250	4500	8500	9500
House C	25,000	8000	13,000	11,500
House D	21,750	5500	9585	9000
House E	18,000	6000	9500	11,000

Q.41 If the cost of consuming 1 KW electricity is Rs 15, then find the total electricity bill for House B.

A. Rs. 6400　　**B.** Rs. 6420

C. Rs. 6450　　**D.** Rs. 6500

E. None of the above

Q.42 How much percent more was the living cost for House C when compared to House E approximately?

A. 25%　　**B.** 20%

C. 28%　　**D.** 31%

E. None of the above

Q.43 If electricity cost is not part of miscellaneous and the cost of 1 KW electricity is Rs. 20, then people of which house are living the most lavish life?

A. House A   **B.** House B   **C.** House C   **D.** House D
E. House E

Q.44 How many houses have rent above the average value?

A. 1   **B.** 2
C. 3   **D.** 4
E. None of the above

Q.45 For the next month, if the electricity cost is Rs. 10500 for House C, then how much should they reduce the miscellaneous cost to keep the overall expense the same as last month? (1KW = Rs. 25)

A. Rs. 10675   **B.** Rs. 11500
C. Rs. 1000   **D.** Rs. 825
E. Rs. 1050

Ques (46-48):Direction: In each of these questions a number series is given. In each series only one number is wrong. Find out the wrong number.

Q.46 4620, 4909, 5134, 5303, 5424, 5505, 5530

A. 5530   **B.** 5424   **C.** 4620   **D.** 5134
E. 5505

Q.47 4, 5, 7, 11, 24, 35, 67

A. 5   **B.** 24   **C.** 67   **D.** 35
E. 7

Q.48 3, 5, 14, 48, 196, 1010, 6072

A. 14   **B.** 1010   **C.** 6072   **D.** 196
E. 5

Ques (49-50):Direction: What will come in place of question mark (?) in the following number series?

Q.49 29, 31, ?, 39, 46, 57

A. 33   **B.** 36
C. 34   **D.** 32
E. None of these

Q.50 47, 23.5, ?, 47, 188, 1504

A. 23   **B.** 35
C. 25   **D.** 23.5
E. None of these

Ques (51-55):Direction: Study the following data and answer the following questions:

Total number of customers of five shops = 3000

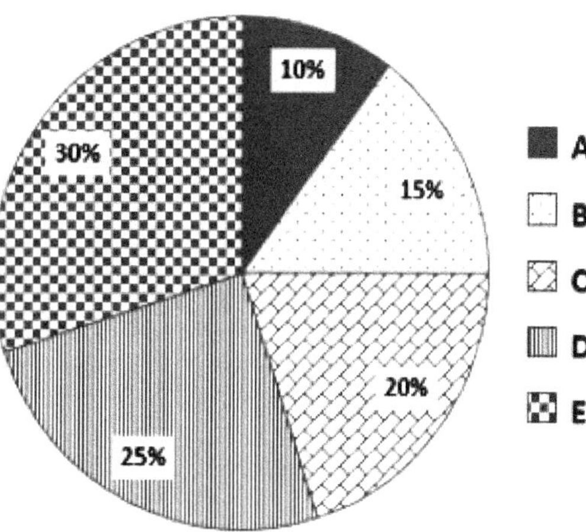

Number of Customers

Q.51 Find the average customers of shops A and C.
A. 300   **B.** 350   **C.** 450   **D.** 500
E. 600

Q.52 Find the difference between the number of customers of shops E and B.
A. 550   **B.** 300   **C.** 250   **D.** 400
E. 450

Q.53 Total customers of Shop D is approximately what percent less than the number of customers of shop E?
A. 12 %   **B.** 19 %   **C.** 14 %   **D.** 20 %
E. 16.66%

Q.54 The ratio between the percentage of degree customers of shop A and B.
A. 2: 5   **B.** 5: 3   **C.** 2: 3   **D.** 5: 2
E. 4: 5

Q.55 The number of customers of shop B is approximately what percent of customers of shop D?
A. 30%   **B.** 20%   **C.** 45%   **D.** 60%
E. 50%

Ques (56-60):Direction: The question below is followed by two statements I and II. You have to determine whether the data given is sufficient for answering the question. You should use the data and your knowledge of mathematics to choose the best possible answer.

Q.56 Find the number of employees in the company.
Statement I: Ratio between male and female is 9 : 11.
Statement II: Out of the total males, 20% belongs to the HR team and 20% of female belongs to the marketing team.

A. Only statement I is sufficient
B. Only statement II is sufficient
C. Statement I and II together is sufficient
D. Any of the above statement alone is sufficient
E. None of the statement together or alone is sufficient

Q.57 What is the rate of interest on the amount Rs. 8000 deposited in a bank?

Statement I: The simple interest for 3 years is 2400.

Statement II: The difference between the SI and CI for 2 years is 80.

A. Only statement I is sufficient

B. Only statement II is sufficient

C. Statement I and II together is sufficient

D. Any of the above statement alone is sufficient

E. None of the statement together or alone is sufficient

Q.58 What is the marked price of the chair?

Statement I: The chair is marked 40% above the cost price.

Statement II: A discount of 60% was given due to which there was a loss of 20%. The cost price of the chair is Rs.800.

A. Only statement I is sufficient

B. Only statement II is sufficient

C. Statement I and II together is sufficient

D. Any of the above statement alone is sufficient

E. None of the statement together or alone is sufficient

Q.59 There are 5 consecutive odd number, find the largest number.

Statement I: Average of the 5 consecutive odd numbers is 15.

Statement II: The difference of highest and lowest number is 8.

A. Only statement I is sufficient

B. Only statement II is sufficient

C. Statement I and II together is sufficient

D. Any of the above statement alone is sufficient

E. None of the statement together or alone is sufficient

Q.60 What is the age of Amit?

Statement I: The ratio of the present age of Anita and Amit is 3: 5.

Statement II: Raman age is double the age of Anita . 6 years hence their age will be in ratio 7: 4.

A. Only statement I is sufficient

B. Only statement II is sufficient

C. Statement I and II together is sufficient

D. Any of the above statement alone is sufficient

E. None of the statement together or alone is sufficient

Ques (61-65):Direction: What approximate will come in the place of the question mark '?' in the following question?

Q.61 33.33% of 659.9 + 25% of 220.31 - 14.28% of 98 = ?

A. 261

B. 240

C. 260

D. 235

E. None of these

Q.62 (69.987 × 2 - 27.872 × ? = 0)

A. 3 **B.** 5 **C.** 7 **D.** 8

E. 9

Q.63 $(36.09\% \text{ of } 950 - 34 \times 3.93 + 10)^{1/3} = ?$

A. 8

B. 7

C. 5

D. 6

E. None of these

Q.64 25.01% of 976.22 × 4.96 = ?

A. 3990

B. 3890

C. 4070

D. 3730

E. None of these

Q.65 $\{40.06\% \text{ of } \frac{2}{5} + 59.97\% \text{ of } \frac{1}{5}\} \times 10^3 + ? = 10^4$

A. 9330

B. 9720

C. 8270

D. 8000

E. None of these

Q.66 If a number is increased by 10% and then reduced by 50%, further increased by 50%, the resulting number would be what percentage of an original number?

A. 80% **B.** 82.5% **C.** 85% **D.** 90%

E. 125%

Q.67 Niharika bought one item for Rs. 600 and another for Rs. 9000. She paid 5% sales tax on the first item and 12.5% sales tax on the second item. How much percentage tax approximately did she pay on average if the two items are taken together?

A. 7% **B.** 8.75% **C.** 12% **D.** 12.5%

E. 17.5%

Q.68 The ratio of male to female employees in an office was 1 : 2. When 2 males and 2 females left the job the new ratio became 1 : 3. Find the new numbers of male and female employees.

A. 4, 12

B. 4, 8

C. 5, 1

D. 2, 6

E. None of the above

Q.69 A mixture contains milk and water in a ratio of 5: 2. If 3 liters of water is added to it, the ratio of milk and water becomes 31: 13. Find the original quantity of milk in the mixture.

A. 160 litres

B. 155 litres

C. 185 litres

D. 215 litres

E. None of these

Q.70 A sum of Rs. 11000 is equally divided and invested at two different rates of interest. The difference between the interests received after 3 years is Rs. 300. What is the difference between the rates of interest?

A. 1.82%

B. 1.75%

C. 1.69%

D. 1.32%

E. None of these

Q.71 A car runs at the speed of 50 kmph when not serviced and runs at 70 kmph, when serviced. After servicing the car covers a certain distance in 4 hours. How much time will the car take to cover the same distance when not serviced?

A. 5.8 hours

B. 6.5 hours

C. 5.6 hours

D. 5.2 hours

E. None of these

Q.72 A square room has a verandah of uniform width of 3 m around it. The area of the verandah is 288 sq. m. Find the cost of flooring the room if the cost of flooring per square meter is Rs. 15.

A. Rs. 6615   **B.** Rs. 8640
C. Rs. 4320   **D.** Rs. 3307
E. None of these

Q.73 Three dies were tossed simultaneously. What is the probability of getting the same number on all three dices?

A. $\frac{1}{6}$ **B.** $\frac{1}{36}$ **C.** $\frac{1}{72}$ **D.** $\frac{1}{44}$

E. $\frac{1}{216}$

Q.74 A Reliance fresh retailer professes to sell his goods at cost price but he uses a weight 920 g instead of a weight of 1 kg. Find his gain percent?

A. 8.6956%   **B.** 8.6356%   **C.** 8.3484%   **D.** 7.6596%
E. 7.2556%

Q.75 Half of a piece of work can be completed if A works for 3 hours and then B works for 2 hours. If A and B together complete the work in 4.8 hours then find the share of B out of Rs. 4500.

A. Rs. 2700   **B.** Rs. 2700   **C.** Rs. 3000   **D.** Rs. 1500
E. Rs. 2000

Ques (76-80):Direction: Two equations I and II are given in each question. On the basis of these equations decide the relation between x and y.

Q.76 I. $3x^2 + 13x + 12 = 0$
II. $2y^2 + 15y + 27 = 0$

A. x > y
B. x ≥ y
C. x < y
D. x ≤ y
E. x = y or the relationship cannot be established

Q.77 I. $2x^2 + 11x + 14 = 0$
II. $2y^2 + 17y + 33 = 0$

A. x > y
B. x ≥ y
C. x < y
D. x ≤ y
E. x = y or the relationship cannot be established

Q.78 I. $x^2 + 3x - 18 = 0$
II. $5y^2 + 7y + 2 = 0$

A. If x < y
B. If x ≤ y
C. If x > y
D. If x ≥ y
E. If x = y or the relationship cannot be established

Q.79 I. $x^2 - 7x + 12 = 0$
II. $2y^2 - 19y + 44 = 0$

A. x < y
B. x ≤ y
C. x > y
D. x ≥ y
E. x = y or no relationship can be obtained

Q.80 I. $x^2 + 11x + 30 = 0$

II. $y^2 + 12y + 36 = 0$

A. if x > y
B. if x ≥ y
C. if < y
D. if x ≤ y
E. if x = y or relationship between x and y cannot be established

// Smart Answer Sheet //

Correct — Percentage of students who answered correctly. **Skipped** — Percentage of students who skipped.

Q.	Ans.	Correct	Skipped
1	C	10.0 %	23.08 %
2	B	11.54 %	58.46 %
3	A	9.23 %	59.23 %
4	A	6.92 %	57.7 %
5	C	7.69 %	60.77 %
6	B	13.08 %	56.15 %
7	D	14.62 %	58.46 %
8	E	12.31 %	59.23 %
9	C	12.31 %	60.77 %
10	A	5.38 %	60.0 %
11	A	37.69 %	41.54 %
12	C	15.38 %	37.7 %
13	C	37.69 %	39.23 %
14	C	31.54 %	45.38 %

Q.	Ans.	Correct	Skipped
15	C	31.54 %	46.92 %
16	C	34.62 %	48.46 %
17	E	30.77 %	49.23 %
18	D	29.23 %	50.0 %
19	D	41.54 %	42.31 %
20	D	26.92 %	45.39 %
21	E	37.69 %	45.39 %
22	B	23.08 %	53.07 %
23	A	20.0 %	56.92 %
24	C	21.54 %	59.23 %
25	D	22.31 %	58.46 %
26	A	22.31 %	55.38 %
27	B	23.08 %	53.07 %
28	C	26.15 %	53.85 %

Q.	Ans.	Correct	Skipped
29	D	22.31 %	53.84 %
30	C	26.92 %	55.39 %
31	C	28.46 %	55.39 %
32	B	9.23 %	67.69 %
33	E	3.85 %	70.77 %
34	C	5.38 %	70.77 %
35	B	3.08 %	70.77 %
36	C	6.92 %	70.0 %
37	A	5.38 %	70.77 %
38	D	4.62 %	73.84 %
39	D	5.38 %	74.62 %
40	E	3.85 %	73.07 %
41	B	33.85 %	51.53 %
42	E	10.77 %	56.15 %

Q.	Ans.	Correct	Skipped
43	C	10.77 %	63.85 %
44	C	19.23 %	58.46 %
45	D	6.15 %	66.93 %
46	A	12.31 %	56.92 %
47	B	26.92 %	53.85 %
48	D	16.15 %	60.77 %
49	C	19.23 %	60.77 %
50	D	9.23 %	61.54 %
51	C	13.08 %	65.38 %
52	E	13.08 %	67.69 %
53	E	9.23 %	68.46 %
54	C	13.85 %	68.46 %
55	D	13.08 %	67.69 %
56	E	21.54 %	54.61 %

Q.	Ans.	Correct	Skipped
57	D	15.38 %	56.16 %
58	B	16.92 %	60.77 %
59	A	16.15 %	56.16 %
60	C	23.85 %	54.61 %
61	A	35.38 %	49.24 %
62	B	40.77 %	48.46 %
63	D	41.54 %	48.46 %
64	E	33.08 %	50.0 %
65	B	31.54 %	50.0 %
66	B	12.31 %	66.15 %
67	C	7.69 %	66.16 %
68	D	10.0 %	59.23 %
69	B	20.77 %	61.54 %
70	A	6.15 %	67.7 %

Q.	Ans.	Correct	Skipped
71	C	13.08 %	68.46 %
72	A	3.85 %	71.53 %
73	B	6.92 %	70.77 %
74	A	6.92 %	70.0 %
75	A	2.31 %	72.31 %
76	B	29.23 %	60.0 %
77	E	23.85 %	62.3 %
78	E	26.15 %	60.77 %
79	B	26.15 %	62.31 %
80	B	21.54 %	63.08 %

Quantitative Aptitude

Q.1 What should come in place of the question mark '?' in the following number series?

2, 9, 39, 161, ?, 2613

A. 643   **B.** 651   **C.** 661   **D.** 673
E. 649

Q.2 What should come in place of the question mark '?' in the following number series?

9, 6, 15, 12, ?,18

A. 15   **B.** 24   **C.** 21   **D.** 22
E. 25

Q.3 What should come in place of the question mark '?' in the following number series?

5, 9, 16, ?, 54, 103

A. 21   **B.** 24   **C.** 27   **D.** 29
E. 31

Q.4 What should come in place of the question mark '?' in the following number series?

28, 30, 27, 37, 22, ?, 13

A. 48   **B.** 46   **C.** 38   **D.** 44
E. 36

Q.5 What should come in place of the question mark '?' in the following number series?

29, 33, 58, ?, 243, 439

A. 139   **B.** 158   **C.** 107   **D.** 117
E. 122

Ques (6-10):Direction: Read the following graph carefully and answer the following questions:

The total population of five cities = 78000

The ratio of the population of cities A, B, C, D and E is 5 : 7 : 8 : 9 : 10.

Percentage of Literate population

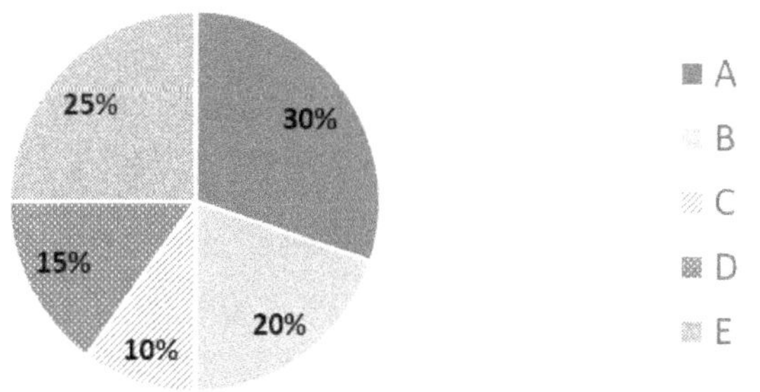

Q.6 The difference between the number of literate population of city A and city B is –

A. 250   **B.** 300   **C.** 150   **D.** 200
E. 100

Q.7 Find the ratio between the illiterate population of city D and city C.

A. 8 : 11   **B.** 21 : 25   **C.** 19 : 22   **D.** 15 : 17
E. 17 : 16

Q.8 The literate population of city A is what percent of total literate population of city E?

A. 60%   **B.** 50%   **C.** 66.67%   **D.** 75%
E. 80%

Q.9 Find the average number of illiterate population of cities C, D, and E.

A. 14700   **B.** 15100   **C.** 14900   **D.** 15300

Q.10 The literate population of city D is how much percent less than the literate population of city A?

A. 15%   **B.** 12%   **C.** 5%   **D.** 10%
E. 20%

Q.11 Selling price of a dress Is Rs 7,500 After allowing two successive discounts of 75% and 70%. Find the marked price.

A. Rs. 100000   **B.** Rs. 75000
C. Rs. 200000   **D.** Rs. 90000
E. Rs. 50000

Q.12 The value of simple interest and compound interest on a certain principal at a certain rate after two years is Rs. 2400 and Rs. 2544 respectively. Find the value of the principal.

A. Rs. 12000   **B.** Rs. 8000
C. Rs. 9000   **D.** Rs. 10000
E. Rs. 15000

Q.13 Manoj can row at the speed of 108 km/hr in still water and he rows the same distance in upstream and downstream which flows at a speed of 5 m/s. Find the average speed throughout the journey.

A. 90 km/hr   **B.** 100 km/hr
C. 102 km/hr   **D.** 105 km/hr
E. None of these

Q.14 Two vessels P and Q of equal capacity contain petrol and water in the ratio 2 : 5 and 6 : 1 respectively. Find the ratio in which these vessels mixed together so that the ratio of petrol and water becomes 7 : 3.

A. 11 : 29   **B.** 12 : 29   **C.** 13 : 31   **D.** 17 : 39
E. 11 : 21

Q.15 Three years from now the age of Abhay will be 62.5% of his father's age. If the sum of their present age is 98 years then find the present age of Abhay.

A. 37 years   **B.** 35 years   **C.** 33 years   **D.** 31 years
E. None

Q.16 In the given question, two equations numbered I and II are given. Solve both the equations and mark the appropriate answer.

I. $x^2 - 35x + 306 = 0$

II. $y^2 - 25y + 144 = 0$

A. x > y

B. x < y

C. x ≥ y

D. x ≤ y

E. x = y or the relationship between x and y cannot be established

Q.17 In the given question, two equations numbered I and II are given. Solve both the equations and mark the appropriate answer.

I. $x^2 + 31x + 240 = 0$

II. $5y^2 + 60y + 135 = 0$

A. x > y

B. x< y

C. x ≥ y

D. x ≤ y

E. x = y or the relationship between x and y cannot be established

Q.18 In the given question, two equations numbered I and II are given. Solve both the equations and mark the appropriate answer.

I. $x^2 + 22x + 120 = 0$

II. $10y^2 + 23y + 12 = 0$

A. x > y

B. x < y

C. x ≥ y

D. x ≤ y

E. x = y or relationship between x and y cannot be established

Q.19 In the given question, two equations numbered I and II are given. Solve both the equations and mark the appropriate answer.

I. $x^2 - 37x + 330 = 0$

II. $y^2 - 28y + 195 = 0$

A. x > y

B. x < y

C. x ≥ y

D. x ≤ y

E. x = y or relationship between x and y cannot be established

Q.20 In the given question, two equations numbered I and II are given. Solve both the equations and mark the appropriate answer.

I. $x^2 + 20x + 64 = 0$

II. $y^2 + 27y + 110 = 0$

A. x > y

B. x < y

C. x ≥ y

D. x ≤ y

E. x = y or relationship between x and y cannot be established

Ques (21-25):Direction: Below bar graph below represents the number of units and their percentage sold online and offline of different products in the market.

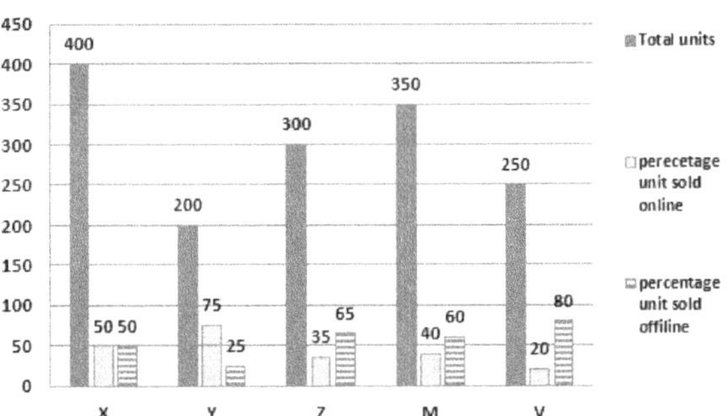

Q.21 Find the total number of units sold offline.

A. 120   **B.** 230   **C.** 855   **D.** 900

E. 810

Q.22 Find the total number of units sold online.

A. 600   **B.** 800   **C.** 200   **D.** 645

E. 125

Q.23 Which product sold maximum number of units off-line?

A. X   **B.** Y   **C.** Z   **D.** M

E. V

Q.24 Which product sold the minimum number of units online?

A. X   **B.** Y   **C.** Z   **D.** M

E. V

Q.25 What is the ratio of total units sold by X to total units sold by Y?

A. 1 : 6   **B.** 2 : 1   **C.** 1 : 3   **D.** 2 : 5

E. 5 : 2

Ques (26-30):Direction: What will come in the place of the question mark '?' in the following question?

Q.26 (44.5 × 4 ÷ 2 + 23.45) = ? - 34 .55

A. 136   **B.** 147   **C.** 123   **D.** 150

E. 154

Q.27 (20% of 65 × 26% of 50) = ? + 23

A. 150   **B.** 192   **C.** 146   **D.** 155

E. 165

Q.28 $(\sqrt{7056} \div 21 \text{ of } 4 \times \sqrt{?}) + 38 = 54$

A. 4   **B.** 256   **C.** 38   **D.** 32

E. 100

Q.29 $(\sqrt{2401} \text{ of } 7 \div \sqrt[3]{343} \times \sqrt[3]{?}) = 67 + 31$

A. 8   **B.** 2   **C.** 4   **D.** 16

E. 22

Q.30 [992 ÷ 32 × 5 + (360 ÷ 45)] =?

A. 160   **B.** 173   **C.** 150   **D.** 163

E. 168

Q.31 A, B and C together earn Rs. 1080 in 6 days. A and C can earn Rs. 600 in 5 days. B and C can earn Rs. 910 in 7 days. How much amount does C can earn per day?

A. Rs. 40   **B.** Rs. 80   **C.** Rs. 60   **D.** Rs. 90
E. Rs. 70

Q.32 A bag contains 26 slips. English alphabets (A to Z) are written on each slip. One slip is drawn randomly. What is the probability that it is vowel?

A. $\frac{7}{52}$ **B.** $\frac{9}{52}$ **C.** $\frac{5}{26}$ **D.** $\frac{7}{26}$
E. $\frac{3}{26}$

Q.33 Hiren, Kishan, and Parth are business partners in a business with a profit-sharing ratio of 2: 1: 5. The business gained Rs. 168000 and by mistakenly they distributed profit equally. What Parth will do?

A. Parth will take 14000 from Hiren and 35000 from Kishan
B. Parth will give 14000 from Hiren and 35000 from Kishan
C. Parth will take 14000 from Kishan and 35000 from Hiren
D. Parth will give 14000 from Kishan and 35000 from Hiren
E. Parth will give 20000 to Kishan and 15000 to Hiren

Q.34 When an express train crosses a platform of 300m long in one minute, a passenger standing there watches a stray dog running at a speed of 15 m/s running in opposite direction. The dog crosses the train in 1/3 minutes. What is the speed of the train?

A. 1200 m/s   **B.** 600 m/s
C. 15 m/s   **D.** 30 m/s
E. None of these

Ques (35-39):Direction: Read the following table carefully and answer the following questions:

The following table shows the number of applications of Males and Females for jobs and the percentage of selected Males and Females.

Year	Applications		Selection percentage	
	Male	Female	Male	Female
2008	4000	6000	40	60
2009	6000	7000	50	55
2010	7000	8000	60	45
2011	9000	12000	55	70
2012	10000	11000	70	75

Q.35 Find the average number of selected males in five years.

A. 4250   **B.** 4050   **C.** 4150   **D.** 4350
E. 3950

Q.36 Find the difference between the number of females selected in five years and the total number of females who rejected in five years.

A. 10800   **B.** 12200   **C.** 9600   **D.** 13200
E. 11400

Q.37 Find the ratio between the total number of males and females who rejected in the year 2008 and in the year 2012 respectively.

A. 84: 95   **B.** 96: 115   **C.** 102: 125   **D.** 114: 135

E. 67: 75

Q.38 The number of rejected males in 2009 and 2012 is what percent of the total number of rejected females in 2008 and 2011?

A. 100%   **B.** 80%   **C.** 120%   **D.** 125%
E. 75%

Q.39 The selected number of selected males in 2010 and 2012 is how much percent less than the number of selected females in 2010 and 2011?

A. 5%   **B.** 6.67%   **C.** 10%   **D.** 8%
E. 3.33%

Q.40 A person uses Jio mobile phone. His April month charge is Rs. 1500 and he used only the internet with that phone for 7hrs/day. For some reason, his phone remained switched off for 5 days in November. How many hrs/day he would have used the mobile to remain the same monthly charge as of April?

A. 6 hrs/day   **B.** 10 hrs/day
C. $9\frac{2}{5}$ hrs/day   **D.** 8.4 hrs/day
E. None of these

Reasoning

Ques (41-45):Direction: Read the information carefully and answer the question asked below.

Eight persons A, B, C, D, E, F, G, and H are sitting around a campfire in a circle. All of them have a unique number of marble stones from 1 to 8. All of them are facing the fire.

Further, the following information is known.

- There are 2 persons sitting between the person 7 marbles and 8 marbles.

- The person with the most number of marbles is sitting adjacent to the person with the least number of marbles.

- The person with the second-highest number of marbles is sitting opposite the person with the least number of marbles and adjacent to the person with the second-lowest number of marbles.

- None of the neighbors of the person with the highest number of marbles has an even number of marbles.

- The person who is sitting opposite the person with 3 marbles has 6 marbles. Neither of them is adjacent to the person with the most number of marbles.

- A is the person with 7 marbles. B is the person with 8 marbles. H and C are neighbors of B. C does not have the least number of marbles. E, who has 4 marbles, is sitting opposite the person with 5 marbles. D is a neighbor of H. G sits opposite to the person with the most number of marbles. F has an odd number of marbles.

Q.41 Who has 6 marbles?

A. G   **B.** C   **C.** D   **D.** H
E. F

Q.42 Who has 5 marbles?

A. G   **B.** C   **C.** D   **D.** H
E. F

Q.43 What is the sum of the number of marbles that the neighbours of the person with the least number of marble have?

A. 15   **B.** 13   **C.** 10   **D.** 14
E. 9

Q.44 How many marbles does G have?

A. 5   **B.** 2   **C.** 6   **D.** 3
E. 1

Q.45 For how many persons can we determine the number of marbles they have?

A. 8   **B.** 6   **C.** 5   **D.** 3
E. 4

Ques (46-47):Direction: In the given questions three statements are followed by two conclusions I and II. You have to assume everything in the statements to be true even if they seem to be at variance with commonly known facts, and then decide which of the given conclusions logically follows from the statements disregarding the commonly known facts.

Q.46 Statements:

No man is handsome.

Some handsome are peoples.

All peoples are mad.

Conclusions:

I. All men being mad is a possibility.

II. No man is a people.

A. Only conclusion I follows
B. Only conclusion II follows
C. Either I or II follows
D. Neither I nor II follows
E. Both conclusions I and II follow

Q.47 Statements:

Some Adidas are Lava.

Some Lava are Iron.

Some Iron are Samsung.

Some Samsung are Rod.

Conclusions:

I. Some Lava are Adidas.

II. Some Samsung are Lava.

[SBI Clerk, 2021]

A. None follows
C. Either I or II
E. None of these
B. Only I
D. Both I and II

Ques (48-50):Direction: Study the information given below carefully and answer the questions that follow.

Sara goes 10 km South from the Market, takes a right turn and goes 24 km to meet Karan. She then goes 15 km North and meets Shaan. She then turns right and goes 30 km to meet Parush. She further goes 9 km South to reach her house and stops there.

Q.48 What is the shortest distance between the market and Karan?

A. 26 km   **B.** 25 km
C. $26\sqrt{2}$ km   **D.** $28\sqrt{2}$ km
E. 27 km

Q.49 What is the shortest distance between Shaan and Sara's House?

A. $3\sqrt{105}$ km   **B.** $2\sqrt{109}$ km
C. $3\sqrt{107}$ km   **D.** $3\sqrt{109}$ km
E. $2\sqrt{107}$ km

Q.50 What is the direction of Parush from the Market?

A. South West   **B.** North East
C. South East   **D.** East
E. North-West

Ques (51-53):Direction: In the question below are given a few statements followed by some conclusions. You have to take the given statements to be true even if they seem to be at variance with commonly known facts. Read all the conclusions and then decide which of the given conclusions logically follows from the given statements, disregarding commonly known facts.

Q.51 Statements:

All flowers are white.

Some whites are beautiful.

Conclusions:

I. All flowers being beautiful is a possibility.

II. At least some white may not be flowers.

A. Only conclusion I follows
B. Only conclusion II follows
C. Either conclusion I or conclusion II follows
D. Neither conclusion I nor conclusion II follows
E. Both conclusion I and conclusion II follow

Q.52 Statements:

10 % population is infected

40 % infected is cured.

Conclusions:

1) Some population is cured

2) 5 % of the infected population is cured

3) Some cured is infected

A. Only conclusion 1 follows
B. Both conclusion 1 and 2 follows
C. Only 3
D. Both 1 and 3
E. None follows

Q.53 Statements:

Some leaves are not poles.

Some pots are poles.

Only few trees are pots.

All pots are branches.

Conclusions:

I. A few pots are not tree.

II. Some branches are leaves is a possibility.

III. Some tree are not pots.
A. Only II follows
B. II and III follows
C. I and II follows
D. All I, II and III follows
E. None follows

Ques (54-56):Direction: Study the following information carefully to answer the given questions:

Step 1: Odd numbers which are a perfect square are written at the right end in descending order.

Step 2: After completing step 1, consonants to be changed to the next letter in alphabetical order.

Step 3: After completing step 2, vowels to be changed to A.

Input: C → K 5 R ÷ 6 N (G © 9 F 4 U T 8) µ M F #

Q.54 How many consonants are followed by a symbol after step 1?
A. 5
B. 4
C. 6
D. 7
E. None of these

Q.55 How many perfect square immediately preceded by a symbol after step 3?
A. 2
B. 3
C. 0
D. 1
E. 4

Q.56 Which element is 4th to the right of the twentie[th] element from the right end after step 2?
A. 0
B. s
C. o
D. ÷
E. 6

Ques (57-61):Direction: Read the following information carefully and answer the questions that follow:

A, B, C, D, E, F, G, and H are sitting around a square table facing away from the table in such a way that four of them sit at the four corners of the square table while the remaining four sit in the middle of each of the four sides. Only three people sit between A and F. C is sitting third to the right of A. F is an immediate neighbour of C and D. H is sitting second to the right of A. H is not an immediate neighbour of G. Both A and F are sitting middle of the table. A is not an immediate neighbour of B.

Q.57 E is related to B. In the same manner, who is related to D?
A. A
B. H
C. F
D. G
E. None of these

Q.58 Four of the following are alike. Which one does not follow the group?
A. C
B. E
C. D
D. B
E. G

Q.59 Who is sitting fourth to the right of F?
A. E
B. A
C. G
D. B
E. D

Q.60 How many people sit between B and F, when counted from left of B?
A. None
B. Two
C. Four
D. Three
E. One

Q.61 What is the position of E with respect to G?
A. Fourth to the right
B. Fifth to the left
C. Second to the right
D. Second to the left
E. Third to the right

Ques (62-63):Direction: In the following question assuming the given statement to be true, find which of the conclusion among the given three conclusions is /are definitely true and then give your answers accordingly.

Q.62 Statements:
X > Y > Z > R; P > Q > R
Conclusions:
I. X > Q
II. R < Y
III. Z = Q
A. Only I and II is true
B. Only II is true
C. Only III is true
D. All of them are true
E. None of them are true

Q.63 Statements:
A = B = C > D > E, C < P < Q
Conclusions:
I. A > E
II. E < B
III. Q < D
A. Only I is true
B. Only I and II are true
C. Only I and III are true
D. Only I and either II or III are true
E. None of them are true

Ques (64-68):Direction: Study the following information and answer the given questions:

Nine persons Sonu, Raju, Monu, Tony, Titu, Sanju, Mohan, Sohan, and Rohan are seated in a row facing North. Mohan is sitting exactly in the middle of the row. Two people sits between Mohan and Raju. Rohan sits to the immediate right of Raju. Sohan sits at one of the extreme ends of the row. One person sits between Sohan and Tony. Titu is not an immediate neighbour of Mohan and Raju. Monu is an immediate neighbour of Tony. Sonu is not an immediate neighbour of Mohan and is not sitting at the end of the row.

Q.64 How many persons are sitting between Rohan and Monu?
A. 4
B. 5
C. 6
D. 1
E. None of these

Q.65 What is the position of Tony with respect to Raju?
A. Sixth to the left
B. Fourth to the left

C. Fifth to the Right   **D.** Fifth to the left
E. None of these

Q.66 Who sits third to the right of Sohan?
A. Tony   **B.** Monu
C. Mohan   **D.** Sonu
E. None of these

Q.67 Who is sitting between Mohan and Sonu?
A. Tony   **B.** Sohan
C. Sanju   **D.** Rohan
E. None of these

Q.68 Which of the following condition is true regarding Titu?
A. Immediate neighbour of Monu
B. Third to the right of Mohan
C. Immediate neighbour Sohan and Tony
D. Fourth to the right of Sanju
E. None of these

Ques (69-70):Direction: Study the given information carefully and answer the following questions.

Sonu is the mother of Amu, who is the only sister of Chan. John is the only son of Dia, who is the wife of Raj. Chan is the only son of Balu, who is the brother of Raj. Lata is the sister of Balu.

Q.69 How is Lata related to Dia?
A. Brother   **B.** Mother
C. Sister-in-law   **D.** Wife
E. Nephew

Q.70 How Amu is related to Lata?
A. Brother   **B.** Niece   **C.** Father   **D.** Wife
E. Nephew

Ques (71-75):Direction: Read the information carefully and answer the question given below.

A, B, C, D, E, F, G, H, I and J are family members. There are three generations in the family. Each member goes for a marriage ceremony in different cities viz. Agra, Haridwar, Delhi, Mumbai, Baroda, Patna, Varanasi, Kolkata, Pune and Hyderabad but not necessarily in the same order. They attend the ceremony in different months namely January, February, March, April and May either on 7th or on 14th of each month. One person attends the ceremony on one given date but not necessarily in the same order.

There is an equal number of male and female in the family. In the family, each female member except B and H has two sisters and one unmarried brother. B has no sister-in-law. I is the father-in-law of F and goes Baroda for wedding in the month having 30 days. No male member goes Hyderabad, Haridwar and Varanasi for the wedding.

Three persons attend wedding between I and G. G who goes Patna is the son-in-law of B. Mother of C goes Haridwar for wedding just before G. D goes Agra, is the unmarried sister of E, who attend wedding in the month having least number of days. E does not go Kolkata for wedding. C is the sister-in-law of F, attends the wedding after her father in an odd number date but does not go Hyderabad.

E is brother in law of G. Father of B is the husband of H and he attends wedding just before H but does not go to Pune. C is a married sister of A, who attends the wedding on odd number date. D attends the wedding before A's husband. Grandparents do not any other city except Pune and Delhi for the wedding.

Q.71 Who among the following goes Pune for the wedding?
A. H   **B.** B   **C.** C   **D.** A

Q.72 On which day unmarried sister of A attends the wedding?
A. 7th April   **B.** 14th April
C. 7th January   **D.** 14th February

Q.73 Which of the following combination is true regarding C?
A. 7th April – Varanasi
B. 7th May – Agra
C. 7th January – Hyderabad
D. 7th May – Varanasi

Q.74 How E is related to the one who attends the wedding on 7th of March?
A. Son   **B.** Son-in-law
C. Grandson   **D.** Grandfather

Q.75 All are same in a certain way and thus form a group. Which of the following does not belong to the group?
A. B   **B.** E   **C.** H   **D.** G

Ques (76-80):Directions: Study the following information carefully and answer the questions following it.

In the NIC company, there are eight persons - Sham, Ramu, Vignesh, Vivek, Mounika, Agarwal, Gupta, and Mishra. Each person holds different posts like - Technical Director, Scientist E, Scientist D, Scientist C, Scientist B, Scientific Officer, Technical Assistant B, and Technical Assistant A. All are arranged in the same order. Technical Director is the senior among all and Technical Assistant A is the junior among all.

Mounika holds the highest post among all. Only one person have post between Mounika and Agarwal. Mishra holds the lowest post among all. Vignesh is senior to only two persons. Two persons have post between Gupta and Sham. The number of persons senior to Vivek is the same as the number of persons junior to Gupta, who is a neighbor of Scientist D and Scientist B. Gupta is senior to Vivek, who is not a Technical Assistant B.

Q.76 Who is Scientist C?
A. Mounika   **B.** Gupta   **C.** Ram   **D.** Sham

Q.77 Who is the scientific Officer?
A. Sham   **B.** Vivek   **C.** Vignesh   **D.** Mishra

Q.78 Which among the following arrangement is True?
A. Scientific Officer, Vivek
B. Scientist B, Vignesh
C. Scientist E, Ramu
D. Technical Assistant B, Mishra

Q.79 Which holds the highest designation?
A. Mounika   **B.** Sham   **C.** Vignesh   **D.** Gupta

Q.80 Which holds the lowest designation?

A. Ramu   **B.** Gupta   **C.** Sham   **D.** Mishra

// Smart Answer Sheet //

Correct Percentage of students who answered correctly.   **Skipped** Percentage of students who skipped.

Q.	Ans.	Correct / Skipped	Q.	Ans.	Correct / Skipped	Q.	Ans.	Correct / Skipped	Q.	Ans.	Correct / Skipped	Q.	Ans.	Correct / Skipped	Q.	Ans.	Correct / Skipped
1	B	6.34 % / 67.32 %	15	A	2.44 % / 90.73 %	29	A	2.44 % / 92.19 %	43	D	11.22 % / 70.73 %	57	A	0.98 % / 92.19 %	71	A	0.49 % / 98.05 %
2	C	7.8 % / 89.76 %	16	A	4.39 % / 90.73 %	30	D	3.9 % / 93.17 %	44	B	11.71 % / 70.24 %	58	D	4.88 % / 92.68 %	72	B	0.49 % / 98.53 %
3	D	3.9 % / 89.76 %	17	B	3.9 % / 91.71 %	31	E	0.98 % / 93.17 %	45	A	11.22 % / 72.19 %	59	B	4.88 % / 92.68 %	73	D	0.49 % / 99.02 %
4	A	0.98 % / 89.75 %	18	B	3.9 % / 92.2 %	32	C	3.9 % / 93.66 %	46	A	3.9 % / 92.2 %	60	E	4.39 % / 92.68 %	74	C	0.49 % / 99.02 %
5	E	3.9 % / 89.76 %	19	C	3.9 % / 92.2 %	33	A	0.49 % / 93.66 %	47	B	6.34 % / 92.2 %	61	C	4.39 % / 92.68 %	75	D	0 % / 100 %
6	D	3.9 % / 89.76 %	20	E	3.9 % / 92.2 %	34	C	1.95 % / 94.15 %	48	A	2.93 % / 92.19 %	62	B	4.88 % / 92.68 %	76	B	0.98 % / 98.04 %
7	E	3.41 % / 90.25 %	21	C	3.9 % / 92.2 %	35	C	1.95 % / 94.15 %	49	D	2.93 % / 92.19 %	63	B	5.37 % / 92.68 %	77	C	0.49 % / 98.53 %
8	A	3.41 % / 90.25 %	22	D	3.41 % / 92.2 %	36	E	1.46 % / 94.15 %	50	B	4.39 % / 92.2 %	64	A	2.93 % / 93.66 %	78	C	0.49 % / 98.53 %
9	C	1.95 % / 90.25 %	23	D	4.39 % / 92.2 %	37	B	1.95 % / 94.64 %	51	E	0.98 % / 92.19 %	65	D	2.44 % / 93.66 %	79	A	0.49 % / 98.05 %
10	D	2.44 % / 90.24 %	24	E	3.41 % / 92.2 %	38	A	0.98 % / 94.63 %	52	C	3.9 % / 92.2 %	66	B	2.93 % / 93.66 %	80	D	0.49 % / 98.05 %
11	A	1.95 % / 90.25 %	25	B	4.88 % / 92.19 %	39	B	1.46 % / 94.15 %	53	B	2.44 % / 92.19 %	67	C	3.41 % / 94.15 %			
12	D	1.95 % / 90.25 %	26	B	5.85 % / 92.2 %	40	D	0.49 % / 94.63 %	54	A	0.49 % / 92.19 %	68	C	3.41 % / 94.64 %			
13	D	1.95 % / 90.73 %	27	C	5.85 % / 92.2 %	41	C	12.68 % / 65.86 %	55	D	0.49 % / 92.19 %	69	C	2.93 % / 94.63 %			
14	A	1.46 % / 90.74 %	28	B	0.98 % / 92.19 %	42	B	10.73 % / 69.27 %	56	E	1.46 % / 92.2 %	70	B	2.44 % / 95.12 %			

Quantitative Aptitude

Q.1 5 years ago, Sam was twice as old as David. 5 years from now, David's age will be two-third of Sam's age. What is the sum of the present ages of David and Sam?

A. 25   **B.** 35   **C.** 40   **D.** 60
E. 75

Q.2 The average age of a man and his son is 40 years. The ratio of their ages is 11:5 respectively. What is the son's age?

A. 28 years   **B.** 32 years   **C.** 35 years   **D.** 36 years
E. 25 years

Q.3 The ratio of the base to the height of a right-angled triangle is 5 : 4. If the area of the right-angled triangle is 160 cm², what is the height of the triangle?

A. 16 cm   **B.** 18 cm   **C.** 20 cm   **D.** 25 cm
E. 12 cm

Ques (4-7):Direction: Study the chart and answer the following questions.

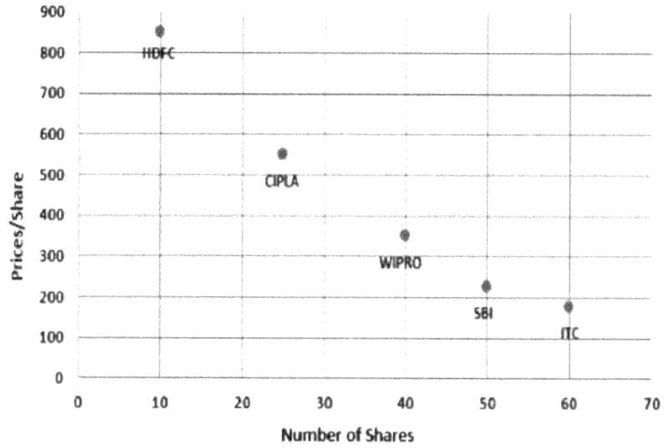

Q.4 What is the difference between the total price of WIPRO shares and SBI shares?

A. Rs. 3200   **B.** Rs. 3500   **C.** Rs. 3000   **D.** Rs. 2500
E. Rs. 4500

Q.5 If the total price of SBI's share is increased by 5%, what is the total price of SBI's share?

A. Rs. 12500   **B.** Rs. 10505
C. Rs. 15050   **D.** Rs. 11550
E. Rs. 12050

Q.6 A man holds 5 shares of ITC, 2 share of HDFC and 10 share of WIPRO. What is the total value of his share?

A. 6000   **B.** 6100   **C.** 5400   **D.** 5900
E. 6400

Q.7 What is the ratio between the total price of 8 shares of HDFC to the 8 shares of WIPRO?

A. 7 : 3   **B.** 10 : 7   **C.** 17 : 7   **D.** 3 : 1
E. 7 : 17

Ques (8-12):Direction: What will come in the place of the question mark '?' in the following question.

Q.8
$$\left(23^2 + 11^3\right) \div 5 + \frac{896}{8} - 17 \times 9 + 12^3 \div \left(3^2 \times 4^2\right) = ?^3$$

A. 7   **B.** 49
C. 343   **D.** 343³
E. None of these

Q.9 $12 \times 3.5 + 12^3 - 32^2 - 119 \times 6 \div 42 = ?^3$

A. 11   **B.** 729
C. 81   **D.** 9
E. None of these

Q.10 $318 \times 2.5 + 64\%$ of $250 + \sqrt[3]{125} = ?^3 - 8 \times 5$

A. 981   **B.** 1000
C. 10²   **D.** 10
E. None of these

Q.11 $(159 + 313) \div 4 + \left(\frac{725}{5}\right) + (413 - 127) \div 11 = ?^2$

A. 19   **B.** 16
C. 289   **D.** 17
E. None of these

Q.12
$$\left\{ \frac{99}{87} \times \frac{87}{99} \div \frac{26}{676} \right\} + \left[\left\{ \left(\frac{71}{97}\right) \times \left(\frac{58}{59}\right) \div \left(\frac{4118}{5723}\right) \right\} + \left(\frac{81}{9}\right) \right] = \sqrt{?}$$

A. 1284   **B.** 1276   **C.** 1396   **D.** 1196
E. 1296

Ques (13-16):Direction: Read the following line graph carefully and answer the questions that follow:

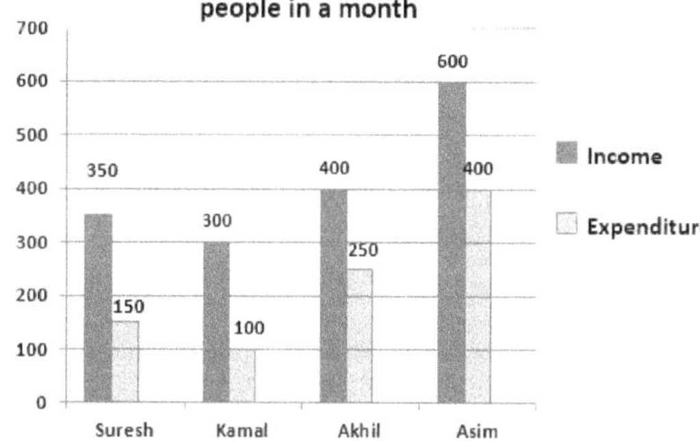

Q.13 What is the average savings of all the 4 people on the above the given chart?

A. 250   **B.** 200   **C.** 187.5   **D.** 185
E. 220

Q.14 What is the difference between the total income of Asim and Kamal together to the savings of Suresh?

A. 650 **B.** 700 **C.** 350 **D.** 350
E. 400

Q.15 Suresh's savings is what percentage of Kamal's savings?

A. 75% **B.** 50% **C.** 25% **D.** 100%
E. 150%

Q.16 If fifth-eight part of the total expenditure of Asim are used to buy goods and rest of this are expend in travel what is the amount are used to expands travel?

A. 180 **B.** 150 **C.** 130 **D.** 100
E. 175

Ques (17-18):Direction: In the following number series, a wrong number is given. Find out the wrong number.

Q.17 31, 102, 165, 256, 345, 446, 562
A. 345 **B.** 31 **C.** 102 **D.** 165
E. 256

Q.18 6, 8, 16, 52, 216, 1096
A. 8 **B.** 16 **C.** 52 **D.** 216
E. 6

Q.19 A shopkeeper has two items both of Rs. 1200. He sells one of the items at a profit of 15% and another at a loss of 20%. Calculate his overall profit or loss.
A. Loss, 2.5% **B.** Profit, 2.5%
C. Loss, 5% **D.** Profit, 5%
E. Profit, 4%

Q.20 Rice worth Rs. 126 per kg and Rs. 134 per kg are mixed with a third variety in the ratio 1 : 1 : 2. If the mixture is worth Rs. 177 per kg, the price of third variety of Rice per kg will be-
A. 236 **B.** 224 **C.** 247 **D.** 216
E. 253

Q.21 The average of 26 articles was found to be 40. On detecting, it was found that two items were wrongly taken as 20 and 18 instead of 40 and 24. Find the correct average.
A. 39 **B.** 40
C. 42 **D.** 41
E. None of these

Q.22 Mr. Kumar spends 20% of his income on food, 18% on luxurious items, 6% on mobile recharge. He donates 4% of his income to the trust. If he spent Rs. 3,600 on luxurious items, then find his saving.
A. Rs. 12,000 **B.** Rs. 11,200
C. Rs. 13,500 **D.** Rs. 10,400
E. None of these

Q.23 When Rajesh reaches the station the train starts running. The train is running with a speed 30 km/hr and Rajesh found that the coach in which he got seat is 125 meters away from the Rajesh. At what speed Rajesh needs to run to catch the train at 30th second.
A. 25 **B.** 35
C. 45 **D.** 40

E. None of these

Q.24 Sam can row his boat at speed of 4 km/h and he finds that the time taken rowing upstream is 3 times the time taken in downstream, then finds the speed of the stream?
A. 8 **B.** 4 **C.** 6 **D.** 2
E. None

Ques (25-29):Direction: Study the following data and answer the following questions:

The following line graph shows the sales of two shops of five products.

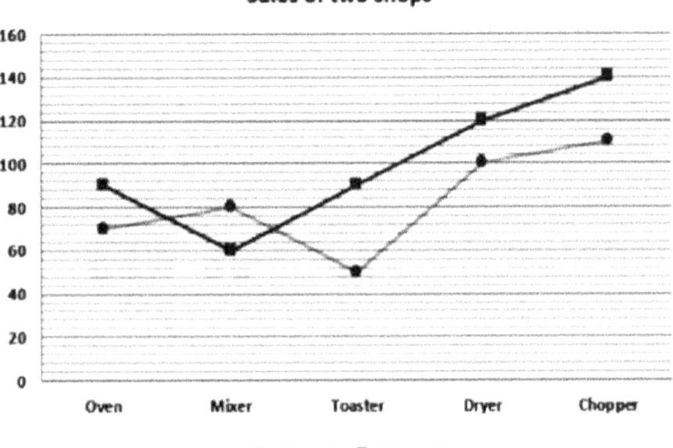

Q.25 Find the difference between the sales of Toasters in shop II and shop I.
A. 60 **B.** 50 **C.** 40 **D.** 90
E. 70

Q.26 Find the average sales of five items in shop II.
A. 90 **B.** 140 **C.** 180 **D.** 100
E. 120

Q.27 The sales of Choppers in a shop I is approximately what percent of total sales of Choppers in both shops?
A. 42% **B.** 44% **C.** 49% **D.** 48%
E. 40%

Q.28 Find the ratio between the sales of Oven in a shop I and shop II.
A. 6 : 7 **B.** 9 : 8 **C.** 7 : 9 **D.** 8 : 7
E. 10 : 11

Q.29 The sales of Dryers of a shop I is what percent more than the sales of Mixer of a shop I?
A. 31% **B.** 25% **C.** 28% **D.** 30%
E. 29%

Ques (30-32):Direction: In the given question, two equations numbered I and II are given. Solve both the equations and mark the appropriate answer.

Q.30 I. $24x^2 + 38x + 15 = 0$

II. $54y^2 + 123y + 65 = 0$

A. $x > y$
B. $x < y$
C. $x \geq y$

D. $x \leq y$

E. x = y or relation between x and y can not be determined

Q.31 $1.2x^2 + 23x + 56 = 0$

II. $12y^2 + 41y + 35 = 0$

A. x > y

B. x < y

C. x ≥ y

D. x ≤ y

E. x = y or relation between x and y can not be determined

Q.32 L. $x^2 - 50x + 225 = 0$

II. $y^2 + 32y - 105 = 0$

A. x > y

B. x < y

C. x ≥ y

D. x ≤ y

E. x = y or relation between x and y can not be determined.

Q.33 Train A and B are 600 km apart. Train A moves toward Train B at a speed of 25 km/hr and Train B moves towards Train A at 35 km/hr. At what distance from the starting point of Train A will they meet?

A. 200 km   **B.** 250 km   **C.** 300 km   **D.** 350 km

E. 400 km

Q.34 6 men can pack 12 boxes in 7 days by working for 7 hours a day. In how many days can 14 men pack 18 boxes if they work for 9 hours a day?

A. 2 days   **B.** 1.8 days   **C.** 3.5 days   **D.** 4 days

E. 9 days

Q.35 The cross section of hand bag is in the shape of trapezium whose top edge is 30 cm and bottom edge is 15 cm. If the area of the trapezium plane is 1125 cm2, the height of bag is _______ m.

A. 25   **B.** 0.25   **C.** 2.5   **D.** 0.5

E. 0.35

Q.36 In how many different ways can the letters of the word 'SECOND be arranged?

A. 720   **B.** 120

C. 5040   **D.** 270

E. None of these

Ques (37-39):Direction: Each question below is followed by two statements I and II. You have to determine whether the data given in the statement is sufficient for answering the question. You should use the data and your knowledge of Mathematics to choose the best possible answer.

Q.37 What is the base of a triangle?

I. Height and base of a triangle are in the ratio of $2:5$.

II. The area of the triangle is 56 m ^{2}, perimeter is 48 m and height is $\dfrac{1^{rd}}{3}$ of the perimeter.

A. If the data in statement I alone is sufficient to answer the question, while the data in statement II alone is not sufficient to answer the question.

B. If the data in statement II alone is sufficient to answer the question, while the data in statement I alone is not sufficient to answer the question.

C. If the data either in statement I alone or in statement II alone is sufficient to answer the question.

D. If the data even in both statements I and II together and not sufficient to answer the question.

E. If the data in both statements I and II together are necessary to answer the question.

Q.38 The difference between the two digits of a two – digit number is 6. What is the number?

I. The digit at unit place is bigger than the ten's digit.

II. The sum of the two digits is 8.

A. If the data in statement I alone is sufficient to answer the question, while the data in statement II alone is not sufficient to answer the question.

B. If the data in statement II alone is sufficient to answer the question, while the data in statement I alone is not sufficient to answer the question.

C. If the data either in statement I alone or in statement II alone is sufficient to answer the question.

D. If the data in both statements I and II together are necessary to answer the question.

E. If the data even in both statements I and II together are not sufficient to answer the question.

Q.39 Is 4X5X9X divisible by 9?

I. x is divisible by 3

II. x is divisible by 9

A. If statement I alone is sufficient to answer the question, but statement II alone is not sufficient.

B. If statement II alone is sufficient to answer the question, but statement I alone is not sufficient.

C. If both the statements I and II together are needed to answer the question.

D. If either statements I alone or statement II alone is sufficient to answer the question.

E. If both the statements together are not sufficient to answer the question.

Q.40 The average age of group of 16 students is 20 years. If 4 more students join the group, the average age rises by 2 years. The average age of the new students is:

A. 29 years   **B.** 25 years

C. 30 years   **D.** 27 years

E. none of these

Reasoning

Ques (41-44):Direction: In the question below are given three statements followed by three conclusions numbered I, II, and III. You have to take the given statements to be true even if they seem to be at variance with commonly known facts. Read all the conclusions and then decide which of the given conclusions logically follows from the given statements disregarding commonly known facts.

Q.41 Statements:

Some men are cow.

All men and cow are genius.

Some men which are not cow are rich.

Conclusion:

I. Some genius are rich.

II. Some rich are cow.

III. Some cow are genius.

A. Only I and II follows

B. Only II and III follows

C. Only I and III follows

D. All follows

E. None follows

Q.42 Statements:

All human are lazy.

Some sleepers are human.

All sleepers are intellectuals.

Conclusion:

I. Some intellectuals are lazy.

II. Some lazy are sleepers.

III. Some intellectuals are human.

A. Only I and II follows

B. Only II and III follows

C. Only I and III follows

D. All I, II and III follows

E. None of these

Q.43 Statements:

Some camphor are rubidium

All bauxite is titanium

All rubidium is bauxite

Conclusions:

I. Some camphor are bauxite

II. All bauxite are rubidium

III. All bauxite is camphor

A. Only I follows

B. Both I and II follows

C. Either I or III follows

D. All follows

E. None follows

Q.44 Statements:

All cats are dogs.

Some dogs are rats.

All rats are pigs.

Conclusions:

I. Some pigs are dogs.

II. Some rats are cats.

III. Some pigs are cats.

A. Only I follows

B. Only II follows

C. Only III follows

D. Only II and III follows

E. None follows

Ques (45-48):Direction: Study the information given below carefully and answer the questions that follow.

There are 6 members in the family. There is one married couple who has only two children. N is grandson of K. P is a daughter of C. D is Paternal Aunt of P. C is maternal uncle of N. K is wife of R who is the father of D.

Q.45 Who is a brother of D?

A. K **B.** C **C.** R **D.** N

E. P

Q.46 How is R related to C?

A. Uncle **B.** Brother

C. Cousin **D.** Father

E. Daughter

Q.47 Which of the following is definitely true?

A. K and R are siblings **B.** D is a daughter of N

C. P is daughter of C **D.** C is father of N

E. C and D are cousins

Q.48 How is R related to P?

A. Grandfather **B.** Grandmother

C. Sister **D.** Aunt

E. Uncle

Q.49 How many pairs of letters are there in the word "MERCHANT" which has as many letters between them as in the English alphabetical series? (in both forward and backward direction)

[SBI PO, 2019]

A. Two **B.** Three

C. Four **D.** More than four

E. One

Q.50 How many meaningful four-letter English words can be formed with the 1st letter, 2nd letter, 4th letter, and 5th letter from the word "EVERYTHING" using "E" twice?

A. One **B.** Two **C.** Three **D.** Four

E. Five

Ques (51-54):Direction: Study the following information carefully and answer the given questions.

In a certain coding language, 'pe na gi' means 'happy is good', 'na se va bo' means 'is nice not great', 'pe se do la' means 'happy nice has love', and 'do fe hi ra' means 'has a lie come'.

Q.51 Which of the following means 'not' in that coded language?

I. va

II. se

III. bo

A. I **B.** II

C. III **D.** Either (I) or (III)

E. Either (II) or (III)

Q.52 Code 'la' is for which word in the given language?

A. love **B.** happy **C.** is **D.** nice

E. great

Q.53 What would be the code for 'not great happy is a lie'?

A. va pe gi na fe ra **B.** va bo pe na fe ra

C. va bo pe na fe gi   **D.** bo na do fe gi pe
E. na se do la ga va

Q.54 In a certain language, 'happy is good but has a lie come' is coded as 'pe na gi ki do fe hi ra'. What is the code for 'but'?

A. na   **B.** do   **C.** ki   **D.** pe
E. fe

Ques (55-57):Direction: Read the instructions carefully and answer the question below.

There are six family members P, Q, R, S, T and U and all of them are of different age. Q is older than T but not as old as U. U is not the oldest. Q's age is not an odd number. The age of P is 24 years. The third youngest person in the family is 27 years old. T is the youngest family member. R's age is not an odd number and not younger than U.

Q.55 Who among the following is the third oldest in the family?

A. P   **B.** Q   **C.** R   **D.** S
E. T

Q.56 What is the possible age of T?

A. 26   **B.** 25   **C.** 28   **D.** 22
E. 35

Q.57 Who among the following is younger than Q but older than P?

A. R   **B.** U   **C.** S   **D.** T
E. None

Ques (58-62):Direction: Study the following information carefully and answer the questions given below.

There are five friends A, B, C, D, and E. They all have different hair colors Black, Brown, Red, White, and Green but not in the same order. Each has a different diet- veg, non-veg, and eggs. Not more than 2 have the same diet. They all study MBA but in different specializations i.e. Finance, Marketing, Human Resources, International Business, and Operations but not necessarily in the same order.

D has black hair, is studying Finance, and eats veg food. B studies Operations but does not eat veg food. E has green hair and eats eggs. A does not have Red or white hair. The person who has white hair eats eggs. C neither eats veg nor non-veg. Neither of the people who eat eggs studies International Business. The person with green-colored hair is not studying Marketing. D is the only person who eats veg.

Q.58 How many people eat non-veg food?

A. 0
B. 1
C. 2
D. Either option (A) or (B)
E. Cannot be determined

Q.59 What is the diet of the person who has brown hair?

A. Veg   **B.** Non-Veg
C. Eggs   **D.** Either (A) or (B)
E. Either (B) or (C)

Q.60 What is the color of B's hair?

A. Brown   **B.** Green   **C.** Black   **D.** White
E. Red

Q.61 What is E studying?

A. Human Resources
B. Finance
C. Marketing
D. Operations
E. International Business

Q.62 What does the person studying International Business eats?

A. Veg
B. Eggs
C. Non-Veg
D. Either (A) or (B)
E. Cannot be determined

Ques (63-64):Direction: In the following question assuming the given statements to be True, find which of the conclusion among given conclusions is/are definitely true and then give your answers accordingly.

Q.63 Statement: P ≥ Q < X; X = Y < R; R > P

Conclusions:

I. X > P

II. Q < R

III. P < Y

A. Only I is True
B. Only II is True
C. Only I and III are True
D. Only III is True
E. I, II, and III all are True

Q.64 Statement: W > T > M ≥ K; P ≥ A = N; Z > U < N; K = P

Conclusions:

I. M > N

II. N = M

A. Only I is True
B. Only II is True
C. Either I and II are True
D. Both I and II are True
E. None is True

Ques (65-69):Direction: Read the following information carefully and answer the questions that follow:

Nine persons are sitting in a row. Some of them are facing north while some are facing south. P sits at the 2nd position from one of the ends. R sits 3rd to the right of P. Only 2 persons sit between R and S. U sits 2ndto the right of S. Immediate neighbours of S are facing the opposite direction to that of S. Immediate neighbours of U faces the opposite direction. T sits second to the right of U. W and T faces the opposite direction. The ones sitting at the ends of the row faces the opposite direction. Q is not a neighbour of U and P. W sits at one of the extreme ends. V sits adjacent to T. X does not face south.

Q.65 Who is sitting at the left end of the row?

[IDBI Bank Assistant Manager, 2021]

A. X **B.** P
C. Q **D.** W
E. None of these

Q.66 How many persons are sitting between P and U?

[IDBI Bank Assistant Manager, 2021]

A. 3 **B.** 2
C. 4 **D.** 1
E. None of these

Q.67 Who is sitting second to the right of V?

[IDBI Bank Assistant Manager, 2021]

A. W
B. T
C. R
D. None of these
E. Cannot be determined

Q.68 Who is sitting in the middle of the row?

[IDBI Bank Assistant Manager, 2021]

A. T **B.** R **C.** U **D.** V
E. P

Q.69 Four of the following five belong to a group following a certain pattern. Who does not belong to the group?

[IDBI Bank Assistant Manager, 2021]

A. PT **B.** TU **C.** UT **D.** US
E. RV

Ques (70-71):Direction: In the question given below, there is a statement followed by two assumptions numbered I and II. An assumption is something supposed or taken for granted. You have to consider the statement and assumptions and then decide which of the assumption(s) is/are implicit in the statement. You have to consider the statements to be true even if they seem to be at variance from commonly known facts.

Q.70 Statement: High fly Airline decided to increases the price of the flight ticket.

Assumption:

I. The number of passengers travelling with High fly airlines increases day by day.

II. They want to earn more profit.

A. If only Assumption I is implicit.
B. If only Assumption II is implicit.
C. If either Assumption I or II is implicit.
D. If neither Assumption I nor II is implicit.
E. If both Assumption I and II are implicit.

Q.71 Statement: The patient's condition would improve after the operation.

Assumption:

I. The patient can be operated upon in his condition.

II. The patient cannot be operated upon in his condition.

A. If only Assumption I is implicit.

B. If only Assumption II is implicit.
C. If either Assumption I or II is implicit.
D. If neither Assumption I nor II is implicit.
E. If both Assumption I and II are implicit.

Ques (72-74):Direction: Study the information given below carefully and answer the questions that follow.

There are seven metro stations T1, T2, T3, T4, T5, T6, and T7 in a city. T1 is 3 km south of T2. T3 is 2 km north of T4. T3 is 4 km east of T2. T7 is 8 km east of T6. T5 is 5 km south of T6. T4 is 6 km west of T5.

Q.72 What is the shortest distance between the metro station T3 and T1?

A. 5 km **B.** 7 km **C.** 8 km **D.** 9 km
E. 10 km

Q.73 In which direction is metro station T4 with respect to metro station T6?

A. South **B.** North
C. South-West **D.** North-East
E. East

Q.74 If a new metro station T8 is built which is 5 km south of T7 then which of the three metro station lie in a straight line?

A. T1, T2, T3 **B.** T2, T3, T4
C. T4, T5, T8 **D.** T5, T6, T7
E. T6, T7, T8

Ques (75-76):Direction: In the following question, a given question is followed by information in two statements. You have to find out the data in which statement(s) is sufficient to answer the question and mark your answer accordingly.

Q.75 Who is the shortest among a group of four friends, Daisy, Sheldon, Rose and Jack?

I. Daisy is shorter than Rose but taller than Sheldon.

II. No one is taller than Jack.

A. The data in statement I alone is sufficient to answer the question, while the data in statement II alone is not sufficient to answer the question

B. The data in statement II alone is sufficient to answer the question, while the data in statement I alone is not sufficient to answer the question.

C. The data in statement I alone or in statement II alone is sufficient to answer the question.

D. The data in both statements I and II are not sufficient to answer the question.

E. The data in both statements I and II together are necessary to answer the question.

Q.76 What is the position of U with respect to Q?

I. Q is north to S.

II. S is left to R and north - east to U.

III. P is east to Q.

A. Only I and II are sufficient
B. Only II and III are sufficient
C. Only I and III are sufficient
D. All the statements are required
E. Insufficient data

Ques (77-80):Direction: Read the following information carefully and answer the questions that follow.

There is a group of seven friends – Ankur, Archana, Aditya, Amit, Subin, Vidya, and Gaurav. All of them have their birthdays in different months from January to July. No two persons share the same birthday month.

Amit's birthday is in January and Subin's birthday is in July. Only one person's birthday comes before Vidya's birthday. There is a gap of two months between Vidya's and Archana's birthdays. Aditya's birthday comes after Archana's birthday. Gaurav's birthday comes before Ankur's birthday.

Q.77 Whose birthday is in the month of June?

A. Archana   **B.** Ankur   **C.** Aditya   **D.** Vidya

E. Gaurav

Q.78 In which month does Vidya have her birthday?

A. February   **B.** March   **C.** April   **D.** May

E. June

Q.79 In which month does Archana have her birthday?

A. February   **B.** March   **C.** April   **D.** May

E. June

Q.80 Whose birthday comes in the month of March?

A. Ankur   **B.** Aditya   **C.** Archana   **D.** Gaurav

E. Vidya

// Smart Answer Sheet //

Correct Percentage of students who answered correctly.   **Skipped** Percentage of students who skipped.

Q.	Ans.	Correct / Skipped	Q.	Ans.	Correct / Skipped	Q.	Ans.	Correct / Skipped	Q.	Ans.	Correct / Skipped	Q.	Ans.	Correct / Skipped	Q.	Ans.	Correct / Skipped
1	C	24.32 % / 22.3 %	15	D	7.43 % / 88.52 %	29	B	2.7 % / 89.87 %	43	A	50.0 % / 41.22 %	57	C	22.97 % / 56.76 %	71	A	6.08 % / 69.6 %
2	E	12.84 % / 65.54 %	16	B	5.41 % / 88.51 %	30	C	0 % / 100 %	44	A	44.59 % / 41.22 %	58	C	23.65 % / 56.76 %	72	A	8.11 % / 70.94 %
3	A	11.49 % / 65.54 %	17	D	1.35 % / 88.51 %	31	B	2.03 % / 89.86 %	45	B	41.22 % / 41.89 %	59	B	22.3 % / 57.43 %	73	C	8.11 % / 70.27 %
4	C	1.35 % / 88.51 %	18	A	1.35 % / 88.51 %	32	A	3.38 % / 89.86 %	46	D	20.27 % / 56.08 %	60	E	22.97 % / 57.44 %	74	C	6.76 % / 70.94 %
5	D	2.03 % / 89.86 %	19	A	2.7 % / 88.52 %	33	B	2.03 % / 91.21 %	47	C	18.24 % / 57.44 %	61	A	10.81 % / 68.24 %	75	E	4.05 % / 70.27 %
6	B	1.35 % / 89.19 %	20	B	0.68 % / 88.51 %	34	C	0.68 % / 92.56 %	48	A	14.19 % / 60.13 %	62	C	8.11 % / 69.59 %	76	A	4.05 % / 68.92 %
7	C	2.03 % / 89.19 %	21	D	2.7 % / 89.19 %	35	D	0.68 % / 92.56 %	49	D	15.54 % / 60.14 %	63	B	12.84 % / 70.27 %	77	C	7.43 % / 72.98 %
8	A	4.05 % / 89.19 %	22	D	2.03 % / 89.19 %	36	A	2.03 % / 92.56 %	50	A	18.24 % / 60.14 %	64	C	12.16 % / 71.62 %	78	A	7.43 % / 75.68 %
9	D	5.41 % / 89.18 %	23	C	0 % / 100 %	37	B	0.68 % / 92.56 %	51	D	48.65 % / 43.24 %	65	D	5.41 % / 70.94 %	79	D	18.24 % / 68.92 %
10	D	4.73 % / 89.19 %	24	D	2.03 % / 89.19 %	38	D	2.7 % / 93.25 %	52	A	46.62 % / 43.92 %	66	A	27.03 % / 56.08 %	80	D	13.51 % / 74.33 %
11	D	5.41 % / 88.51 %	25	C	6.08 % / 89.19 %	39	D	1.35 % / 93.24 %	53	B	34.46 % / 46.62 %	67	E	25.0 % / 55.41 %			
12	E	2.03 % / 88.51 %	26	D	3.38 % / 89.86 %	40	C	1.35 % / 97.97 %	54	C	32.43 % / 53.38 %	68	B	26.35 % / 55.41 %			
13	C	8.11 % / 88.51 %	27	B	2.03 % / 89.19 %	41	C	50.0 % / 38.51 %	55	B	25.68 % / 55.4 %	69	D	24.32 % / 55.41 %			
14	B	6.08 % / 88.51 %	28	C	5.41 % / 89.86 %	42	D	27.7 % / 39.87 %	56	D	25.0 % / 56.76 %	70	E	26.35 % / 57.43 %			

Quantitative Aptitude

Ques (1-5):Direction: Study the following information carefully and answer the questions given below.

The table below gives partial info on data of revenue generated by different e-commerce platforms among Flipkart, Amazon, Paytm, Shopclue, and Myntra. The percentage of revenue contribution for a particular company by different product categories among – Mobile Phone, Clothing, TV, AC, and Healthcare is also shown in the table.

	Total revenue (In crore)	Mobile Phone	Clothing	TV	AC	Healthcare
Flipkart	324	25%	15%		10%	20%
Amazon	652		20%	15%	25%	10%
Paytm	570	18%	28%	12%		27%
Shopclue	266	15%		30%	30%	5%
Myntra		24%	11%	16%	18%	

Additional information:

a) All the listed e-commerce platforms sell only products among given categories.

b) Total revenue generated by all the companies together is Rs. 2162 crore.

Q.1 What is the approx percentage contribution to total revenues generated by all companies by the sale of TV?
A. 26%   **B.** 30%   **C.** 34%   **D.** 38%
E. 42%

Q.2 Revenue generated by Myntra by selling Healthcare products is approx. how much percent more/less than the revenue generated by Paytm by selling AC?
A. 33.1% less   **B.** 20.4% more
C. 26.2% less   **D.** 22.8% more
E. No change

Q.3 What is the absolute difference in revenue generated by Shopclues by selling clothing products and by Flipkart by selling TV?
A. Rs. 48.2 crore   **B.** Rs. 51.3 crore
C. Rs. 57.3 crore   **D.** Rs. 62.3 crore
E. Rs. 66.5 crore

Q.4 Revenue generated by selling Healthcare products by all companies together is approx how many percent more than the total revenue generated by selling AC by all companies together?
A. 97%   **B.** 100%   **C.** 105%   **D.** 95%
E. 102%

Q.5 Revenue generated by Myntra by selling TV is how many approx. percent more than the revenue generated by Flipkart by selling the mobile phone?
A. 29.6%   **B.** 34.4%   **C.** 27.1%   **D.** 24.7%
E. 21.5%

Q.6 If the simple interest on a certain sum of money for 4 years is one–fifth of the sum, then find the rate of interest per annum?
A. 4%   **B.** 5%   **C.** 6%   **D.** 8%
E. 10%

Q.7 The perimeter of a rectangle is 8936 m and the area is 4203987 sq. m Given that the length of the rectangle is greater than the breadth, what is the ratio of the length to the breadth?
A. 3111 : 1357   **B.** 3121 : 1347
C. 2922 : 1546   **D.** 2546 : 1922
E. Can't be determined

Q.8 A and B are mixed in 3:5 to obtain X. A and B are mixed in 7:4 to obtain Y. In what ratio should X and Y be mixed so that the resultant mixture has A and B in ratio 3:2?
A. 4 : 9   **B.** 2 : 9   **C.** 5 : 2   **D.** 3 : 4
E. 1 : 3

Q.9 150 kgs of an alloy of gold and silver in the ratio 1:4 is mixed with x kgs of an alloy of gold and silver in the ratio 7:3. If the overall alloy should contain between 40% and 50% gold, what is the range of values x can take?
A. $90 \leq x \leq 220$ **B.** $135 \leq x \leq 245$
C. $100 \leq x \leq 225$ **D.** $80 \leq x \leq 195$
E. $95 \leq x \leq 210$

Q.10 A racing truck is running at a speed of 72 kmph. At this speed, what distance will it cover in 22 seconds?
A. 440 meters   **B.** 550 meters
C. 350 meters   **D.** 250 meters
E. None of these

Q.11 Sachin got married 21 years ago and his present age is $\frac{7}{4}$ times the age at the time of his marriage. If his brother was 4 years younger than him at the time of Sachin's 18th birthday, then find the age of Sachin brother.
A. 45 years   **B.** 49 years   **C.** 53 years   **D.** 56 years
E. 55 years

Q.12 A cricket team has to select a captain and a vice-captain from 12 of its players. In how many ways can this be done?
A. 126   **B.** 125   **C.** 132   **D.** 180
E. 123

Q.13 In how many ways can a group of 6 men and 4 women can be made out of a total of 9 men and 6 women.

A. 720 **B.** 640 **C.** 1280 **D.** 1260
E. 1560

Q.14 Two integers are selected at random from the set {1, 2, ..., 11}. Given that the sum of selected numbers is even, the conditional probability that both the numbers are even is:

A. $\frac{7}{10}$ **B.** $\frac{1}{2}$ **C.** $\frac{2}{5}$ **D.** $\frac{3}{5}$
E. $\frac{2}{10}$

Q.15 The volume of a cylinder is twice of the volume of a cone. If their base radius are the same then what is the ratio of the height of the cylinder to the height of the cone?

A. 2 : 5 **B.** 2 : 3
C. 1 : 3 **D.** 2 : 1
E. None of these

Q.16 The efficiency of Nitish is 80% more than Paras and Paras takes 45 days to complete a piece of work. Nitish started work alone and then Paras joined him 9 days before the actual completion of work. For how many days Nitish worked alone?

A. 20 **B.** 15 **C.** 11 **D.** 17
E. 12

Q.17 If B exceed A by 25%, then A is less than B by-

A. $33\frac{1}{3}$% **B.** $16\frac{2}{3}$% **C.** 20% **D.** 50%
E. 30%

Q.18 Two friends Ravi and Kishan invested Rs. 65000 and Rs. 95000 respectively in a business. After one year, they had got some profit, which they had invested in a bank at the rate of 6% per quarter at simple interest. If they got Rs. 3968 after one year, what would have been the difference of their share of profit had they not invested it again in the bank?

A. Rs. 600 **B.** Rs. 744
C. Rs. 3300 **D.** Rs. 1984
E. None of these

Q.19 A number, when reduced by 10%, gives 27 as result. The number is:

A. 30 **B.** 35 **C.** 40 **D.** 33
E. 35

Q.20 What will come in place of question mark (?) in the following equation?

$950 + 50 \times 15 - 14 \times 22 + \sqrt{?} = 11^3 + 9^2$

A. 200 **B.** 240 **C.** 320 **D.** 400
E. 420

Q.21 What will come in place of question mark '?' in the following question?
74% of 159 − [36.5% of 142 + 25.4% of 203] = 13.5% of ? − 10.5% of 120

A. 129.05 **B.** 149.22
C. 179.03 **D.** 199.02
E. None of the above

Q.22 What should come in place of question mark (?) in the following questions? (You do not have to calculate the exact value.)

$17^4 + \sqrt{2400.5} + 50.67 + 17\%$ of $400 + \sqrt{528.9} = (?) + 44$

A. 38128 **B.** 98728
C. 50488 **D.** 83668
E. None of these

Q.23 What should come in place of the question mark '?' in the following question?

$9\frac{10}{2} \times \left(\frac{3}{8} \times \frac{16}{9}\right) - 6\frac{5}{3} = 5\frac{5}{2} + 4\frac{1}{2} - ?$

A. $\frac{14}{3}$ **B.** $\frac{31}{3}$ **C.** $\frac{28}{3}$ **D.** $\frac{33}{5}$
E. $\frac{31}{5}$

Q.24 What will come in place of ? in the following equation?
$3^8 \times 3^4 \div 243 = 9 \times 3 \times 81 \times 3^4 \div ?$

A. 27 **B.** 4 **C.** 1 **D.** 81
E. 3

Q.25 In the following question, two equations are given. You have to solve these equations and determine the relation between a and b.

I. $\frac{131a^2}{7} + 29a + \frac{240}{7} = \frac{89a^2}{7} - \frac{5}{7}$

II. $2b^2 + 9(b + 1) = \frac{5b+5}{6}$

A. a < b
B. a > b
C. a ≤ b
D. a ≥ b
E. a = b or the relationship cannot be determined

Q.26 In this question two quadratic equations are given. Solve them and choose the applicable option.

I. $x^2 - 2\sqrt{3}x + 1 = 0$

II. $y^2 + \sqrt{3}(\sqrt{6} - 1)y + 4 - \sqrt{6} = 0$

A. x > y
B. x < y
C. x ≥ y
D. x ≤ y
E. x = y or relation cannot be established

Q.27 In the following question two equations are given in variables x and y. You have to solve these equations and determine relation between x and y.

I. $\frac{4}{\sqrt{x}} + \frac{23}{\sqrt{x}} = \sqrt{x}$

II. $y^6 - \frac{(-3)^{\frac{39}{2}}}{\sqrt{y}} = 0$

A. x > y
B. x < y
C. x ≥ y
D. x ≤ y
E. x = y or relation cannot be established

Q.28 In the following question two equations are given in variables x and y. You have to solve these equations and determine relation between x and y.

I. $x^2 + 2x - 5.9696 = 0$

II. $2y^2 + 4y + 1.1808 = 0$

A. x > y

B. x < y

C. x ≥ y

D. x ≤ y

E. x = y or relation cannot be established

Q.29 In the following question two equations are given in variables x and y. You have to solve these equations and determine relation between x and y.

I. $\dfrac{3^3 + 6^2}{7} = x^2$

II. $17y^3 = (15 \times 9) + 12y^3$

A. x > y

B. x < y

C. x ≥ y

D. x ≤ y

E. x = y or relation cannot be established

Q.30 In the following series one number is wrong, Find out the wrong number.

1, 6, 13, 46, 130, 398, 1181

A. 130   **B.** 1181   **C.** 6   **D.** 46

E. 398

Q.31 In the following number series, the wrong number is given. Find out the wrong number.

0, 15, 48, 105, 192, 305

A. 15   **B.** 305   **C.** 0   **D.** 48

E. 192

Q.32 What should come in place of the question mark '?' in the following number series?

66, ?, 180, 1593, 42930

A. 63   **B.** 198   **C.** 60   **D.** 129

E. 130

Q.33 What should come in place of question mark '?' in the following number series?

242, 288, 338, ?, 450, 512

A. 225   **B.** 676   **C.** 392   **D.** 451

E. 454

Ques (34-38):Direction: Study the following line graph carefully and answer the questions given below:

Assuming that there is no fixed component and all the units produced are sold in the same year.

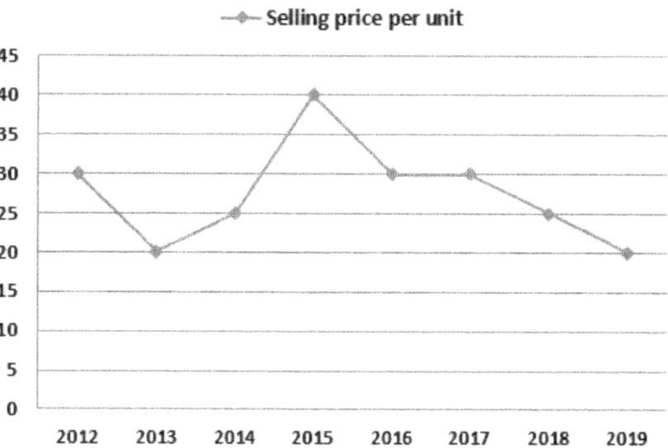

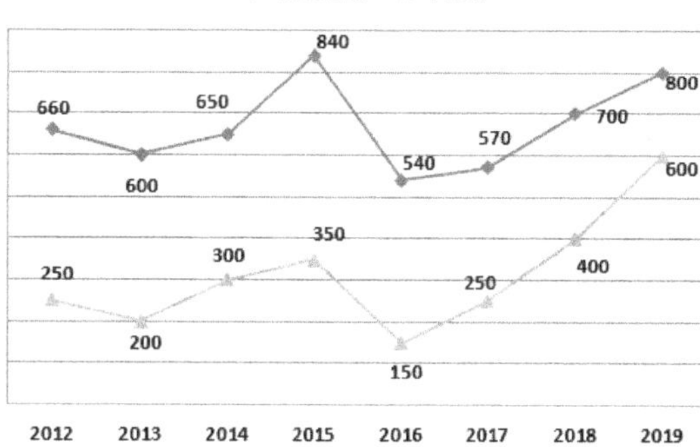

Q.34 If the Selling Price per unit decreased by 20 % during 2012 to 2015 and the Cost price per unit increased by 20% during 2016 to 2019 then the cumulative profit for the entire period 2012 to 2019 decreased by

A. 842   **B.** 862   **C.** 665   **D.** 792

E. 762

Q.35 What is the average of quantities sold during the period 2014 to 2018?

A. 28.4   **B.** 23.8   **C.** 22.4   **D.** 27.6

E. 26.2

Q.36 If the Selling Price per unit decreases by 30% during 2012 to 2015 and the cost per unit increases by 30% during 2016 to 2019 then during how many years is there no profit no loss?

A. None   **B.** 1   **C.** 3   **D.** 4

E. 2

Q.37 What is the average cost during the period of 2012 to 2019?

A. 298.75   **B.** 467.5   **C.** 412.25   **D.** 357.5

E. 368.75

Q.38 In which of the following years is the per unit cost the maximum?

A. 2014   **B.** 2015   **C.** 2013   **D.** 2017

E. 2018

Q.39 A, B, and C started a business with a capital of Rs. $80000, 120000$ and 150000 respectively and they decided to share their profit according to the ratio of their capital but A is working also and takes 12.5% of the total profit as salary. If C withdraws his capital after 6 months and profit after one year is Rs. 88000 then find the share of A?

A. Rs. 22400 **B.** Rs. 33600

C. Rs. 33400 **D.** Rs. 21000

E. None of these

Q.40 Kunal bought 40 bananas at the rate of 2 Rs. per banana and he again bought 50 bananas at the rate of Rs. 1.6 per banana. He mixed them and sold them at the rate of Rs. 1.8 per banana. Find his profit or loss percent?

A. 2.5%   **B.** 2.25%

C. 1.5%   **D.** 1.25%

E. None of these

Reasoning

Ques (41-45):Direction: Study the following information carefully and answer the question given below.

There are seven friends A, B, C, D, E, F, and G. The seven friends have a different number of coins with them. The number of coins with them are consecutive numbers.

Further, it is known that,

1. The sum of the coins with all of them is 35.

2. The number of coins with C is the average of the number of coins with F and E.

3. G has as many coins less than B as E has less than F.

4. D has the least number of coins.

5. The sum of the coins with G and A is equal to the number of coins with C.

Q.41 Who has the highest number of coins?

A. B

B. F

C. A

D. C

E. Cannot be determined

Q.42 How many coins does E have?

A. 9

B. 5

C. 6

D. 2

E. Cannot be determined

Q.43 F has how many more coins than D?

A. 6

B. 4

C. 5

D. 3

E. Cannot be determined

Q.44 If all the friends stand from left to right in the ascending order of number coins with them, who stands third from the left?

A. G

B. F

C. D

D. A

E. Cannot be determined

Q.45 How many people have more coins than B?

A. 0

B. 2

C. 3

D. 4

E. Cannot be determined

Ques (46-49):Direction: In these questions, the relationship between different elements is shown in the statements. These statements are followed by two conclusions. Study the conclusions based on the given statement(s) and select the appropriate answer.

Q.46 Statement:

All cars are bikes.

Some boats are bikes.

No car is a boat.

Conclusions:

I. All bikes can be boats.

II. All bikes cannot be cars.

A. Only conclusion I follows

B. Only conclusion II follows

C. Either conclusion I or II follows

D. Neither of the conclusions follow

E. Both the conclusions follow

Q.47 Statements:

Some skies are blue.

No blue is red.

Some red are water.

Conclusions:

I. Some blue can be water.

II. All water cannot be skies.

A. Only conclusion I follows

B. Only conclusion II follows

C. Either conclusion I or II follows

D. Neither of the conclusions follow

E. Both the conclusions follow

Q.48 Statements:

All dogs are dragons.

All cats are dragons.

No dragon is a lion.

Conclusions:

I. No dog can be a lion.

II. No cat can be a lion.

A. Only conclusion I follows

B. Only conclusion II follows

C. Either conclusion I or II follows

D. Neither of the conclusions follow

E. Both the conclusions follow

Q.49 Statements:

No tree is a herb.

Some shrubs are grass.

No grass is a herb.

Conclusions:

I. No shrub can be a herb.

II. No grass can be a tree.

A. Only conclusion I follows

B. Only conclusion II follows

C. Either conclusion I or II follows

D. Neither of the conclusions follow

E. Both the conclusions follow

Q.50 Direction: In the following question, the symbols #, @, $, % are used with the following meaning illustrated.

'P # Q' means 'P is neither smaller than nor equal to Q'

'P @ Q' means 'P is neither greater than nor equal to Q'

'P $ Q' means 'P is not smaller than Q'

'P * Q' means 'P is not greater than Q'

'P & Q' means 'P is neither greater than nor smaller than Q'

Now in each of the following questions assuming the given statements to be true, find which of the four conclusions given below them is/are definitely true and give your answer accordingly.

Statement:

U @ V $ W * X, W & Y $ Z

Conclusion:

I. Z $ X

II. U # W

III. V $ Z

IV. U * Y

A. Only III is true

B. Only either II or IV are true

C. Only III and either II or IV are true

D. Only II, III and IV are true

E. Only III and I are true

Ques (51-55):Direction: Read the following information carefully and answer the questions that follow.

Five people Tarun, Megha, Krishna, Dilip, and Sarika participated in a 100 m race. Each of them finished the race in different times and were accordingly ranked 1-5, 1 being the first person to finish the race. Each of the five participants was from a different department among Computer, Electronics, Civil, Electrical, and Mechanical.

The following information is also known:

(i) Krishna finished the race before Megha, who in turn finished the race before Sarika.

(ii) Tarun is from Mechanical while Dilip is from Electronics.

(iii) The person from the Electrical department finished the race 4th.

(iv) Tarun was one of the first three to finish the race.

(v) Sarika was from either Civil or Computer.

(vi) The person from Mechanical finished the race before the person from Electronics but not before the person from Computer.

Q.51 Who finished the race in the first place?

A. Megha

B. Krishna

C. Dilip

D. Sarika

E. Cannot be determined

Q.52 Which person belongs to the Civil Department?

A. Megha

B. Krishna

C. Sarika

D. Either (A) or (C)

E. Either (B) or (C)

Q.53 Megha is from which department?

A. Electrical

B. Computer

C. Civil

D. Electronics

E. Cannot be determined

Q.54 Which of the following correctly matches the person with his/her department and rank?

A. Megha - Civil - 4

B. Tarun - Mechanical - 3

C. Sarika - Computer - 3

D. Dilip - Electronics - 3

E. Krishna - Computer - 2

Q.55 For how many people can the department and rank be uniquely determined?

A. 1   **B.** 2   **C.** 3   **D.** 4

E. 5

Ques (56-58):Direction: Study the information given below carefully and answer the questions that follow.

A is 6m east of B. Q is 2m north of B. H is 6m west of M. A is 2m south of H. R is 5m west of P. D is 2m east of F. T is 8m south of R. M is 6m north of D. F is 8m south of P.

Q.56 What is the position of M with respect to Q?

A. East   **B.** West

C. North   **D.** South

E. None of these

Q.57 What is the position of B with respect to D?

A. South   **B.** North-West

C. North-East   **D.** West

E. South-East

Q.58 If a person travel directly from D to R, then how much distance he has to travel?

A. $\sqrt{111}$ **B.** $\sqrt{122}$ **C.** $\sqrt{113}$ **D.** $\sqrt{117}$

E. $\sqrt{120}$

Q.59 Direction: In the following question assuming the given statements to be true, find which of the conclusion among given conclusions is/ are definitely true and then give your answers accordingly.

Statement: P > Q > R; R < S > T; T = U > V

Conclusions:

I. R = V

II. P > S

A. Only I is true

B. Only II is true

C. Either I or II is true

D. Neither I nor II is true

E. Both I and II are true

Q.60 Direction: In a certain language, 'brown black are colors' is coded as 'po ta to la'. 'black dog is fast' is coded as 'cu da la tu'. 'fox and dog are friends' are coded as 'na da po hi pi'. 'brown fox is quick' is coded as 'pi to ra cu'.

What is the code for 'black'?

A. to

B. la

C. cu

D. ra

E. Cannot be determined

Q.61 If in a certain code language, 'MIND' is written as 'KGLB' and 'ARGUE' is written as 'YPESC'. Then, how will the word 'DIAGRAM' be written in the same code language?

[Haryana Primary Teacher (PRT), 2020]

A. BGYEYPK

B. BGYEPYK

C. GLPEYKB

D. BGEPYLK

E. GBGEPYLK

Q.62 If ABCDEF is coded ZYXWVU, then how is MERCEDES coded?

A. IVNXVHVW

B. XNVIWVHV

C. WHVVNXIV

D. NVIXVWVH

E. NNVIXVWVH

Q.63 If MEDICINE is coded EOJDJEFM, then how is COMPUTER coded?

A. RFUVQNPC

B. RFUVNQPC

C. RFVUQNPC

D. RFVUNQPC

E. FRFVUNQPC

Ques (64-65):Directions: Read the following information carefully and answer the question given below-

When a word and number arrangement machine is given an input line of words and numbers, it arranges them following a particular rule. The following is an illustration of input and its rearrangement.

Input: waste 43 hat 55 ant 19 nest 13 gap 27

Step I: 13 waste 43 hat 55 19 nest gap 27 ant

Step II: 19 13 waste 43 hat 55 nest 27 ant gap

Step III: 27 19 13 waste 43 55 nest ant gap hat

Step IV: 43 27 19 13 waste 55 ant gap hat nest

Step V: 55 43 27 19 13 ant gap hat nest waste

Step V is the last step of the above arrangement as the intended arrangement is obtained.

As per the rules followed in the above steps, find out in each of the following questions the appropriate step for the given input.

Input: fly 92 high 48 bird 74 tree 62 green 56

Q.64 Which element is exactly between '92' and '74' in Step III?

A. green

B. bird

C. tree

D. high

E. None of these

Q.65 What is the difference between the number which is fourth from the left end in Step III and the number which is second from the right end in Step I?

A. 23   **B.** 24   **C.** 29   **D.** 25

E. 36

Ques (66-70):Direction: Read the following information carefully and answer the question given below.

Eight friends Moin, Manoj, Mahesh, Mukesh, Mridul, Mani, Mari and Manu are sitting around a circular table, facing outside the center and the distance between them is same.

Also, Moin is second to the right of Mridul. Mridul is neighbor of both Mahesh and Mari. Mukesh is not the neighbor of Moin. Mari is the neighbor of Mani. Manoj does not sit between Mukesh and Manu. Manu does not sit between Mani and Mukesh.

Q.66 How many different seating arrangements are possible?

A. 1   **B.** 2   **C.** 3   **D.** 4

E. 6

Q.67 The position of how many people can be determined?

A. 6

B. 8

C. 5

D. 4

E. None of these

Q.68 What is the position of Maari with respect to Mahesh?

A. Second to the right

B. Second to the left

C. Immediate right

D. Immediate left

E. Cannot be determined

Q.69 Who sits next to the right of Manu?

A. Mahesh

B. Mani

C. Mukesh

D. Manoj

E. Cannot be determined

Q.70 What is the position of Mahesh with respect to Moin?

A. Next to the right

B. Next to the left

C. Second to the right

D. Second to the left

E. Cannot be determined

Q.71 Directions: The question below consists of a question and two statements numbered I and II given below it. You have to decide whether the data provided in the statements are sufficient to answer the question. Read both the statements and give the answer.

In a certain code, '14' means 'stop whispering' and '68' means 'it's irritating'. What do '8' and '6' mean respectively in that code?

Statements:

I. '167' means 'stop irritating me'.

II. '4982' means 'it's sound like whispering'.

A. Statement I alone is sufficient while II alone is not sufficient.

B. Statement II alone is sufficient while I alone is not sufficient.

C. Either statement I or II is sufficient.

D. Neither statement I nor II is sufficient.

E. Both statement I and II are sufficient.

Ques (72-74):Direction: Study the given information carefully and answer the following questions. A word arrangement machine when given an input of words, rearranges them following a particular rule in each step. The following is an illustration of input and steps rearrangement.

INPUT: Valour Punctual Courage Motivation Sensitive Fearless

STEP 1: Courage Valour Punctual Motivation Sensitive Fearless

STEP 2: Courage Fearless Valour Punctual Motivation Sensitive

STEP 3: Courage Fearless Motivation Valour Punctual Sensitive

STEP 4: Courage Fearless Motivation Punctual Sensitive Valour

This is the final arrangement and step 4 is the last step. As per the rules followed in the given steps, answer the questions given below for the following input.

Input: Spunk Resolve Mettle Pluck Daring Heroism

Q.72 How many words are there before "Resolve" in step 3?

A. 3   **B.** 2   **C.** 5   **D.** 1
E. 4

Q.73 How many steps are there?

A. 5   **B.** 3
C. 4   **D.** 6
E. Either 4 or 5

Q.74 Which comes exactly between "Daring" and "Spunk" in step2?

A. Resolve   **B.** Heroism
C. Plunk   **D.** Either 1 or 2
E. Either 2 or 3

Ques (75-76):Direction: Study the following information carefully and answer the questions given below.

For two men P and Q, the following symbols denote their relationship:

P+Q means that P is the elder brother of Q.

P*Q means that P is the father of Q.

P$Q means that P is the son of Q's sister.

P%Q means that P is the son of Q's brother.

P#Q means that P is the son of Q.

Q.75 If R*F$B, how is R related to B?
A. Nephew   **B.** Cousin
C. Brother   **D.** Brother-in-law
E. Father-in-law

Q.76 Which of the following denotes that E and F are cousins?
A. F$C*E   **B.** F$C%E
C. F#C+E   **D.** F%C+E
E. E$D%B+F

Q.77 Directions: The question below consists of a question and two statements numbered I and II given below it. You have to decide whether the data provided in the statements are sufficient to answer the question. Read both the statements and give answer.

On which day of the week did Haritha visit the zoo?

Statements:

I. Haritha did not visit zoo either on Tuesday or on Thursday.

II. Haritha visited zoo two days before her mother reached her house which was a day after Tuesday.

A. I alone is sufficient while II alone is not sufficient

B. II alone is sufficient while I alone is not sufficient

C. Either I or II is sufficient

D. Neither I nor II is sufficient

E. Both I and II are sufficient

Q.78 Direction: A statement is given followed by two inferences I and II. You have to consider the statement to be true even if it seems to be at variance from commonly known facts. You have to decide which of the given inferences, if any, follow from the given statement.

Statement: Security of the building was increased after the incident at the old lady's apartment.

Assumptions:

I. Something dangerous happened at the old lady's apartment.

II. The old lady was an easy target.

A. Only assumption I is implicit

B. Only assumption II is implicit

C. Both assumption I and II are implicit

D. None of the assumptions are implicit

E. Either I or II is implicit

Ques (79-80):Direction: In the following questions, the symbols #, @, $, % are used with the following meaning illustrated.

'P # Q' means 'P is neither smaller than nor equal to Q'

'P @ Q' means 'P is neither greater than nor equal to Q'

'P $ Q' means 'P is not smaller than Q'

'P * Q' means 'P is not greater than Q'

'P & Q' means 'P is neither greater than nor smaller than Q'

Now in each of the following questions assuming the given statements to be true, find which of the four conclusions given below them is/are definitely true and give your answer accordingly.

Q.79 Statement:

A @ B, C $ B, D & C, D # E

Conclusion:

I. D # A

II. B # E

III. B @ E

IV D * B

A. Only I and II are true

B. Only I and either II or III are true

C. Only I and IV are true

D. Only IV is true

E. Only I is true

Q.80 Statement:

M $ N, N & O, P & O # Q, R @ Q

Conclusion:

I. N @ R

II. O * M

III. R @ N

IV M # Q

A. Only II is true

B. Only either I or III are true

C. Only II and III are true

D. Only II, III and IV are true

E. Only III and IV are true

// Smart Answer Sheet //

Correct — Percentage of students who answered correctly. **Skipped** — Percentage of students who skipped.

Q.	Ans.	Correct / Skipped	Q.	Ans.	Correct / Skipped	Q.	Ans.	Correct / Skipped	Q.	Ans.	Correct / Skipped	Q.	Ans.	Correct / Skipped	Q.	Ans.	Correct / Skipped
1	B	42.2 % / 40.34 %	15	B	44.28 % / 47.99 %	29	D	40.24 % / 52.7 %	43	A	66.79 % / 32.3 %	57	B	50.11 % / 46.01 %	71	C	61.25 % / 33.53 %
2	D	68.75 % / 30.17 %	16	C	21.05 % / 76.11 %	30	A	65.71 % / 31.38 %	44	D	58.92 % / 34.57 %	58	C	46.82 % / 34.72 %	72	E	66.13 % / 31.88 %
3	C	60.41 % / 35.97 %	17	C	50.35 % / 46.95 %	31	B	50.78 % / 41.59 %	45	C	41.45 % / 56.7 %	59	D	53.48 % / 30.58 %	73	A	59.63 % / 30.35 %
4	B	55.43 % / 30.39 %	18	A	48.18 % / 43.72 %	32	A	62.68 % / 36.11 %	46	B	59.83 % / 38.22 %	60	B	11.48 % / 72.73 %	74	B	44.66 % / 51.36 %
5	A	41.81 % / 43.08 %	19	A	46.12 % / 53.62 %	33	C	54.27 % / 40.04 %	47	A	55.36 % / 42.52 %	61	B	57.15 % / 38.78 %	75	D	48.0 % / 43.01 %
6	B	40.48 % / 59.13 %	20	D	65.54 % / 30.8 %	34	D	57.57 % / 35.52 %	48	E	68.93 % / 30.42 %	62	D	62.76 % / 34.36 %	76	A	55.36 % / 32.71 %
7	B	87.48 % / 10.28 %	21	D	50.66 % / 30.82 %	35	C	49.98 % / 33.46 %	49	D	61.59 % / 37.87 %	63	A	60.05 % / 32.65 %	77	B	40.9 % / 41.9 %
8	B	56.98 % / 34.47 %	22	D	57.16 % / 40.74 %	36	C	41.04 % / 51.64 %	50	C	62.9 % / 33.96 %	64	D	46.03 % / 38.34 %	78	A	64.95 % / 30.45 %
9	C	49.34 % / 35.96 %	23	B	52.54 % / 35.19 %	37	D	67.64 % / 31.14 %	51	B	50.2 % / 38.76 %	65	E	44.23 % / 42.8 %	79	E	68.74 % / 31.11 %
10	A	84.94 % / 12.02 %	24	D	40.21 % / 33.26 %	38	B	55.6 % / 34.01 %	52	C	61.46 % / 34.64 %	66	B	59.91 % / 32.83 %	80	D	56.27 % / 33.2 %
11	A	47.41 % / 40.8 %	25	C	57.95 % / 39.94 %	39	C	58.83 % / 32.43 %	53	A	23.79 % / 71.31 %	67	C	67.48 % / 31.39 %			
12	C	66.79 % / 32.83 %	26	A	61.0 % / 37.1 %	40	D	57.47 % / 34.0 %	54	D	49.84 % / 47.04 %	68	B	49.16 % / 47.86 %			
13	D	58.25 % / 32.94 %	27	A	66.19 % / 32.68 %	41	D	62.67 % / 31.62 %	55	E	29.68 % / 67.25 %	69	C	44.29 % / 49.0 %			
14	C	48.74 % / 35.58 %	28	E	65.66 % / 30.9 %	42	C	52.72 % / 36.17 %	56	A	59.62 % / 37.57 %	70	A	52.41 % / 41.91 %			

Reasoning

Ques (1-5):Direction: Follow the given information to answer the questions.

'He loves his family' is written as 'sup rup mup cup'.

'My family likes him' is written as 'mup lup hup bup '.

'Everyone loves him' is written as 'rup hup xup'.

'He likes animals' is written as 'sup tup bup'.

Q.1 What is the code for 'animals'?

A. hup   **B.** cup   **C.** lup   **D.** bup
E. tup

Q.2 The code 'hup' is used for which of the following?

A.   his
B.   him
C.   he
D.   None of these
E.   Cannot be determined

Q.3 What is the code for 'family'?

A.   sup
B.   rup
C.   cup
D.   mup
E.   Cannot be determined

Q.4 The code 'lup' is used for which of the following?

A. My   **B.** family
C. likes   **D.** him
E. None of these

Q.5 What is the code for 'Everyone'?

A.   rup
B.   hup
C.   xup
D.   None of these
E.   Cannot be determined

Ques (6-10):Direction: Study the following information carefully to answer the questions given below-

Ten boxes are placed in an almirah such that the box which is at lowest place is numbered as 1st, and the box just above it is numbered as 2nd and so on till the topmost box is numbered as 10th position. Four boxes placed between J and K which is placed on an odd numbered position. The box K is placed below the box J. The box M is placed below the box K. Two boxes are placed between K and L which is placed just below Q box. Box B is placed below the box M. Q box is placed on 7th position. The box I is placed on an even numbered position but above the box P. The box A is placed immediate above the box R.

Q.6 Which box is placed at the bottom?

A. J   **B.** K
C. I   **D.** Data inadequate
E. None of these

Q.7 Which box is placed at the 9th position?

A. J   **B.** P
C. Q   **D.** Data inadequate
E. None of these

Q.8 How many boxes are placed between L and B box?

A. Three   **B.** Two
C. Four   **D.** Seven
E. None of these

Q.9 Four of the following five are alike in a certain way, based on their position. Which of the following does not belongs to that group?

A. B   **B.** L   **C.** K   **D.** A
E. Q

Q.10 Choose the correct option?

A.   J box is placed just above L box.
B.   Two boxes are placed between P and Q.
C.   R box is placed at an even numbered position.
D.   K box is placed on at 4th number position.
E.   None of the given option true.

Ques (11-12):Directions: Study the information given below carefully and answer the questions that follow.

Point E is 5 km to the South of point A. Point I is 5 km to the East of point E and point O is 5 km to the South of point I. Point U is 2 km to the West of point O while point V is 3 km to the south of point U. Point W is 3 km to the West of point V and point X is 5 km to the north of point W.

Q.11 What is the distance between A and X?

A. 6 km   **B.** 8 km   **C.** 10 km   **D.** 9 km
E. 12 km

Q.12 What is the direction of point I with respect to point W?

A. North-West   **B.** West
C. North- East   **D.** East
E. South-East

Ques (13-17):Directions: Study the following information carefully and answer the questions given below:

Certain number of person is sitting in a row facing towards north direction. Following information is known about them:

Only two persons are sitting between H and C, who is sitting 5th to the right of B. C, is sitting 3rd from the right end. D is sitting at left most end of the row and there are only two persons sitting between D and A. F is sitting just in the middle of A and B and 2nd to the right of A.

Not more than two persons are sitting between B and G and G is sitting just next to H. There are only one person is sitting between G and C.

Q.13 how many persons are sitting in the row?

A. 10 **B.** 12
C. 14 **D.** 15
E. None of these

Q.14 How many people are sitting between A and B?

A. 1 **B.** 2 **C.** 3 **D.** 4
E. 5

Q.15 How many persons are unknown in a row out of total members?

A. 7 **B.** 8
C. 9 **D.** 5
E. None of these

Q.16 How many persons are sitting to the left of person which is 3rd to the right of H?

A. 10 **B.** 11 **C.** 12 **D.** 13
E. 14

Q.17 How many persons are sitting between F and H?

A. 2 **B.** 3 **C.** 4 **D.** 5
E. 6

Ques (18-22):Directions: In the following question assuming the given statements to be True, find which of the conclusion among given conclusions is/are definitely true and then give your answers accordingly.

Q.18 Statements: R ≤ P ≤ Q; R ≥ S > T ≤ M = U

Conclusions:

I. Q > T

II. R ≥ M

A. Only II is True
B. Only I is True
C. Both I and II are True
D. Either I or II is True
E. None is true

Q.19 Statements: P < R < D < A < N; P > F = S

Conclusions:

I. A = F

II. F < A

A. Only II is True
B. Only I is True
C. Both I and II are True
D. Either I or II is True
E. None is true

Q.20 Statements: P < Q ≥ G; G ≥ I ≥ E; C ≤ P; C > U

Conclusions:

I. U > I

II. P ≤ E

A. Both I and II are True
B. Only II is True

C. Either I or II is True
D. Only I is True
E. Neither I nor II is true

Q.21 Statements: Y = O ≤ G ≤ K = U > L > P; Y = A ≥ R

Conclusions

I. U > R

II. R = U

A. Only II is True
B. Only I is True
C. Both I and II are True
D. Either I or II is True
E. None is true

Q.22 Statements: N ≥ T > P = A ≥ Z = K; N = B > D

Conclusions

I. D ≥ Z

II. B > K

A. Only II is True
B. Only I is True
C. Both I and II are True
D. Either I or II is True
E. None is true

Ques (23-27):Directions: Study the following information carefully and answer the questions given below.

9 friends A, B, C, D, E, F, G, H, and I are sitting around a circular table of which 4 are facing the center while others are facing outside. 3 people are sitting between A who is sitting to the immediate left of E and I who is facing outside. F and D are immediate neighbors of I and are facing the opposite direction. The equal number of persons sits between A and H and A and B. B and D are the immediate neighbors and facing the opposite direction. G sits between A and B and facing outside. C sits third to the right of A and facing the same direction as of G. I is sitting third to the right of H who faces the same direction as that of D.

Q.23 What is the position of the person who is sitting second to the left of F?

A. Third to the right of G
B. Third to the right of C
C. Third to the left of A
D. Fourth to the right of E
E. Immediate left of B

Q.24 How many people are sitting between H and D if counted from the left of D?

A. 5 **B.** 2 **C.** 4 **D.** 3
E. 6

Q.25 Which of the following is true?

A. F is the immediate neighbor of B.
B. D is facing the same direction as that of E.
C. B is third to the right of E.
D. A, E, H and F are facing towards the center.
E. A is sitting forth to the right of I.

Q.26 What is the position of F with respect to B?

A. Third to the left   **B.** Immediate left
C. Third to the right   **D.** Fifth to the right
E. Sixth to the right

Q.27 Who is sitting exactly between G and F?
A. D   **B.** H   **C.** B   **D.** E
E. I

Q.28 How many such pairs of letters are there in the word GRANDEUR each of which has as many letters between them in the word as in the English alphabet (considering both ways).
A. 1   **B.** 2   **C.** 3   **D.** 4
E. 5

Q.29 6 person, "A, B, C, D, E, F" goes for a movie on 6 different days from Monday to Saturday. A goes 2 days after D but before Friday. There is a 3 days gap between C and E. B goes on Saturday. F goes immediately before A. Who goes on Wednesday?
A. E   **B.** B   **C.** D   **D.** F
E. A

Q.30 Directions: Read the following information carefully and answer the given question.

In a number '85214796' if 2 is added to all odd numbers and 1 is subtracted from all even numbers, then what will be the difference between the first digit from left end and the first digit from the right end?
A. 7   **B.** 6   **C.** 5   **D.** 2
E. 3

Q.31 In the given word 'EXPATRIATE' if the vowels are changed to the next letter and the consonants are changed to the previous letters as per the alphabetical series, then which letter/letters are repeated more than once?
A. J, O   **B.** O, Q   **C.** W   **D.** Q, J
E. B, F, S

Ques (32-36):Directions: Answer the following questions according to the given statements:

There are eight persons A, B, C, D, E, F, G, and H, who live on four different floors among floor 1, floor 2, floor 3 and floor 4. Each floor has two different flats viz. flat 1 and flat 2.

There are 2 flats on each floor flat 1 – flat 2 from left to right in such a way that flat 1 of the fourth floor is exactly above flat 1 of the third floor and flat 1 of the third floor is exactly above flat 1 of the second floor and other flats are situated in the same way.

C lives one floor above the floor on which B lives. F lives with B who lives two floors below D. B lives on the second floor. E lives in flat 2 of the first floor. G lives on the third floor but not in flat 1. H does not live on the fourth floor but in flat 1. B lives in even-numbered flat. A and C live in flat 1 but on different floors.

Q.32 Who live in the flat 1 of floor 2?
A. B   **B.** C   **C.** F   **D.** A
E. G

Q.33 Who lives two floor below the floor on which G lives in the same flat number?
A. A   **B.** F
C. C   **D.** E
E. None of these

Q.34 Who lives on the same floors?
A. H and G   **B.** F and B
C. C and B   **D.** E and D
E. None of the above

Q.35 Who live on the fourth floor of flat 2?
A. H   **B.** C   **C.** A   **D.** E
E. D

Q.36 Which of the following given pair is different from rest?
A. H and C   **B.** G and E   **C.** C and F   **D.** E and G
E. B and D

Ques (37-40):Direction: Read the given information and answer below questions.

There are seven persons A, B, C, D, E, F and G sitting in a row facing north direction but not necessarily in the same order. Each one has a different age (in years), i.e., 4, 15, 17, 19, 21, 23 and 40 but not necessarily in the same order.

The person whose age is 19 years is sitting between C and F. F is sitting 3rd to the right of E whose age is 6 years more than that of B. A sits just immediately left of B whose age is a multiple of 5 but not more than 20. Age of F is the sum of the ages of E and G. There is only one person who sits to the immediate right of F. C whose age is a two digit prime number sits 3rd to the right of the person whose age is 4 years. Age of D is two years less than the age of G.

Q.37 How many people sit between A and D?
A. 5   **B.** 4
C. 3   **D.** 2
E. None of the above

Q.38 What is the age of F?
A. 21 years   **B.** 40 years   **C.** 17 years   **D.** 15 years
E. 19 years

Q.39 Which of the following is correct?
A. A sits third to the right of C
B. Age of F is 19 years
C. Sum of the age of A and B is same as that of G
D. Only one person sits between F and D.
E. Age of C is not a prime number.

Q.40 Four of the following are alike in a certain way and so form a group. Which of the following does not belong to the group?
A. BC   **B.** GD   **C.** GE   **D.** AE
E. CF

Quantitative Aptitude

Ques (41-46):Direction: What should come in place of the question mark '?' in the following number series?

Q.41 3.5, 7, 14, 24.5, 38.5, ?
A. 42   **B.** 56   **C.** 52.5   **D.** 77
E. 49

Q.42 287, ?, 71, 35, 17, 8
A. 144   **B.** 143   **C.** 142   **D.** 141
E. 140

Q.43 19, 20, 42, 129, ?, 2605
A. 512   **B.** 543   **C.** 555   **D.** 520
E. 536

Q.44 3.5, 2.5, 3, 6, 20, ?
A. 91   **B.** 82   **C.** 93   **D.** 84
E. 95

Q.45 106, 101, 90, 73, 50, ?
A. 31   **B.** 21   **C.** 36   **D.** 27
E. 41

Q.46 20, 60, 25, 65, 30, ?
A. 35   **B.** 70   **C.** 84   **D.** 95
E. 55

Ques (47-52):Directions: Read the following Pie chart carefully and answer the following questions:-

The pie chart shows the percentage of candidates in 6 different shifts of an examination.

Total number of candidates = 5500

Percentage of candidates

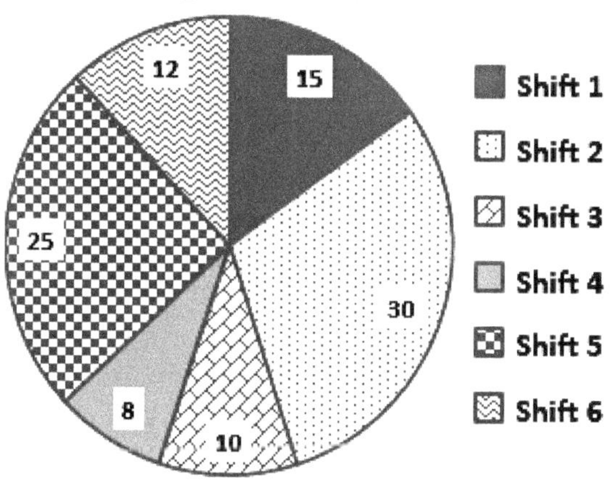

Q.47 Number of candidates in shift 6 is what percentage more/less than number of candidate in shift 4?
A. 20%   **B.** 50%
C. 30%   **D.** 10%
E. None of these

Q.48 If 215 candidates in shift 2 were absent, then find the number of candidates present in the same shift.
A. 1200   **B.** 1050   **C.** 1435   **D.** 915
E. 1285

Q.49 If ratio of male to female candidates in shift 3 is 6 : 5, then find number of female candidates in shift 3.

A. 350   **B.** 225
C. 435   **D.** 250
E. None of these

Q.50 Find the average number of candidates in shift 2, shift 3 and shift 4 together in the examination.
A. 700   **B.** 660   **C.** 880   **D.** 910
E. 750

Q.51 The number of candidates in shift 1 is how much more than the number of candidates in shift 4?
A. 260   **B.** 385
C. 425   **D.** 360
E. None of these

Q.52 If 40% candidates in shift 6 were failed, then find the number of candidates passed the examination in the same shift.
A. 369   **B.** 228   **C.** 426   **D.** 264
E. 396

Q.53 A invest 80% of his income on mutual fund, real estate and insurance in the ratio of 3 : 5 : 7 respectively. Find his saving, if his investment on the mutual fund is Rs. 24,000.
A. Rs. 1,00,000   **B.** Rs. 50,000
C. Rs. 30,000   **D.** Rs. 40,000
E. Rs. 80,000

Q.54 A cylinder of radius 14 cm and height 5 cm is melted and recast into cubes of edge length 2 cm. How many identical cubes will be obtained?
A. 462   **B.** 385   **C.** 352   **D.** 429
E. 484

Q.55 A boat takes 2 hours more to travel 45 km upstream than to travel the same distance downstream. If the ratio of the speed of current to the speed of boat is 1 : 4, then find the speed of the current.
A. 5 km/hr   **B.** 9 km/hr
C. 4 km/hr   **D.** 6 km/hr
E. None of these

Q.56 A mixture contains 15 kg of rice at Rs. 60 per kg and 25 kg of rice at X per kg are mixed and sold at Rs. 97.5 per kg. The profit earned by the seller is 30%. What will be the value of x?
A. 72   **B.** 84   **C.** 80   **D.** 77
E. 70

Q.57 If 3 coins are tossed simultaneously, what is the probability of getting at least 2 heads?
A. $\frac{1}{3}$ **B.** $\frac{1}{2}$ **C.** $\frac{1}{8}$ **D.** $\frac{7}{8}$
E. $\frac{2}{3}$

Q.58 A and B on working together can complete a work in 4 days. A alone takes 6 days less than B alone takes. In how many days C alone can complete the work if he is 50% more efficient than B?
A. 8   **B.** 16   **C.** 12   **D.** 14
E. 20

Q.59 A shopkeeper marked his article 1500 more than its cost price and gives a discount of 12.5% on it. If the selling price of the article is Rs. 3500, then find profit per cent made by the shopkeeper.

A. 10%   **B.** 20%   **C.** 25%   **D.** 30%
E. 40%

Ques (60-64):Direction: In the given question, two equations numbered I and II are given. Solve both the equations and mark the appropriate answer.

Q.60 I. $x^2 - 11x + 30 = 0$

II. $y^2 + 12y + 36 = 0$

A. x > y
B. x < y
C. x ≥ y
D. x ≤ y
E. x = y or the relationship between x and y cannot be established.

Q.61 I. $x^2 + 9x + 20 = 0$

II. $8y^2 - 15y + 7 = 0$

A. x > y
B. x < y
C. x ≥ y
D. x ≤ y
E. x = y or the relationship between x and y cannot be established.

Q.62 I. $x^3 = 64$

II. $y^2 = 16$

A. x > y
B. x < y
C. x ≥ y
D. x ≤ y
E. x = y or the relationship between x and y cannot be established.

Q.63 I. $x^2 - 20x + 91 = 0$

II. $y^2 + 16y + 63 = 0$

A. x > y
B. x < y
C. x ≥ y
D. x ≤ y
E. x = y or the relationship between x and y cannot be established.

Q.64 I. $6x^2 + 5x + 1 = 0$

II. $2y^2 - y - 1 = 0$

A. x > y
B. x < y
C. x ≥ y
D. x ≤ y
E. x = y or the relationship between x and y cannot be established.

Q.65 In a school class A have 320 students and class B have 240 students. In class A 40% students not passed and in class B 30% students not passed. Find the overall pass percentage(approximate) of the school.

A. 64%   **B.** 35%   **C.** 62%   **D.** 37%
E. 48%

Q.66 Two trains of same length moving in opposite direction. Speed of $train_1$ is 54 km/hr and Speed of $train_2$ is 18 km/hr. First train takes 30 seconds to cross the second train. Find the time taken by first train to cross 450 m long platform.

A. 58 sec   **B.** 64 sec   **C.** 60 sec   **D.** 50 sec
E. 75 sec

Q.67 6 years ago age of A and B are in the ratio of 7 : 10. 10 years after the sum of ages A and B is 100 years. C is 12 years elder than B. Find the present age of C.

A. 28 years   **B.** 39 years   **C.** 58 years   **D.** 42 years
E. 45 years

Q.68 A starts from point x at a speed of 15 km/hr and B starts towards A from point y at a speed of 25 km/hr and meet each other after 2 hours at point z. Find the difference in distance between point xz and point yz.

A. 20 km   **B.** 30 km
C. 60 km   **D.** 45 km
E. None of these

Q.69 A shop of mobile phones is closed on Tuesday. The average sale per day for remaining six days of a week is Rs.1564 and the average sale of Wednesday to Sunday is Rs. 1412.4. The sales on Monday is:

A. 2232   **B.** 2792   **C.** 2562   **D.** 2342
E. 2322

Q.70 Three pipes A, B and C were opened to fill a tank. Working alone A, B and C requires 12 minutes, 15 minutes and 20 minutes respectively. Another pipe D, which is outlet pipe, can empty the fully filled tank in 30 minutes working alone. What is the total time taken to fill the tank if all the pipes are simultaneously opened?

A. 3 minutes   **B.** 12 minutes
C. 6 minutes   **D.** 8 minutes
E. 5 minutes

Ques (71-75):Direction: Given below are two quantities named I and II. Based on the given information, you have to determine the relation between the two quantities. You should use the given data and your knowledge of Mathematics to choose among the possible answers.

Q.71 Quantity I: A and B completes the work in 15 days while working together. The ratio of their time is 3 : 5. In how many days B alone can complete the work.

Quantity II: 45 days

A. Quantity I > Quantity II
B. Quantity I < Quantity II
C. Quantity I ≥ Quantity II
D. Quantity I ≤ Quantity II
E. Quantity I = Quantity II or No relation

Q.72 Quantity I: In a mixture of 80 litre, Milk and water are in the ratio of 7 : 1. If 30% of the mixture is taken out, Find the quantity of the water left in the mixture.

Quantity II: 7 litre

A. Quantity I > Quantity II
B. Quantity I < Quantity II
C. Quantity I ≥ Quantity II
D. Quantity I ≤ Quantity II
E. Quantity I = Quantity II or No relation

Q.73 Quantity I: Age of A is 5 times of his son, after 15 years the ratio of age of A and son is 13 : 5, find the age of A (in years)?

Quantity II: 45

A. Quantity I > Quantity II
B. Quantity I < Quantity II
C. Quantity I ≥ Quantity II
D. Quantity I ≤ Quantity II
E. Quantity I = Quantity II or No relation

Q.74 Quantity I: The average age of a group of students is 24 years. When the age of their teacher is also included, the average age increases by 1 year. If the age of the teacher is 36 years, find the number of students in the group.

Quantity II: 11

A. Quantity I > Quantity II
B. Quantity I < Quantity II
C. Quantity I ≥ Quantity II
D. Quantity I ≤ Quantity II
E. Quantity I = Quantity II or No relation

Q.75 Quantity I: A train takes 10 seconds to cross a 120 m long platform and takes 8 seconds to cross another 84 m long platform. What is the length of the train?

Quantity II: 50 m

A. Quantity I > Quantity II
B. Quantity I < Quantity II
C. Quantity I ≥ Quantity II
D. Quantity I ≤ Quantity II
E. Quantity I = Quantity II or No relation

Ques (76-80):Direction: Study the following information carefully and answer the given questions.

The table shows the total number of invited person and the percentage of person who attended the events (A, B, C, D, E) respectively.

Events	Invited Person	Person who attended the event (in %)
A	360	50%
B	240	60%
C	420	80%
D	120	75%
E	300	50%

Q.76 What is the ratio of the number of persons who attended event B to the number of persons who attended the event C?

A. 3 : 7
B. 3 : 8
C. 4 : 3
D. 4 : 7
E. None of these

Q.77 What is the average of number of persons who attended the events C, D and E?

A. 195
B. 194
C. 192
D. 198
E. None of these

Q.78 Find the percentage of persons who attended the event A is how much more than the number of persons who attended the event D.

A. 80%
B. 100%
C. 90%
D. 75%
E. None of these

Q.79 Find the difference between the number of persons who attended the events C and D and the number of persons who attended the events B and E.

A. 130
B. 134
C. 136
D. 132
E. None of these

Q.80 Find the ratio of number of persons who did not attend the event B to the total number of persons who were invited for event D.

A. 2 : 3
B. 4 : 5
C. 2 : 5
D. 15 : 16
E. 3 : 5

// Smart Answer Sheet //

Correct — Percentage of students who answered correctly.   **Skipped** — Percentage of students who skipped.

Q.	Ans.	Correct	Skipped	Q.	Ans.	Correct	Skipped	Q.	Ans.	Correct	Skipped	Q.	Ans.	Correct	Skipped	Q.	Ans.	Correct	Skipped	Q.	Ans.	Correct	Skipped
1	E	58.22 %	31.64 %	15	B	46.3 %	40.45 %	29	D	67.31 %	30.79 %	43	D	57.67 %	33.4 %	57	B	69.79 %	30.0 %	71	B	59.58 %	38.25 %
2	B	68.11 %	30.99 %	16	C	40.37 %	40.02 %	30	D	48.35 %	42.67 %	44	E	47.11 %	38.26 %	58	A	54.0 %	37.31 %	72	E	54.59 %	33.06 %
3	D	61.13 %	36.25 %	17	B	57.03 %	34.53 %	31	E	50.02 %	43.87 %	45	B	60.18 %	36.64 %	59	E	41.47 %	44.05 %	73	A	59.57 %	39.61 %
4	A	57.73 %	38.48 %	18	B	41.46 %	30.47 %	32	C	65.54 %	31.1 %	46	B	55.17 %	31.82 %	60	A	40.49 %	45.75 %	74	E	67.23 %	31.62 %
5	C	69.36 %	30.4 %	19	A	65.41 %	34.11 %	33	D	63.87 %	35.87 %	47	B	55.87 %	35.84 %	61	B	46.1 %	51.4 %	75	A	52.94 %	33.65 %
6	E	50.04 %	30.18 %	20	E	63.05 %	31.6 %	34	B	51.77 %	39.93 %	48	C	55.63 %	39.42 %	62	C	62.57 %	33.84 %	76	A	46.27 %	34.5 %
7	B	60.72 %	32.76 %	21	D	63.26 %	30.98 %	35	E	68.57 %	30.5 %	49	D	51.26 %	35.32 %	63	A	62.96 %	33.2 %	77	C	53.98 %	43.04 %
8	C	52.7 %	34.36 %	22	A	54.1 %	44.22 %	36	C	43.71 %	45.81 %	50	C	67.32 %	31.16 %	64	E	57.67 %	31.85 %	78	B	54.41 %	42.83 %
9	B	46.36 %	50.06 %	23	C	62.23 %	33.63 %	37	A	66.14 %	31.52 %	51	B	57.79 %	37.21 %	65	A	58.81 %	34.83 %	79	D	45.82 %	34.7 %
10	C	59.95 %	31.57 %	24	D	46.21 %	49.39 %	38	B	46.51 %	38.46 %	52	E	48.35 %	46.82 %	66	D	57.2 %	39.78 %	80	B	62.36 %	34.02 %
11	B	47.0 %	31.47 %	25	B	61.06 %	31.07 %	39	C	45.46 %	45.31 %	53	C	69.25 %	30.51 %	67	C	42.48 %	47.8 %				
12	C	63.95 %	33.63 %	26	C	66.5 %	32.3 %	40	C	68.78 %	30.48 %	54	B	47.8 %	41.0 %	68	A	63.51 %	35.89 %				
13	D	62.54 %	35.92 %	27	A	52.33 %	46.75 %	41	B	40.56 %	38.82 %	55	E	50.56 %	41.68 %	69	E	62.11 %	37.52 %				
14	C	48.7 %	32.29 %	28	B	62.28 %	34.11 %	42	B	51.53 %	41.34 %	56	B	40.89 %	50.04 %	70	C	47.58 %	38.87 %				

Reasoning

Ques (1-5):Direction: Read the following given information carefully and answer the questions.

Eight people A, B, C, D, E, F, G, and H were born on the same date but in different years viz. 1972, 1980, 1958, 1960,1968, 1988,1999, and 1962. (Calculating all ages with respect to the year 2019)

G was born eight years after B. A was born in an even number of years. Only one person was born in the odd number year whose age is multiple of 2. H is the youngest among all. C is not younger than A. The difference between the age of B and the person who was born in the year 1958 is 2 years. B is not older to the F whose age is 61. The age difference between D and E is 10 years. D is 10 years older than the one who is four years younger than G.

Q.1 Who is the oldest among all?
A. C
B. D
C. F
D. B
E. None of the above

Q.2 How many persons were born between H and F?
A. 4
B. 6
C. 2
D. 5
E. None

Q.3 What is the sum of age of persons born between the age of 35 and 60?
A. 304
B. 320
C. 253
D. 299
E. None of these

Q.4 B is how many years older than C?
A. 18
B. 25
C. 20
D. 15
E. None of these

Q.5 Ten years before D was same age of.
A. E
B. C
C. A
D. H
E. None of these

Ques (6-7):Directions: Pranav and Pranjal starts from the same point. Pranav moves 10 m towards North then takes a right and moves 5 m ahead and finally halt after moving 2 m towards his right. Pranjal walked towards West for 10 m, then he takes a left and moves for next 10 m, then he again turns to his left and moves for 15 m and finally stops after moving 5 m towards his left.

Q.6 If Pranav cannot see Pranjal shadow then what might be the time, and what is the distance between both of them?
A. 10 am, 13 m
B. 3 pm, 15 m
C. 9 am, 15 m
D. 12 pm, 13 m

E. 9 am, 13 m

Q.7 If Pranav's shadow is to the right of Pranjal then what might be the time?
A. 12 am
B. 3 pm
C. 9 am
D. 12 pm
E. Cannot be determined

Ques (8-11):Directions: Study the following information carefully and answer the given questions:

In a certain code language,

'he who knows Sam' is written as 'ma co he mx'.

'Sam is a bad doctor' is written as 'mx mh la sa ox'.

'Ravi knows Sam' is written as 'mx he kl'.

'who is doctor under Ravi' is written as 'kl mh co ze ox'.

Q.8 What is the code for 'he' in the given code language?
A. ma
B. he
C. co
D. mx
E. mh

Q.9 What does the code 'co' stand for?
A. who
B. knows
C. he
D. Sam
E. Either (A) or (C)

Q.10 In the given code language, which of the following means 'a bad doctor'?
A. la sa mh
B. sa la ox
C. os sa mh
D. Either (A) or (B)
E. mx mh la

Q.11 What is the code for 'doctor'?
A. kl
B. ox
C. mh
D. ze
E. Either (B) or (C)

Q.12 Directions: Study the following information carefully and answer the given questions.

There are seven persons A, B, C, D, E, F and G. Each of them has different heights. B is taller than A and E but not the tallest. F is taller than only G. Equal number of persons are shorter and taller than C.

Who among the following is the tallest?
A. A
B. E
C. F
D. D
E. None of the above

Ques (13-17):Direction: Read the following information carefully and answer the questions that are given below.

There are eight persons namely A, B, C, D, E, F, G and H sitting around a square table. Four persons are sitting on the corner of the square table and are facing inside, and four persons are sitting on the edge of the square table and are facing outside. No two consecutive alphabets are sitting next to each other, for example A is not sitting next to B, B is not sitting next to A and C and so on.

B and D are sitting opposite to each other. H sits third to the left of C. A sits on one of the corners. B does not sit on the edge of the square table. A and H are to the immediate right of each other. H is not near to B. E and G are sitting opposite to each other.

Q.13 Who is sitting second to the left of G?

A. B   **B.** F   **C.** A   **D.** H
E. C

Q.14 How many persons are sitting between D and F when counted from the left of D?

A. Three   **B.** Two   **C.** Four   **D.** Five
E. One

Q.15 Who is sitting immediately to the right of B?

A. C   **B.** F   **C.** A   **D.** E
E. H

Q.16 Who is sitting opposite to H?

A. F   **B.** A   **C.** G   **D.** C
E. E

Q.17 How many persons are sitting between F and A when counted from the left of F?

A. Five   **B.** One   **C.** Four   **D.** Three
E. Two

Ques (18-19):Direction: In the question below are given two statements followed by two conclusions numbered I and II. You have to take the given statements to be true even if they seem to be at variance with commonly known facts. Read all the conclusions and then decide which of the given conclusions logically follows from the given statements disregarding commonly known facts.

Q.18 Statement:

Only a few Pens are Boats.
All Boats are Ships.

Conclusion:

I. A few Pens are Ships.
II. All Ships being Pens is a possibility.

A. Only I follows
B. Only II follows
C. Either I or II follows
D. Neither I nor II follows
E. Both I and II follow

Q.19 Statement:

Only a few Photos are Paints.
Some Paints are Colours.

Conclusion:

I. All Colours can be Paints is a possibility.
II. Some Photos are not Colours.

A. Only I follows
B. Only II follows
C. Either I or II follows
D. Neither I nor II follows
E. Both I and II follow

Q.20 Directions: In the question below there are three statements followed by three conclusions I, II and III. You have to take the three given statements to be true even if they seem to be at variance from commonly known facts and then decide which of the given conclusions logically follows from the given statements disregarding commonly known facts.

Statements:

I. Some owls are peacock.
II. Some peacocks are hawks.
III. No hawks are squirrels.

Conclusions:

I. No owls are hawks.
II. Some peacocks are not squirrels.
III. Some owls are squirrels.

A. Only conclusion II follows
B. Either conclusion I or II follows
C. Only conclusion III follows
D. Both conclusion II and conclusion III follow
E. None of the above

Ques (21-22):Directions: In the question below are given two statements followed by two conclusions I, II. You have to take the given statements to be true even if they seem to be at variance from commonly known facts. Read all the conclusions and then decide which of the given conclusions logically follows from the given statements disregarding commonly known facts.

Q.21 Statements:

No bulb is a tubelight.
No fan is a bulb.

Conclusions:

I. Some bulb is a fan.
II. No tubelight is a fan.

A. Only I follows
B. Only II follows
C. None follows
D. Both I and II follow
E. Either I or II follows

Q.22 Statements:

All reds are black.
No white is red.

Conclusions:

I. Some white is black.
II. All black are red.

A. Only II follows
B. Only I follows
C. Either I or II follows
D. Neither I or II follows
E. Both I and II follow

Ques (23-27):Direction: Read the following information carefully and answer the questions that are given below.

There are seven persons namely M, N, O, P, Q, R, and S. They all are sitting in a row facing north. They all belong to seven different cities namely, Delhi, Mumbai, Chennai, Kolkata, Bangalore, Pune and Hyderabad.

The one who belongs to Bangalore sits in the middle of the row. The one who belongs to Delhi sits second from one of the ends of the row. The one who belongs to Mumbai sits third to the right of M. Equal number of persons sit to the left and right of N. M belongs to Delhi. P sits on the right end of the row and belongs to Pune. Three persons are sitting P and Q. R belongs to Hyderabad and sits two places away to the left of Q. The one who belongs to Chennai sits exactly in between the one who belongs to Mumbai and R. S does not sit next to P.

Q.23 Who is sitting second to the right of N?
A. P   **B.** S   **C.** O   **D.** M
E. R

Q.24 How many persons are sitting between O and M?
A. Five   **B.** Four   **C.** Two   **D.** Three
E. One

Q.25 Who belongs to Chennai?
A. M   **B.** Q
C. S   **D.** O
E. None of these

Q.26 Who is sitting second to the left of M?
A. R   **B.** Q   **C.** N   **D.** O
E. No one

Q.27 Which pair of name – place is not correct?
A. O – Kolkata   **B.** P – Pune
C. Q – Chennai   **D.** M – Bangalore
E. R – Hyderabad

Q.28 How many pairs of letters are there in the word EXTREME according to the English alphabetical series (both in the forward and backward direction)?
A. Three   **B.** Four   **C.** Two   **D.** One
E. None

Q.29 There are 6 persons in a family namely A, B, C, D, E and F, they all are related to each other in some or the other way. B is the only daughter of C. E is the sister-in-law of B, but is not married to F. F is the son of A. A has three children. C is the wife of A. How is D related to B?
A. Sister   **B.** Sister-in-law
C. Brother   **D.** Mother
E. Father

Q.30 There are six persons namely M, N, O, P, Q and R. They all take leave from office on any one day of the week starting from Monday to Saturday. Only one person takes leave on one day. C is the first person to take a leave. Three persons take leave between D and C. F takes leave just after D. E takes leave on Wednesday. B takes a leave after A. Who takes a leave on Thursday?

A. A   **B.** D   **C.** E   **D.** B
E. F

Ques (31-35):Direction: In the following question, assuming the given statements to be true, find which conclusion among the given conclusions is/are definitely true and then give your answers accordingly.

Q.31 Statements: F = L; K < L; K ≥ D; M < D
Conclusions:
I. F ≥ M
II. L > D
A. Both I and II are True
B. Only II is True
C. Only I is True
D. Either I or II is True
E. Neither I nor II is true

Q.32 Statements: H = G > F; A < B ≥ X; B ≤ F
Conclusions:
I. H ≥ A
II. X < F
A. Both I and II are True
B. Only II is True
C. Either I or II is True
D. Only I is True
E. Neither I nor II is true

Q.33 Statements: A > B ≥ C; E = D ≤ C
Conclusions:
I. B ≥ D
II. A > E
A. Only II is True
B. Only I is True
C. Both I and II are True
D. None is True
E. Either I or II follows

Q.34 Statements: Q ≤ A < D < K ≤ M = J = F > Z
Conclusions:
I. K > Q
II. F ≥ K
A. Only II Is True
B. Only I is True
C. Both I and II are True
D. Either I or II is True
E. None is true

Q.35 Statements: P = Q ≤ R; T = P; T > S
Conclusions:
I. Q < S
II. R < S
A. Only I is True
B. Only II is True
C. Both I and II are True
D. Either I or II is True
E. None is True

Ques (36-40):Direction: Read the following information carefully and answer the questions.

Nine boxes – B_1, B_2, B_3, B_4, B_5, B_6, B_7, B_8, B_9 are placed one above the other not necessarily in the same order. More than three boxes are placed between B_2 and B_9. B_5 is the lowermost box which is not kept immediately below B_2. Only four boxes are kept between B_3 and B_7 which is not the topmost box. Only two boxes are kept between B_7 and B_6. Less than three boxes are kept below B_3. B_9 is placed two places below B_8 which is kept immediately below B_4. B_4 is placed on one of the places above B_1.

Q.36 Which box is placed immediately below B_1?

A. B_5

B. B_3

C. B_4

D. B_8

E. Either (A) or (D)

Q.37 How many boxes are placed below B_3?

A. None

B. Two

C. Three

D. One

E. None of these

Q.38 If B_7 is related to B_2 and B_3 is related to B_9 in a certain way, then B6 is related to?

A. B_8

B. B_4

C. B_1

D. B_3

E. B_5

Q.39 How many boxes are placed between B_7 and B_8?

A. Three

B. More than three

C. One

D. Two

E. Either (A) or (D)

Q.40 Which of the following box is kept second from the top?

A. B_8

B. B_4

C. B_1

D. B_3

E. B_7

Quantitative Aptitude

Ques (41-45):Direction: Find the missing number in the given series:

Q.41 1000, 100, 20, 8, 6.4, ?

A. 10

B. 10.34

C. 10.24

D. 10.14

E. 10.44

Q.42 2, 6, 33, 49, 174, ?

A. 220

B. 210

C. 200

D. 190

E. 180

Q.43 14, 8, 9, 14.5, 30, ?

A. 67

B. 69

C. 71

D. 74

E. 76

Q.44 77, 85, 69, 101, 37, ?

A. 165

B. 110

C. 150

D. 180

E. 135

Q.45 20, 29, 54, 103, 184, ?

A. 290

B. 295

C. 300

D. 305

E. 310

Ques (46-50):Direction: The given bar graph shows the number of pens sold by two shops A & B in four consecutive months. Study the following data and answer the following questions:

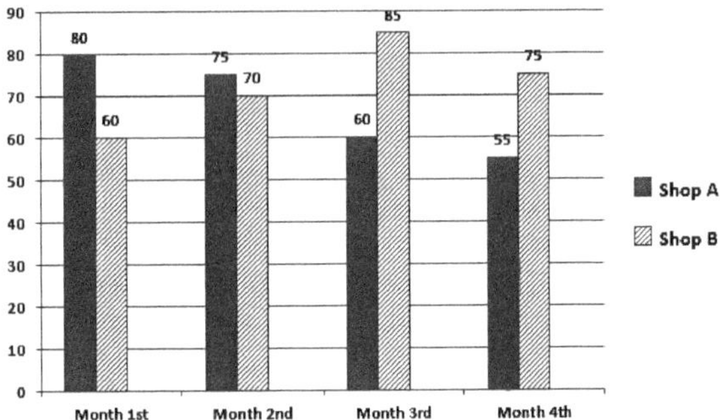

Q.46 Find the ratio of the number of pens sold by shop A in months 1st and 3rd together to the number of pens sold by shop B in months 2nd and 4th together.

A. 27 : 28

B. 28 : 29

C. 29 : 30

D. 26 : 27

E. None of these

Q.47 Find the average of the number of pens sold by shop A in 1st and 3rd months and the number of pens sold by shop B in 3rd and 4th month together.

A. 75

B. 85

C. 72

D. 78

E. None of these

Q.48 Find that the number of pens sold by shop A in 1st month is how much percent more than the number of pens sold by shop A in 3rd month.

A. 37.5%

B. 42.5%

C. 33.33%

D. 47.5%

E. None of these

Q.49 What is the difference between the number of pens sold by shop A and B together in month 3th and 4th?

A. 25

B. 15

C. 20

D. 10

E. None of these

Q.50 Find the ratio of the number of pens sold by shop A in 1st month to the number of pens sold by B in 3rd month.

A. 13 : 14

B. 14 : 15

C. 15 : 16

D. 16 : 17

E. None of these

Q.51 A sum of money is invested on simple interest at 1.5% p.a for 8 years yields interest Rs.3000. What will be the simple interest on the same sum at 5% for 6 years.

A. 8000

B. 7500

C. 9500

D. 6000

E. None of these

Q.52 The average of 5 term is 50. If the first 4 terms are 45, 37, 80 and 43 what will be the last term?

A. 70

B. 80

C. 75

D. 45

E. 55

Q.53 The ratio between the present age of two friends Arvind and Mahesh is 5 : 6. After 8 years the ratio of their ages will be 7 : 8. Find their sum of Arvind and Mahesh ages after 10 years.

A. 45   **B.** 60
C. 64   **D.** 74
E. None of these

Q.54 An article was purchased for Rs.93645. Its price was marked up by 30%. It was sold at a discount of 20% on the marked up price. What was the profit percentage on the cost price?

A. 5%   **B.** 10%   **C.** 7%   **D.** 4%
E. 8%

Ques (55-59):Direction: Given below are two quantities named I and II. Based on the given information, you have to determine the relation between the two quantities. You should use the given data and your knowledge of Mathematics to choose among the possible answers.

Q.55 Quantity I: A certain invested for 2 years at the rate of 12% simple interest. If the simple Interest is Rs.1200. Find the Principal.

Quantity II: Rs. 6000

A. Quantity I > Quantity II
B. Quantity I < Quantity II
C. Quantity I ≥ Quantity II
D. Quantity I ≤ Quantity II
E. Quantity I = Quantity II

Q.56 Quantity I: An article was sold at Rs. 450. If the profit earned by selling the article is 20%. Find the Cost price.

Quantity II: Rs. 350

A. Quantity I > Quantity II
B. Quantity I < Quantity II
C. Quantity I ≥ Quantity II
D. Quantity I ≤ Quantity II
E. Quantity I = Quantity II

Q.57 Quantity I: A coin is tossed 3 times. What is the probability of getting a tail each time?

Quantity II: $\dfrac{1}{16}$

A. Quantity I > Quantity II
B. Quantity I < Quantity II
C. Quantity I ≥ Quantity II
D. Quantity I ≤ Quantity II
E. Quantity I = Quantity II

Q.58 Quantity I: If A goes with $\dfrac{4}{5}$th of his actual speed he reaches the distance 1.5 hours late. What was his actual time (in hours)?

Quantity II: 6

A. Quantity I > Quantity II
B. Quantity I < Quantity II
C. Quantity I ≥ Quantity II
D. Quantity I ≤ Quantity II

E. Quantity I = Quantity II

Q.59 Quantity I: The income of A and B are in the ratio 4 : 3 and their expenditures are in the ratio 2 : 1. If each saves Rs. 200, then what will the sum of their incomes?

Quantity II: 500

A. Quantity I < Quantity II
B. Quantity I > Quantity II
C. Quantity I ≥ Quantity II
D. Quantity I ≤ Quantity II
E. Quantity I = Quantity II

Ques (60-65):Direction: What approximate value should come in the place of x in the following question?

Q.60 $1027.96 = 20\%$ of $4999.98 + 7\%$ of $\left(\dfrac{199.95}{x}\right)$

A. 0.05   **B.** 5   **C.** 0.5   **D.** 50
E. 2

Q.61 $257.12 + 187.99x = (49.99)^2 + 390.09$

A. 16   **B.** 14   **C.** 20   **D.** 18
E. 22

Q.62 $\left(\dfrac{2.99}{3.99}\right) \times \sqrt[3]{511.99} + 123.9\%$ of $650.11 = x$

A. 901   **B.** 812   **C.** 821   **D.** 832
E. 841

Q.63 $24.002 \times 14.005 - 7.995 \times 5.96 = x$

A. 280   **B.** 272   **C.** 266   **D.** 255
E. 288

Q.64 $\sqrt{784.01} \times 7.042 + 351.99 \times 24.98\% = x$

A. 264   **B.** 244   **C.** 284   **D.** 266
E. 224

Q.65 $\left(\dfrac{15.96}{11.99}\right) \times 143.68 + 29.93\%$ of $439.96 - 155.65 = x$

A. 145   **B.** 168   **C.** 196   **D.** 230
E. 285

Q.66 The diameter of the circle is twice the length of the rectangle. The ratio between their areas is 11 : 7 respectively. Then what will be the ratio between the length and breadth of the rectangle?

A. 1 : 2   **B.** 1 : 4   **C.** 1 : 7   **D.** 2 : 1
E. 7 : 1

Q.67 In a mixture the ratio of milk to water is 4 : 1. If 30 litre of water is added then new ratio becomes 14 : 11. Calculate the initial mixture?

A. 20 litre   **B.** 65 litre   **C.** 70 litre   **D.** 10 litre
E. 30 litres

Q.68 A and B together can do the work in X days. A takes 12 days less than B to complete the whole. If time taken by A to complete the whole working alone is 9 days, then find X.

A. 6.3 days   **B.** 7 days   **C.** 5 days   **D.** 5.5 days
E. 7.2 days

Q.69 Age of A is 1.5 times of B. The ratio of their ages after 10 years is 4 : 3. then what is the current age of B?

A. 15 **B.** 45 **C.** 30 **D.** 20
E. 25

Q.70 A man rows 10km upstream and the same distance downstream. The difference in time taken by the man in rowing upstream and downstream is 5min. If the speed of boat is 35km/hr, what is the speed of the stream?

A. 13 km/ hr **B.** 5 km/hr
C. 10 km/hr **D.** 7.5 km/hr
E. 3 km/hr

Q.71 There is a 50% increase in an amount in 5 years at certain rate of simple interest. What will be the compound interest of Rs. 15000 for 2 years at the same rate?

A. 1795 **B.** 3065 **C.** 3150 **D.** 1815
E. 1875

Q.72 A started a business with Rs.10000 after 6 months B joins with Rs.12000. At the end of the year total profit is Rs.96000. Find the share of A in the profit.

A. Rs. 50000 **B.** Rs. 40000
C. Rs. 80000 **D.** Rs. 45000
E. Rs. 60000

Q.73 Two trains, each having a length of 320 meters moving in the same direction crossed each other in 18 seconds. If the slower train crosses the 200 meters long platform in 26 seconds. Then find the speed in km/hr of the faster train.

A. 180 km/hr **B.** 176 km/hr
C. 200 km/hr **D.** 182 km/hr
E. 264 km/hr

Q.74 To fill the tank Pipe A and Pipe B takes 12hours. Pipe B and Pipe C takes 9 hours to fill the tank and Pipe C and Pipe A together take 15 hours to fill the tank. Find the time taken to fill the tank when Pipe A, Pipe B and Pipe C opened together (approximately).

A. 5 hours **B.** 8 hours **C.** 9 hours **D.** 11 hours
E. 6 hours

Q.75 Three numbers A, B and C are in the ratio of 12 : 15 : 25. If sum of these numbers is 312, Find the difference between A and C.

A. 72 **B.** 78 **C.** 65 **D.** 52
E. 96

Ques (76-80):Direction: Read the following table carefully and answer the following questions:

The table shows the total number of students and the number of girls in three schools A, B & C in two consecutive years.

Years →	1999		2000	
School	Total number of students	Number of girls	Total number of students	Number of girls
A	500	270	600	350
B	400	160	50	25
C	600	270	800	700

Q.76 Find the number of boys in year 1999 is how much percent more than the number of boys in year 2000 together in all the three schools.

A. 50% **B.** 40%
C. 33.33% **D.** 30%
E. None of these

Q.77 Find the ratio of the total number of boys of school A and B together in year 1999 to the number of boys of school B and C together in 2000.

A. 35 : 47 **B.** 37 : 45
C. 45 : 37 **D.** 47 : 35
E. None of these

Q.78 Find the average number of boys of all the schools in year 2000.

A. 200 **B.** 250
C. 300 **D.** 175
E. None of these

Q.79 If the total number of students of school B in the year 2001 is 20% more than that of school B in the year 2000 and the number of boys in 2001 is 50% more than that of school B in the year 2000, then find the average number of girls in the year 2001 in all the school together. (The strength of school A and C are constant for year 2000 and 2001).

A. 525 **B.** 425
C. 325 **D.** 350
E. None of these

Q.80 If the total number of boys of school C in the year 2001 is $\left(\dfrac{300}{11}\right)$% more than that of school C in the year 1999 and the number of girls of school C in the year 2001 is 100% more than that of school C in the year 1999, then find the ratio of number of boys of school C in 2001 to the number of girls of school C in 2001.

A. 7 : 9 **B.** 3 : 7
C. 5 : 7 **D.** 5 : 9
E. None of these

// Smart Answer Sheet //

Correct — Percentage of students who answered correctly. **Skipped** — Percentage of students who skipped.

Q.	Ans.	Correct	Skipped	Q.	Ans.	Correct	Skipped	Q.	Ans.	Correct	Skipped	Q.	Ans.	Correct	Skipped	Q.	Ans.	Correct	Skipped	Q.	Ans.	Correct	Skipped
1	C	69.16 %	30.61 %	15	D	45.79 %	45.55 %	29	C	40.78 %	51.56 %	43	E	56.1 %	34.62 %	57	A	51.95 %	40.62 %	71	C	52.51 %	34.08 %
2	B	64.13 %	31.61 %	16	A	79.93 %	16.3 %	30	D	56.35 %	31.88 %	44	A	56.25 %	30.99 %	58	E	47.58 %	37.19 %	72	E	41.81 %	47.19 %
3	C	58.93 %	40.84 %	17	E	48.24 %	34.19 %	31	B	43.56 %	43.09 %	45	D	58.65 %	35.28 %	59	B	51.61 %	40.91 %	73	C	53.78 %	32.15 %
4	C	66.12 %	33.7 %	18	E	62.35 %	31.9 %	32	E	64.72 %	30.32 %	46	B	60.84 %	37.65 %	60	C	58.02 %	35.06 %	74	B	22.26 %	70.41 %
5	A	49.9 %	48.58 %	19	A	55.29 %	36.47 %	33	C	67.63 %	31.69 %	47	A	60.71 %	39.04 %	61	B	43.65 %	44.87 %	75	B	81.92 %	14.73 %
6	D	64.68 %	31.17 %	20	A	23.19 %	71.87 %	34	C	44.86 %	37.43 %	48	C	68.53 %	31.21 %	62	B	50.52 %	39.51 %	76	C	59.17 %	33.12 %
7	B	45.51 %	34.81 %	21	C	67.0 %	32.45 %	35	E	51.12 %	31.08 %	49	B	46.1 %	38.66 %	63	E	65.12 %	30.47 %	77	D	44.14 %	35.14 %
8	A	50.1 %	45.07 %	22	D	65.5 %	32.06 %	36	A	58.89 %	36.27 %	50	D	56.89 %	42.0 %	64	C	52.16 %	39.8 %	78	A	49.52 %	44.87 %
9	A	67.63 %	30.11 %	23	C	53.54 %	43.15 %	37	B	45.26 %	53.73 %	51	B	53.77 %	36.11 %	65	B	60.2 %	31.25 %	79	B	49.6 %	34.46 %
10	D	61.89 %	30.85 %	24	D	59.31 %	30.47 %	38	A	66.34 %	31.49 %	52	D	67.26 %	31.55 %	66	A	48.46 %	36.62 %	80	A	45.44 %	48.46 %
11	E	68.96 %	30.74 %	25	B	45.35 %	37.42 %	39	C	50.68 %	44.62 %	53	C	27.27 %	68.71 %	67	C	56.24 %	36.7 %				
12	D	42.63 %	47.65 %	26	E	40.79 %	36.13 %	40	E	63.22 %	33.64 %	54	D	40.03 %	50.69 %	68	A	58.52 %	41.05 %				
13	B	66.25 %	31.96 %	27	D	67.23 %	32.23 %	41	C	41.21 %	33.18 %	55	B	42.0 %	55.68 %	69	D	49.42 %	32.5 %				
14	C	52.84 %	37.57 %	28	E	69.31 %	30.08 %	42	B	69.3 %	30.32 %	56	A	65.69 %	30.49 %	70	B	67.48 %	31.66 %				

Reasoning

Ques (1-5):Direction: Study the following information carefully and answer the given questions:

In a certain code language,

'people visit many auditorium' is written as 'bh oa pu ki',

'many places like visit' is written as 'pu mh jk oa',

'people like discover places' is written as 'bh jk eg mh'

'auditorium visit discover things' is written as 'ki oa eg qw'.

Note that all the codes are of two letters.

Q.1 What is the code for the word 'discover' in this language?

A. mh 　　　　　　　**B.** eg
C. qw 　　　　　　　**D.** either mh or eg
E. oa

Q.2 Which of the following word is coded as 'ki' in the given coding language?

A. many 　　　　　　**B.** visit
C. auditorium 　　　**D.** people
E. things

Q.3 What is the code for the word 'visit' in the given language?

A. mh 　　　　　　　**B.** oa
C. jk 　　　　　　　**D.** either 'mh' or 'jk'
E. bh

Q.4 What will the code for 'discover grievance' in the given coding language?

A. eg qw 　　**B.** jk mh 　　**C.** ki pb 　　**D.** bh oa
E. pb eg

Q.5 Which of the following word is coded as 'bh' in the given coding language?

A. people 　　**B.** many 　　**C.** things 　　**D.** places
E. visit

Q.6 If it's possible to make a meaningful word from 1st, 4th, 5th and 8th letters of the word DOMINANT, then which will be the third letter of the word from the left side? Mark 'X' if no such word can be formed, 'Y' if more than 1 such word can be formed.

A. T 　　　　**B.** N 　　　　**C.** X 　　　　**D.** D
E. Y

Ques (7-11):Direction: Read the given information carefully and answer the questions that are given below.

There are 10 persons namely J, K, L, M, N, P, Q, R, S, and T. They stay in a five floored building. The bottom floor is numbered 1 and the top floor is numbered 5. Each floor of the building has two flats namely flat A and flat B. Flat A is to the west of flat B. Flat A of floor 2 is immediately above the flat A of floor 1 and

immediately below the flat A of floor 3 and flat B of floor 2 is immediately above the flat B of floor 1 and immediately below the flat B of floor 3, it is similar for all the other floors. Here, the same flat type means if one person stays in flat A then the other person also stays in flat A if they are staying in the same flat type.

Q stays in flat A of an odd numbered floor, but not the topmost floor. There are two floors between the floor of N and R. J stays just above Q. S and N are in different flat types on different floors. S stays on the topmost floor. There is no one to the east of R. M is to the north-east of L. N and R stay in the same flat type. P stays on one of the floors below Q, but not immediately below. R's floor is just below the floor of S. M does not stay on the fifth floor. T stays below K.

Q.7 Who is staying to the west of M?

A. S 　　　**B.** L 　　　**C.** J 　　　**D.** Q
E. R

Q.8 How many floors are there between T and K?

A. 　One
B. 　Two
C. 　Three
D. 　They are on the same floor
E. 　Zero

Q.9 Who stays second above L on the same type of flat as that of L?

A. R 　　　**B.** K 　　　**C.** S 　　　**D.** P
E. J

Q.10 Who stays immediately below K?

A. S 　　　**B.** M 　　　**C.** R 　　　**D.** T
E. P

Q.11 Which pair of persons stays on the fourth floor?

A. S and K 　　**B.** Q and M 　　**C.** R and L 　　**D.** J and R
E. P and N

Ques (12-16):Direction: In the following question assuming the given statements to be True, find which of the conclusion among given conclusions is/are definitely true and then give your answers accordingly.

Q.12 Statements: C > W; G < N; W = T; N ≤ T
Conclusions:

I. C > G

II. W ≥ N

A. 　Only II is True
B. 　Neither I nor II is true
C. 　Both I and II are True
D. 　Either I or II is True
E. 　Only I is True

Q.13 Statements: A < B ≥ C; D > E > A; C = F > G

Conclusions:

I. D ≥ C

II. B > G

A. Only II is True

B. Only I is True

C. Both I and II are True

D. None is true

E. Either I or II is True

Q.14 Statement: A > B = C, D < M, M ≤ C

Conclusion:

I. B > M

II. D < A

A. None is true

B. Only II is true

C. Only I is true

D. Both I and II are true

E. Either I or II is true

Q.15 Statements: Y = O ≤ G ≤ K = U > L > P; Y = A ≥ R

Conclusions:

I. U > R

II. R = U

A. Only II is True

B. Only I is True

C. Both I and II are True

D. Either I or II is True

E. None is true

Q.16 Statements: L > B < J ≤ Q; T = O < L; P = Q

Conclusions:

I. T < L

II. P ≥ J

A. Only II is True

B. Only I is True

C. Both I and II are True

D. None is true

E. Either I or II is True

Ques (17-21):Direction: Read the given information carefully and answer the questions that are given below.

There are seven persons in a company namely A, B, C, D, E, F and G. They have different designations starting from clerk, PO, assistant manager, manager, deputy general manager, general manager, and managing director. Starting from the managing director being the highest post and the clerk being the lowest post. They all like different colours namely red, blue, white, black, green, orange, and yellow.

The one who likes red has the highest post. Only three persons have posts lower than that of B, who likes blue. F likes yellow and has a post higher than that of B. There are two posts between B and E, who likes white colour. The one who likes black colour has a post which is just higher than that of E. F is not the general manager. A likes green colour and is senior to G, who is assistant manager and likes orange colour. C does not have the highest post.

Q.17 Who likes black colour?

A. E

B. A

C. F

D. The one who is the PO

E. The one who is the manager

Q.18 How many persons have posts lower than A?

A. Six   **B.** Four   **C.** Three   **D.** Two

E. Five

Q.19 Who has the designation of deputy general manager?

A. C   **B.** B   **C.** D   **D.** A

E. F

Q.20 How many persons are there who have their posts in between D and the one who likes orange color?

A. One   **B.** Three   **C.** Four   **D.** Five

E. Two

Q.21 Which of the following pair of name – designation – colour is correct?

A. D – General Manager – Yellow

B. B – Assistant Manager – Blue

C. E – PO – White

D. A – General manager – Green

E. G – manager – orange

Q.22 How many pairs of letters are there in the word "SECURITY" each of which has as many letters between them in the word (in the forward and backward direction) as they have between them in the English alphabetical order?

A. One   **B.** Two

C. Three   **D.** None

E. More than Three

Q.23 If 2 is added to each even digit and 1 is subtracted from each odd digit in the number 321754, then which number/numbers are repeated more than once?

A. Only 4   **B.** Both 4 and 6

C. 4, 6, 8   **D.** Only 6

E. None

Ques (24-28):Direction: Read the given information carefully and answer the questions that are given below.

There are nine persons namely, J, K, L, M, N, O, P, Q, and R. They all are sitting in a row. Some are facing north and some are facing south. The person facing in the same direction means that if one person faces in the north direction then the other also faces north direction. If persons are facing opposite directions then if one is facing north then the other faces in the south direction and vice-versa. The number of persons facing south is more than the number of persons facing north.

The one who is sitting in the middle of the row faces in the north direction. The persons sitting on the extreme ends are facing in opposite directions. J sits on one of the extreme ends. The person sitting second to the right of the one who is on the extreme left end is facing opposite to the one who is sitting on the extreme left end. N faces in the north direction. The person

sitting on the extreme right end faces south. Two persons are sitting between N and Q. P is sitting immediately to the right of J, and faces in the opposite direction to that of J. K is sitting third from the left end. Q is sitting in the middle of the row. J does not face the south. R is near to N. Three persons are sitting between K and L, and both are facing in the same direction. Immediate neighbours of Q are facing in the opposite direction. O and N is facing in the same direction and there is only one person between O and N.

Q.24 Who is sitting third to the left of K?

A. N **B.** J **C.** Q **D.** O
E. L

Q.25 How many persons are not facing north?

A. Four **B.** Five **C.** Two **D.** Three
E. Six

Q.26 Who is sitting third from the right end?

A. K **B.** M **C.** L **D.** O
E. Q

Q.27 How many persons are sitting to the left of L?

A. Four **B.** Six **C.** Two **D.** Three
E. Seven

Q.28 Which of the following pairs of 'Name – Face direction' is correct?

A. L - North **B.** M - South
C. K - North **D.** N - South
E. J - South

Ques (29-31):Direction: Read the given information carefully and answer the questions that are given below.

There are seven persons in a family namely, D, G, J, K, N, M, and P. N is the mother of J. D is the son-in-law of N. G is the son of D. K is the only aunt of G. D does not have any brother-in-law. N and M are a married couple. D has only one brother.

Q.29 How is P related to G?

A. Aunt **B.** Paternal Uncle
C. Father **D.** Mother
E. Grandfather

Q.30 How many female members are there in the family?

A. Two **B.** One **C.** Four **D.** Three
E. Five

Q.31 How is M related to D?

A. Father **B.** Mother
C. Sister **D.** Son-in-law
E. Father-in-law

Ques (32-36):Direction: Study the given information carefully and answer the following questions.

Ten Boxes A, B, C, D, E, F, G, H, I and J are placed one above the other in any particular order. Box number 1 is at the top and Box number 10 is at the bottom. There are three boxes between Box A and Box B. Box I is placed on an even numbered position. Box J is immediately above F and immediately below C. Box G is placed between the Box D and Box H. There are

three boxes between Box D and Box I. Box B is neither at the top nor at the bottom. Box F is at ninth position. Box G is immediately above Box H.

Q.32 Which box is placed at the top?

A. A **B.** C **C.** D **D.** I
E. B

Q.33 Which of the following box is placed at the position number 3?

A. A **B.** G **C.** D **D.** I
E. B

Q.34 Which of the following box is placed immediately below I?

A. A **B.** G **C.** D **D.** I
E. C

Q.35 Four among the five are alike in certain way. Find the one that does not belong to that group.

A. G **B.** B **C.** C **D.** J
E. F

Q.36 What is the Box number of Box H?

A. 6 **B.** 2 **C.** 4 **D.** 5
E. 3

Ques (37-40):Direction: Study the following information carefully and answer the question given below.

Certain numbers of persons are sitting in a row. All are facing in the north direction. M sits third to the left of N. Five people sit between M and K. S sits second to the right of K. O sits fifth to the right of R who is an immediate neighbor of M. L sits second to the left of O. K sits third from one of the extreme ends. O is not an immediate neighbor of N. Number of people sit between R and L is same as the number of people sits to the right of O.

Q.37 How many people are sitting in the given row?

A. 18 **B.** 15 **C.** 17 **D.** 19
E. 13

Q.38 If Q sits between R and N then what is the position of S with respect to Q?

A. Fifth to the right **B.** Fifth to the left
C. Sixth to the right **D.** Sixth to the left
E. Seventh to the right

Q.39 The number of people sits to the left of S is same as the number of people sits to the right of _______?

A. N **B.** L
C. O **D.** R
E. None of these

Q.40 How many people sit between O and K?

A. Two **B.** Seven **C.** Nine **D.** Eleven
E. Thirteen

Quantitative Aptitude

Ques (41-46):Direction: Find the wrong number in the following series.

Q.41 40320, 5040, 720, 120, 30, 6, 2
A. 720　　**B.** 5040　　**C.** 30　　**D.** 6
E. 120

Q.42 66, 56, 65, 57, 64, 58, 61
A. 56　　**B.** 65　　**C.** 57　　**D.** 58
E. 61

Q.43 8, 17, 35, 71, 145, 287, 575
A. 145　　**B.** 35　　**C.** 575　　**D.** 287
E. 71

Q.44 3, 5, 7, 11, 13, 17, 23
A. 7　　**B.** 5　　**C.** 17　　**D.** 23
E. 13

Q.45 545, 537, 521, 489, 425, 297, 43
A. 521　　**B.** 537　　**C.** 43　　**D.** 297
E. 489

Q.46 210, 206, 197, 181, 156, 121, 71
A. 71　　**B.** 121　　**C.** 181　　**D.** 156
E. 206

Q.47 10 men can do $\frac{2}{5}$ part of a work in 10 days. Find time taken by 25 men to complete the whole work.
A. 10 days　　**B.** 20 days　　**C.** 15 days　　**D.** 8 days
E. 12 days

Q.48 A, B and C started a business by investing the sum of money in the ratio of 3 : 4 : 2 and after one year the profit earned by B is Rs. 20,000, then find the total profit which was earned by all three after one year.
A. Rs. 42000　　　　**B.** Rs. 45000
C. Rs. 38000　　　　**D.** Rs. 50000
E. Rs. 40000

Q.49 A sum of money invested for 2 years at 20% compounded annually and similar money invested for 3 years on simple interest at 10% per annum. If the difference between interests is Rs. 280, then find the sum of money.
A. Rs. 2500　　**B.** Rs. 3000　　**C.** Rs. 4000　　**D.** Rs. 2000
E. Rs. 1500

Q.50 Total surface area of a sphere is 400π m². If length of a rectangle is equal to diameter of sphere and breadth of rectangle is 3 metre smaller than its length, then find the area of rectangle.
A. 360 m²　　**B.** 320 m²　　**C.** 380 m²　　**D.** 280 m²
E. 340 m²

Q.51 In a mixture the ratio of liquid A and liquid B is 3 : 2. If 5 litre mixture is drown out and in final mixture the quantity of liquid A is 12 litre more than liquid B, then find the initial quantity of liquid A in the mixture.
A. 36 litre　　**B.** 39 litre　　**C.** 32 litre　　**D.** 45 litre
E. 42 litre

Ques (52-56):Direction: Read the given information carefully and answer the following questions.

Three streams Arts, Science, and Commerce are offered in 3 colleges A, B, and C.

(1) There are 1750 students in college A. The number of Commerce students in college A is 400 more than that of in Science in college A. the ratio of the number of students in college A in Arts and Science is 23 : 2.

(2) There are 3250 students in Arts in all colleges. The number of students in Science in all colleges is 37.5% less than that of in Commerce in all colleges.

(3) The number of Arts students in college C is 10% more than that of in college B. the ratio of the number of students in Science in college B to that of in college C is 3 : 4.

(4) The number of students in Commerce in college B is 30% less than that in college A. total number of students in college B is 280 less than that of in college C.

Q.52 The total number of students in college B is what percent more/less than that of in Science in all colleges?
A. 106.25%　　**B.** 141.25%　　**C.** 118.75%　　**D.** 96.96%
E. 105.50%

Q.53 If 30 students from Science of college A are shifted to the respective streams in college C then what would be the difference between the number of students in Science in college A and C?
A. 300　　**B.** 360　　**C.** 330　　**D.** 240
E. 270

Q.54 If the number of students in Science in college B increased by 10% then what would be the ratio of the number of students in Science in college A to that of in college B?
A. 10 : 27　　**B.** 13 : 30　　**C.** 4 : 11　　**D.** 1 : 3
E. 10 : 33

Q.55 What is the average number of students in Commerce in colleges B and C?
A. 550　　**B.** 465　　**C.** 425　　**D.** 390
E. 350

Q.56 What is the ratio of the number of students in Arts in college A and B together to that of in Science in college B and C together?
A. 43 : 4　　　　**B.** 43 : 14
C. 3 : 1　　　　**D.** 21 : 5
E. None of the above

Ques (57-61):Direction: In the following question, two equations numbered I and II are given. You have to solve both the equations and give the answer:

Q.57 I. $x^2 - x - 12 = 0$
II. $y^2 + 5y + 6 = 0$
A. $x > y$
B. $x \geq y$
C. $x < y$
D. $x \leq y$

E. x = y or the relation cannot be determined

Q.58 I. $y^2 = 49$

II. $(x - y)^2 = 0$

A. x > y

B. x ≥ y

C. x < y

D. x ≤ y

E. x = y or the relation cannot be determined

Q.59 I. $x^2 - 28 + 3x = 0$

II. $8y^2 - y - 9 = 0$

A. x > y

B. x ≥ y

C. x < y

D. x ≤ y

E. x = y or the relation cannot be determined

Q.60 I. $x^2 + 13x + 40 = 0$

II. $y^2 + 7y + 10 = 0$

A. x > y

B. x ≥ y

C. x < y

D. x ≤ y

E. x = y or the relation cannot be determined

Q.61 I. $4x^2 - 3x - 1 = 0$

II. $2y^2 - 7y - 9 = 0$

A. x > y

B. x ≥ y

C. x < y

D. x ≤ y

E. x = y or the relation cannot be determined

Q.62 Length of first train is 300 meter and its speed is 25 km/h and length of second train is 200 metre and both the trains are running towards each other. If higher speed train crosses the lower speed train in 45 seconds, then find the speed of second train in km/h.

A. 12 km/h   **B.** 10 km/h   **C.** 15 km/h   **D.** 22 km/h

E. 18 km/h

Q.63 A boat covers 36 km downstream in 4 hours and 18 km upstream in 6 hours. Find the speed of boat.

A. 12 km/hr   **B.** 9 km/hr   **C.** 6 km/hr   **D.** 5 km/hr

E. 3 km/hr

Q.64 Two unbiased dice are rolled simultaneously. Find the probability of getting sum greater than 5.

A. $\frac{13}{18}$ **B.** $\frac{23}{36}$ **C.** $\frac{7}{9}$ **D.** $\frac{5}{9}$

E. $\frac{11}{18}$

Q.65 3 years ago, the ratio of age of A and B is 1 : 3 and the ratio of present age of B and C is 2 : 7. Find the C's age after 3 years if sum of present age of A and B is 34 years.

A. 81 years   **B.** 87 years   **C.** 78 years   **D.** 89 years

E. 85 years

Q.66 A person invests 10% of his income on mutual fund and expends 70% of the remaining on groceries and transport. The ratio of expenditure on groceries and that of transport is 2 : 7. Find the total income if the expenditure on groceries is Rs.2800.

A. Rs. 30000   **B.** Rs. 15000

C. Rs. 24000   **D.** Rs. 20000

E. Rs. 28000

Ques (67-71):Direction: Read the Graph carefully and answer the following questions:

The following Line graph shows the number of Fruits (Apple and Banana) sold in five different years.

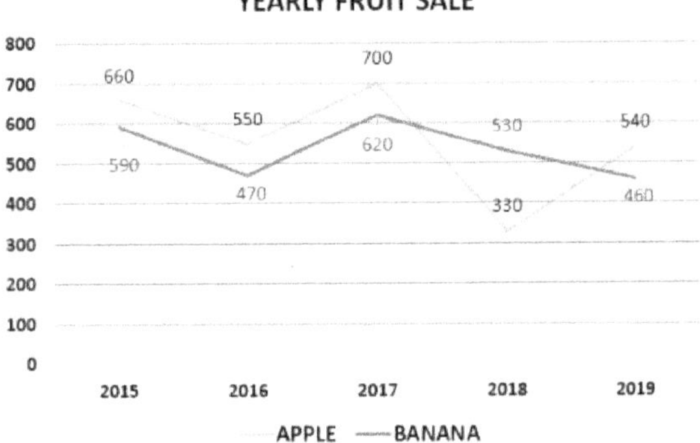

Q.67 What is the overall average sale of banana?

A. 524   **B.** 528   **C.** 538   **D.** 542

E. 534

Q.68 What is the ratio between the sales of apple in 2016 to banana in 2018?

A. 52 : 41   **B.** 56 : 47   **C.** 55 : 53   **D.** 65 : 61

E. 62 : 49

Q.69 In which year is the difference between the sale of apple and banana recorded the most?

A. 2015   **B.** 2016   **C.** 2017   **D.** 2018

E. 2019

Q.70 The total number of sale of banana in 2017 is what percent of the total number of sale of apple in 2017?

A. 88.5%   **B.** 87.5%   **C.** 92.5%   **D.** 96.5%

E. 82.5%

Q.71 What percent more is the sale of banana to that of apple in 2018?

A. 62.6%   **B.** 63%   **C.** 60.6%   **D.** 64.2%

E. 66.66%

Q.72 The marked price of an article is 150% more than the cost price and the discount given on the marked price is 30%. If the difference between selling price and cost price is Rs.525, find the cost price of the article.

A. Rs. 500   **B.** Rs. 550   **C.** Rs. 650   **D.** Rs. 700

E. Rs. 750

Q.73 A invest Rs.3000 and B invest x amount in a partnership. After 6 months, C replaced B with some amount in his hand. If

A's share in profit at the end of the year is Rs.2000, find the amount that B invested.

A. Rs. 2000
B. Rs. 2500
C. Rs. 3500
D. Cannot be determined
E. Rs. 4000

Q.74 The average of the seven numbers is 45. We replace two numbers 65 and 54 with 56 and 35. Then find the new average.

A. 41   **B.** 43   **C.** 47   **D.** 45
E. 39

Q.75 If the ratio of the speed of the boat in downstream and speed of the stream is 7 : 2 and the speed of the boat in still water is 35 km/hr. What would be the distance travelled in upstream by boat in 5 hours?

A. 100 km   **B.** 90 km
C. 110 km   **D.** 105 km
E. None of these

Ques (76-80):Direction: Read the following table carefully and answer the questions given below:-

The given the table is showing the number of students in different school.

Name of School	Total number of girls out of total number of students	Total number of boys out of total number of students
A	420	58%
B	450	70%
C	350	65%
D	550	45%

Q.76 Find the average number of girls in schools B, C, and D.

A. 400   **B.** 350   **C.** 450   **D.** 500
E. 600

Q.77 Find the ratio between the total number of boys in school D and the total number of girls in school A.

A. 11 : 9   **B.** 12 : 7   **C.** 15 : 14   **D.** 17 : 13
E. 14 : 11

Q.78 The total number of girls in school B is what percent of the total number of boys in school D?

A. 80%   **B.** 120%   **C.** 125%   **D.** 75%
E. 100%

Q.79 Find the ratio between the average number of girls in school B and D together and the average number of boys in school B and C together.

A. 8 : 15   **B.** 7 : 16   **C.** 9 : 20   **D.** 8 : 13
E. 10 : 17

Q.80 Find the total number of girls in school A is how much percent more or less than the total number of boys in school B.

A. 66.66%   **B.** 50%   **C.** 75%   **D.** 60%
E. 40%

// Smart Answer Sheet //

Correct Percentage of students who answered correctly.   **Skipped** Percentage of students who skipped.

Q.	Ans.	Correct / Skipped	Q.	Ans.	Correct / Skipped	Q.	Ans.	Correct / Skipped	Q.	Ans.	Correct / Skipped	Q.	Ans.	Correct / Skipped	Q.	Ans.	Correct / Skipped
1	B	50.53 % / 30.41 %	15	D	44.99 % / 45.01 %	29	B	81.42 % / 15.61 %	43	A	57.06 % / 34.8 %	57	E	86.55 % / 11.94 %	71	C	78.57 % / 17.88 %
2	C	62.17 % / 37.11 %	16	C	45.73 % / 54.16 %	30	D	85.64 % / 12.12 %	44	D	77.15 % / 11.77 %	58	E	81.42 % / 13.27 %	72	D	58.94 % / 31.04 %
3	B	42.63 % / 43.94 %	17	D	45.47 % / 39.69 %	31	E	80.76 % / 10.27 %	45	C	30.19 % / 69.48 %	59	E	65.11 % / 34.22 %	73	D	14.98 % / 77.11 %
4	E	64.23 % / 34.37 %	18	E	49.7 % / 30.63 %	32	A	63.01 % / 30.2 %	46	B	57.31 % / 37.55 %	60	D	69.12 % / 30.8 %	74	A	49.43 % / 46.89 %
5	A	55.13 % / 34.15 %	19	E	45.48 % / 34.56 %	33	B	43.29 % / 47.02 %	47	A	68.01 % / 30.31 %	61	E	60.52 % / 36.9 %	75	D	59.95 % / 33.99 %
6	E	50.48 % / 47.96 %	20	D	43.81 % / 44.64 %	34	E	50.41 % / 43.53 %	48	B	84.95 % / 11.47 %	62	C	12.51 % / 68.09 %	76	C	61.24 % / 31.11 %
7	D	32.27 % / 67.65 %	21	D	60.26 % / 35.9 %	35	D	52.34 % / 32.72 %	49	D	40.57 % / 52.04 %	63	C	84.02 % / 10.82 %	77	C	49.27 % / 44.46 %
8	B	30.79 % / 67.22 %	22	C	81.59 % / 14.9 %	36	C	52.39 % / 30.81 %	50	E	47.64 % / 47.64 %	64	A	51.71 % / 30.31 %	78	E	62.85 % / 30.39 %
9	E	25.75 % / 71.31 %	23	B	84.6 % / 14.47 %	37	C	42.26 % / 33.9 %	51	B	47.36 % / 45.89 %	65	B	30.81 % / 68.83 %	79	E	49.43 % / 41.02 %
10	C	27.72 % / 72.01 %	24	D	47.45 % / 49.48 %	38	D	68.89 % / 30.18 %	52	A	26.39 % / 70.69 %	66	D	49.86 % / 48.95 %	80	D	57.24 % / 40.48 %
11	D	23.57 % / 72.94 %	25	B	67.49 % / 30.72 %	39	B	56.93 % / 40.71 %	53	B	17.62 % / 81.42 %	67	E	85.0 % / 14.58 %			
12	C	57.04 % / 36.74 %	26	C	42.83 % / 44.6 %	40	D	66.96 % / 31.33 %	54	E	25.89 % / 67.43 %	68	C	80.42 % / 18.1 %			
13	A	41.83 % / 49.76 %	27	C	44.46 % / 30.56 %	41	C	45.41 % / 36.22 %	55	D	22.49 % / 77.45 %	69	D	40.23 % / 35.44 %			
14	B	62.08 % / 34.45 %	28	B	56.03 % / 40.85 %	42	E	82.12 % / 10.03 %	56	B	20.03 % / 69.65 %	70	A	88.74 % / 11.1 %			

// Notes //

// Notes //